Interpreting News

Also by Graham Meikle

Future Active: Media Activism and the Internet (2002)

Interpreting News

Graham Meikle
University of Stirling

palgrave
macmillan

First published 2009 by
PALGRAVE MACMILLAN

Palgrave Macmillan in the UK is an imprint of Macmillan Publishers Limited, registered in England, company number 785998, of Houndmills, Basingstoke, Hampshire RG21 6XS.

Palgrave Macmillan in the US is a division of St Martin's Press LLC, 175 Fifth Avenue, New York, NY 10010.

Palgrave Macmillan is the global academic imprint of the above companies and has companies and representatives throughout the world.

Palgrave® and Macmillan® are registered trademarks in the United States, the United Kingdom, Europe and other countries.

ISBN-13: 978–1–4039–3382–9 hardback
ISBN-10: 1–4039–3382–0 hardback
ISBN-13: 978–1–4039–3383–6 paperback
ISBN-10: 1–4039–3383–9 paperback

This book is printed on paper suitable for recycling and made from fully managed and sustained forest sources. Logging, pulping and manufacturing processes are expected to conform to the environmental regulations of the country of origin.

A catalogue record for this book is available from the British Library.

A catalog record for this book is available from the Library of Congress.

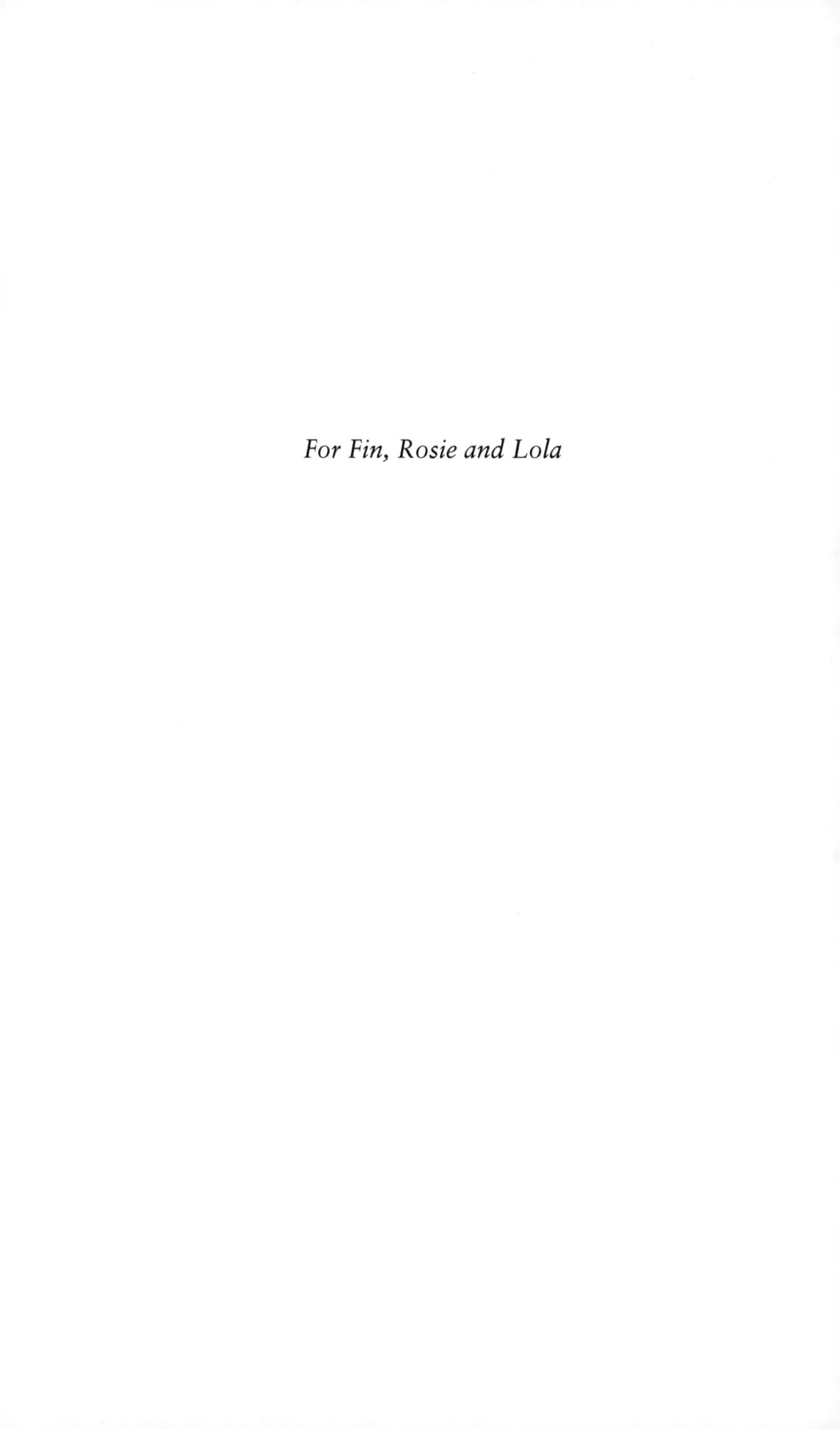

For Fin, Rosie and Lola

Contents

Acknowledgments

Thanks to the many friends and colleagues who helped in many crucial ways while I was writing this book. Particular thanks go to Chris Atton, Neil Blain, Steve Collins, Camille Durand, Gerard Goggin, Phil Hayward, Christine Jones, Stephanie Marriott, John Potts, McKenzie Wark and Sherman Young.

Thanks to students in MAS 203 News and Current Affairs at Macquarie University in Sydney in 1999, 2003, 2004, 2006 and 2007.

And, above all, thanks to Fin, and our daughters Rosie and Lola. You're the business.

Introduction: News and Symbolic Power

A news story should answer 'w' questions — who, what, where, when, how, and all too rarely, why. This book asks 'w' questions of news. It asks 'who' questions, of the roles of journalists, owners, sources and audiences. It asks 'what' questions, of the nature of news stories, news texts, of news values and narratives. It asks 'where' and 'when' questions, of the development of different news industries and forms. It asks 'how' questions, of the distribution and reception of news, from the printing press to SMS. And it asks 'why' a lot. This is not a book about putting news together, but about taking it apart.

Many readers of *Interpreting News* are likely to be undergraduate students, and yet I'm conscious that many such students aren't all that interested in the news. I don't mean that they're uninterested in issues — I mean that they're uninterested in the established news media. Newspapers, for example, struggle to appeal to teenagers and university students. In 2004 the *Washington Post* held focus groups to find out why they were having so much trouble attracting younger readers — those interviewed said that they didn't like the thought of piles of old newspapers cluttering up the house, and that they wouldn't be interested in a subscription to the paper even if it were free (*Wired News*, 24 November 2004). The *New York Times* reported similar findings, with one 22-year-old complaining that newspapers 'are so clunky and big' (22 January 2006, p. 1). One 2006 survey found that 27% of Americans under the age of 30 had got *no news at all* from TV, radio, newspapers or the Net on the day before being interviewed (Pew Research Center for the People & the Press 2006: 9). Back in the 1980s leading scholars could write that news was 'high-status' (Fiske 1987: 281) and that it enjoyed 'a privileged and prestigious position in our culture's hierarchy of values' (Hartley 1982: 5). But in the early twenty-first century, as Graeme Turner suggests, the very idea of news 'looks increasingly old-fashioned' (2005: 13).

And yet this picture is a complicated one, with the traditional news media still far from being replaced by newer ones. For instance, students I talk to often say that they don't read the papers or watch the TV bulletins, but prefer to go online for news. But when I ask for details, this often turns out to mean they go to the websites of the main newspapers or TV news providers. Some students say they prefer the experience of blogging or participatory news networks such as Indymedia <http://www.indymedia.org> to that of consuming news — but here again the agenda for discussion is often that set by the traditional news media. Others are happier with the blend of news and entertainment and satirical commentary offered by a website like *The Onion* <http://www.theonion.com> or by an irreverent video blog like *Rocketboom* <http://www.rocketboom.com>. They may prefer TV shows such as *The Daily Show* or *The Colbert Report* in the US (and beyond, with episodes widely shared online), *Have I Got News For You?* in the UK, or *The Chaser's War on Everything* in Australia. And yet here again, the content of these sites and shows — the menu of topics available to satirize — is often set by the current concerns of the traditional news media.

So this book starts from the claim that a thorough understanding of news remains central to an understanding of contemporary media, which is in turn central to an understanding of contemporary society and culture. News, notes McQuail, deserves particular attention in the study of media content, as it is 'one of the few original contributions of the mass media to the range of cultural forms of expression' (2000: 337). News deserves attention for many other reasons too. Being in the news business can confer a privileged legal and regulatory status upon media organizations. Moreover, news confers credibility and respectability upon media organizations (despite the success of *The Simpsons,* Rupert Murdoch is not the head of Cartoon Corporation but of News Corporation). And this credibility allows them to accumulate and exercise a particular form of power.

The mediascape is, as Castells argues, 'the social space where power is decided' (2007: 238). The media enable an arena for the defining of reality. James Carey once argued that reality is 'a scarce resource' (1989: 87). In this, the ability to define reality is also, as Carey puts it, a 'fundamental form of power' (p. 87). This 'fundamental form of power' is what Bourdieu calls *symbolic* power — 'Symbolic power is a power of constructing reality' (1991: 166). This is the ability 'to intervene in the course of events, to influence the actions of others and indeed to create events, by means of the production and transmission of symbolic forms' (Thompson 1995: 17). Thompson distinguishes symbolic power from other dimensions of power — the coercive power of the military or the law, the political power of governments, and the economic power of corporations. Coercive power works through the use or threat of force; political power through the coordination and regulation of individuals and groups; economic power through productive activity, the transformation of raw material, the creation of services and goods (1995: 12–18).

What might we mean by a phrase like 'the production and transmission of symbolic forms'? We would mean the creation and distribution of ideas and images, stories and songs, information and entertainment. Institutions such as the media, universities, schools, government and religious organizations are all in the symbolic power business — they are, as Hartley has it, 'sites of knowledge-production and meaning-exchange' (1999: 6). The news media are central players in this. Their work is the exercise of symbolic power — the creation and distribution of symbolic content; the exchange of shaped information; the expression of cultural skills and values. Symbolic power, as Bourdieu puts it, is the power of 'making people see and believe' (1991: 170). In a society in which information is central, argues Melucci, 'the power of information is essentially the *power of naming*' (1996: 228, emphasis in original). Symbolic power is the power to name, to define, to endorse, to persuade. The news media are among the most important of those institutions that exercise such symbolic power. News matters.

Symbolic power is about defining reality. It's not separate from other forms of power, but bound up with them — political power generates resources of symbolic power; economic power can be expressed as symbolic power; coercive power can be demonstrated through the exercise of symbolic power. Not everyone is able to exercise this power in the same kinds of way or with the same kinds of success. Certain types of institution, and certain individuals, have greater resources than others — schools and universities; churches, temples and mosques; and media organizations. These are the main centres of symbolic power — and each, as Hartley argues (1998, 1999), is built around *teaching*, a positive activity.

But all kinds of teaching are messy — the difference between what gets taught and what gets learned can be a big one. The exercise of symbolic power isn't a simple, one-way transaction — like all forms of power, it's expressed within relationships, and so is not entirely predictable; it is, as Foucault has it, 'exercised from innumerable points, in the interplay of nonegalitarian and mobile relations' (1978: 94). Audiences can respond in many ways. Communication of this sort is a dynamic process — even, in some accounts, a chaotic one (McNair 2006). News organizations may have far greater resources of symbolic power than you or me, but the news itself is a volatile process. We live in an increasingly global, digital, always-on media environment, in which the live broadcast of an event can change the outcome of that event (Friedland 1992, Wark 1994). We live in a mediascape where the people we somehow persist in calling audiences can now collaborate and intervene in the news agenda in new ways — ask former CBS anchor Dan Rather, who retired early with his credibility badly damaged, after bloggers mobilized to debunk a CBS story about George W. Bush's service record (Allan 2006: 94–8).

Is 'symbolic power' just another way of saying 'ideology'? No, although as part of the problem with the word 'ideology' is that it means very different things to different people, some overlap is not out of the question (Williams 1983, Thompson 1990, Eagleton 2007). Ideology has been a central concept in much media and cultural theory (such as Glasgow University Media Group 1976, 1995a, 1995b, Hall *et al* 1978, Herman & Chomsky 1988). This is particularly the case for those working in the Marxist tradition, exploring whether control of the means of production is the same thing as control of the production of meaning (Gramsci 1971, Althusser 1984, Marx & Engels 2006). But this tradition of ideological analysis rather lost its way — 'in a sea of methodological doubt' as two leading scholars put it (Atton & Couldry 2003: 580; see also Curran 2002: 107–13). The influence of Foucault's approach to power (1978, 1980, 2000) became more central, while post-modernist critics announced that 'grand narratives' were over (Lyotard 1984). For our present purposes, however, ideology and symbolic power should be distinguished: the key distinction to make is that ideology, as Thompson (1990) argues, is best seen as a subset of symbolic power relations — those concerned with *domination*. With this distinction made, symbolic power can be seen to describe a wider field of communication, some aspects of which may well be dominant or even repressive, but other aspects of which are not.

Do we need to be journalists to talk about the news with any authority? No — this book is about the social and cultural importance of news. News is central to the experience of all of us — not just those who work for companies that sell it. More importantly, the news and its creators need to be subjected to the same scrutiny to which they subject others. Reporters routinely demand access and answers in the name of the people, claim to speak on our behalf, and ask questions in the name of 'the public interest'. The news media claim for themselves formidable power to scrutinize everyone else's business. But those same news media are now themselves among the ranks of the powerful that they claim to scrutinize — and so they ought to be called to account too, in the same ways and on the same grounds. As Michael Schudson writes (1995: 3): 'Everyone in a democracy is a certified media critic, which is as it should be.' News is too important to be left only to journalists.

What's going on

This book interprets the news — and the critical literature on news — in terms of symbolic power. As Couldry observes, the concept of symbolic power is 'surprisingly underdeveloped' (2003: 39); this book develops this concept by examining its relevance to the production, distribution and reception of news. It maps out the key kinds of actors who exercise symbolic power in and through the news, the principal contexts in which they do this, and the importance of particular media forms in enabling the exercise of symbolic power. It concentrates mainly on the UK, US and Australia, and emphasizes certain news forms (principally TV news, newspapers and the Net) over others (radio, news magazines, documentaries and current affairs programming). The book can also be read as an introduction to the main ways in which news has been theorized and understood in the various traditions that converge as Media Studies. News matters, as I've said already, but so does the study of news, which has been approached from a wide range of traditions — textual analysis, critical theory, journalism history, medium theory, political economy and others. If the study of the media means the study of that-which-is-in-the-middle, it is a virtue of Media Studies that it too is in-the-middle, with much of the best work being done in the interstices between humanities and social sciences, between established traditions and new approaches. The study of media is by its very nature interdisciplinary (perhaps even anti-disciplinary) — Media Studies is less a discipline than it is an *un*discipline. This makes some people uncomfortable, but it can also be a source of invention and creative energy.

If news is an arena and a vehicle for the exercise of symbolic power, who gets to exercise this power? *Interpreting News* identifies four kinds of groups or individuals who do this in various unequal ways. First, *media organizations and their owners* — this book discusses a number of key media organizations in detail, including News Corporation, Reuters, the BBC, CNN, Al Jazeera and Indymedia. Second, *journalists*, who are licenced by news organizations to exercise symbolic power and who draw their authority from those organizations. Third, those *sources* of information who have the capacity to influence and direct the news by providing (or withholding) high-status information — politicians and their staffers are central sources, although they do not only exercise symbolic power but are also vulnerable to its use by others (through scandal, leak, gaffe and smear, for example); other people with official status of some kind can also exploit their positions as sources of news. And fourth, *audiences* — readers, viewers and users of news, whose interpretations, responses to (or outright rejections of) the news are a fundamental daily dimension of symbolic power.

Chapter 1, 'Defining News', builds a definition of news that runs through the discussion in the rest of the book (an attempted exercise of symbolic power in itself, as is true of every definition — and every book). It argues that news has to be understood as both a particular kind of product or text, and also as particular kinds of processes of production, distribution and reception.

Chapter 2, 'Know Your Product', starts from the position that a basic truth of the news is that it is overwhelmingly produced and marketed by large media organizations. These organizations have symbolic power resources that are far greater and more concentrated than those of the other actors in the news processes. Indeed, their symbolic power is so great, their capacity to define reality so extensive, that we may take it for granted and not notice it (Bourdieu 1991, Couldry 2000, 2003) — which in turn increases their symbolic power still further. This chapter sets large commercial news organizations as the first context for a consideration of news and symbolic power, emphasizing those organizations' capacity to define reality by defining what counts as news. It also discusses the issues surrounding the increasingly concentrated ownership of news organizations (to complement this, public service broadcasters are discussed in Chapter 7, alternative news organizations in Chapter 8).

Chapter 3, 'True Stories', sets the preceding discussion in a wider cultural context. It examines some of the principal ways in which news is shaped by (and in turn shapes) our expectations of story-telling and of visual culture. It focuses first on print news stories, second on news photographs, and third on television (the Net is discussed in Chapters 4 and 8).

Chapter 4, 'From Coffee-House To Cyber-Café', focuses on journalists and their changing status. Journalists are licenced agents of symbolic power. Their social and cultural roles are underwritten by their claim to Fourth Estate status. This chapter traces the emergence of this and its current, most pressing, challenge from the opening up of the new media environment of blogging.

Chapter 5, 'Pay No Attention To That Man Behind The Curtain', turns to attempts to influence the news agenda. It discusses the roles of sources — powerful or official or otherwise established groups and individuals who are able to exercise symbolic power through the news media by having their concerns presented as news. This chapter discusses the staged pseudo-event, the tactics of spin, and the concept of moral panic.

Chapter 6, 'Here We Are, Now Entertain Us', introduces the fourth crucial set of actors in the processes of news — audiences, readers, viewers, and users of news. The chapter surveys the most important perspectives on media audiences, and places these within the context of debates around information and entertainment, of tabloid media and celebrity culture. The chapter also draws on the critical theory concept of the public sphere. The history of the development of audience research, from the mid-twentieth century on, can be read as a very gradual recognition that audiences are not only subject to symbolic power but are also able to exercise it. This is of critical importance in the digital media environment, in which audiences have unprecedented opportunities to create, circulate and remix media content of their own. For many people, the media are no longer just what they read, watch or listen to — the media are now also what they *do*.

Chapters 7 and 8 approach our topic from the angle of examining some of the technological possibilities that enable and extend the exercise of symbolic power. New media create new opportunities for new kinds of player (this is not just true of our contemporary sense of 'new media', but of all media when they were new).

Chapter 7, 'Totally Wired', examines the relationships between communication technologies and news institutions. It traces how the adoption and adaptation of new technical possibilities can enable new kinds of news institutions, able to exercise symbolic power in new ways. It looks first at the telegraph, and how this was taken up in the development of global news agencies such as Reuters; second, at broadcasting, and the emergence of public service broadcasters such as the BBC; and third, at satellite and cable news channels such as CNN and Al Jazeera, and their strategy of continuous live news.

Chapter 8, 'News 2.0?', picks up the discussion of Internet news begun in Chapter 4, and examines some of the most important dimensions of online news. In one sense, online news is being shaped by processes of convergence, the coming together of things that were previously separate — industries and technologies, texts and audiences, models and modes of news. But in another sense, it's also being shaped by processes of divergence, the coming apart of things that were previously stable and settled — an unravelling and rethinking of approaches to making and taking news; new possibilities for distribution; new types of author and audience.

Chapter 1

Defining News

> 'News is more easily pursued than defined, a characteristic it shares with such other enthralling abstractions as love and truth' (Roshco 1975: 9)

What is news? What makes news on a typical day?

Click. A Sydney man steals a tank and uses it to demolish half a dozen mobile phone towers while being chased, very slowly, by police (ABC News).

Click. Russia suspends a Cold War arms control treaty, in protest at the installation of US missile defence systems in Eastern Europe (BBC News).

Click. Controversy about a Georgia district attorney distributing copies of a teen sex tape used as evidence (CNN).

Click. Republican senators pressuring President Bush on a plan to withdraw US forces from Iraq (*New York Times*).

Click. The death of a Native American leader and activist (Indymedia).

Click. Posh and Becks arrive in LA ('American Idol!') (*The Sun*)

These headlines don't offer us a simple definition. They show news as local, and national, and global; as politics and as entertainment; as sport and as war. The range and diversity of these stories suggests that the answer to the question 'what is news?' is not an obvious one. McQuail notes that many journalists would see the question as 'metaphysical', an attempt to over-theorize a straightforward common-sense category (2000: 337; see also Zelizer 1993). Yet the news, as we'll see throughout this book, is anything but a common-sense category, and any definition has to capture a wide range of complex factors. This is why, as Roshco observes, news is easier to pursue than define (1975: 9). The scholarly literature offers a range of definitions — some presented formally, others occurring almost as asides in the pursuit of different discussions. In this section I'll canvass some of the most useful definitions, distinguish between news and journalism, and finally offer a definition of my own that underpins the discussion in the rest of the book.

Technologies, stories, organizations

Let's begin with one contemporary definition from a major textbook. Media historian Mitchell Stephens defines news as 'new information about a subject of some public interest that is shared with some portion of the public' (2007: 4). This definition takes us part of the way, but is rather too broad — as well as news, for instance, it could also accommodate both advertisements and personal telephone calls. And it raises more questions than it answers: where does this 'new information' come from? What is the 'public interest' here? What 'portion of the public' is concerned? Moreover, some central elements are missing; I'll highlight three — technologies, stories, and news organizations.

First, technologies — in what ways is the information 'shared'? The principal forms of media used for news (television, print, radio, the Net) have important points of difference from each other, as well as from other media forms (such as cinema or videogames), and from other forms of communication (private conversation, phone calls, meetings). The specifics of the different news media are central to what news is, not incidental. Take print, for instance: the newspaper and the modern conception of news both have their origins in the introduction of printing to western Europe in the 1450s. The OED notes that the English word 'news' only came into common usage from 1500, gradually replacing the older English term 'tidings'. The word 'news' itself, then, is closely linked to the *printed* word (Hartley 1982: 18). Moreover, the newspaper as a media form depends on mass production: on multiple copies of identical texts distributed through a given territory for near-simultaneous use — all of this needed the printing press to become possible. The different technical media involved in the news process are intrinsic to the nature of news (we'll look at this point in more detail in Chapters 4, 7 and 8).

Second, stories — what forms does Stephens's 'new information' take? News stories and news genres have quite different conventions from those of sitcoms, horror movies or online role-playing games — most obviously, news *stories* are presented as being *true*. I emphasized the words 'true' and 'stories' in that sentence, because together they point to one of the basic tensions in the news that runs throughout this book — that on the one hand, information in the news is presented as fact, while on the other hand, it has to be shaped into certain story formats (and formulas). As one argument has it: 'While news is not fiction, it is a story about reality, not reality itself' (Bird & Dardenne 1997: 346). The implicit claim in every news story that what it says is true is a central part of the news as symbolic power.

Third, organizations — who does the 'sharing' in Stephens's definition? News certainly has important social dimensions — gossip, blogging, word-of-mouth, family viewing — but for the most part news is not so much shared as marketed. News is produced and distributed by news organizations, from the local paper to the BBC. Moreover, news is not something that occurs in nature, and nor does it lie around in the streets waiting to be collected. Rather, news is a product, something created and marketed, packaged and distributed, by (and for) news organizations and institutions. Those organizations have unique concentrations of symbolic power. Reuters' internal *International Style Guide* in 1988 answered the question of 'what is news?' by effectively declaring that news is whatever they say it is. Anything that Reuters report automatically becomes news — 'we give it the Reuter hallmark and it rises above the status of a mere report to that of news' (Read 1999: 440).

Early definitions

As early as 1922 Walter Lippmann argued that news was an institutional product whose characteristics were shaped by the requirements of media organizations: not, then, a naturally-occurring category to which reporters addressed themselves, but rather a product of the selection criteria and bureaucratic conventions of the news-gathering apparatus. The bureaucratic machinery of news gathering is able to recognize particular aspects of particular events at particular times — but may not be able to recognize events until they are rendered in a form that the institution can manage. News, according to Lippmann, 'is not a mirror of social conditions, but the report of an aspect that has obtruded itself' (1922: 216). Lippmann's argument echoes through a number of important strands of media scholarship that have developed since, including work that emphasizes the importance of powerful sources in influencing the news agenda (Boorstin 1961, Molotch & Lester 1974, Herman & Chomsky 1988), and work that examines the importance of the news organization and its operational requirements in shaping the nature of news (Galtung & Ruge 1965, Tuchman 1978, Golding & Elliott 1979, Fishman 1980, Schlesinger 1987 [1978]).

What about other earlier definitions? How has news been approached throughout the development of the study of media? In 1940 Robert Park examined news as a kind of knowledge. Park distinguished between systematic, scientific knowledge (which he called 'knowledge about') and individual experience, intuition and instinct (which he called 'acquaintance with'). News, Park argued, could be understood as a special type of knowledge in the middle of the continuum bounded by 'knowledge about' and 'acquaintance with'. In Park's analysis, news was distinctive because of, among other things: its emphasis on isolated events, not linked in causal sequences; its concern with the present time; and its ephemeral nature. News, Park wrote, 'does not so much inform as orient the public, giving each and all notice as to what is going on' (1967: 42). Of particular interest is the way in which Park drew attention to social uses of news: 'The first typical reaction of an individual to the news is likely to be a desire to repeat it to someone' (p. 42). Conversation turns to discussion, but in that discussion the news event ceases to be news and the discussion turns to the issues raised rather than the news itself. So in this way, there is a sense in which the news disappears through everyday use.

Park also argued that events and stories — 'the incidents and the chances that turn up in the game of life' (p. 45) — can be seen as contributions to popular heritage, like legends or ballads. Park concluded that 'news, as a form of knowledge, contributes from its record of events not only to history and to sociology but to folklore and literature' (p. 46). This emphasis on the cultural uses of news has often been echoed since Park. News has been analysed for its dramatic qualities, its particular textual features and conventions. Golding and Elliott point out that 'News stories are, as the term suggests, stories as well as news' (1979: 115), while for James Carey 'news is not information but drama' (1989: 21). Some of the implications of these observations are explored in Chapter 3, but I'll also return to this emphasis on drama later in this section. In particular, I'll build upon a remark by sociologist Charles Bantz. In an essay on conflict within news organizations, Bantz describes news as the 'daily creation of nonfiction drama' (1997: 133). This captures some important aspects of news in an economical phrase; nevertheless, some aspects of the news processes are still absent from this characterization, as I'll discuss below.

News as mosaic

Other approaches to defining news emphasize the forms of the specific media used, as in Marshall McLuhan's typically idiosyncratic and provocative discussion of the newspaper as a cultural form. He contrasts the newspaper with the book, seeing the latter as 'a private confessional form that provides a "point of view"' (1964: 221). The newspaper, in contrast is 'a group confessional form that provides communal participation' (p. 221). What is distinctive about the newspaper, McLuhan suggests, is the 'mosaic' organization of different stories on a single page. For McLuhan, the concept of 'human interest' arises out of the juxtaposition of different topics on a single sheet, and our daily exposure to them as a community.

Take, for instance, the 'world news' page from a random issue of Sydney's *Daily Telegraph* (Saturday 21 August 2004, p. 24). It's a mosaic of five stories. In one we learn of developments in the post-invasion insurgency in Iraq; in another we are told of new allegations against singer Michael Jackson. A third story reports how seven American children have been found somehow abandoned in an orphanage in Nigeria and flown home to Texas, while a fourth relates the details of how Argentinean soccer star Diego Maradona has been captured on video snorting coke while in a rehab clinic. The last story informs us that a Cambodian baby, born with a 10 cm tail, has become the chief family breadwinner, as crowds of people pay money to see her.

What these stories have in common, as the newspaper tells us with a handy label at the top of the page, is that they are all *world* news. It may be hard to believe that they all happened in the *same* world, but they do illustrate McLuhan's observation that the defining characteristic of the newspaper is its mosaic form of organization. This form, McLuhan writes, captures the 'discontinuous variety and incongruity of ordinary life' (1964: 225). McLuhan's point about the newspaper is not restricted to that medium, because newspaper organization has had a huge influence on the structure of broadcast and Internet news as well. The newspaper, suggests McQuail, is 'arguably the archetype as well as the prototype of all modern mass media' (2000: 337), with regular news (organized in mosaic form) at the centre of the structure of radio and television organizations, and of many new media ventures as well.

As Benedict Anderson writes: 'Reading a newspaper is like reading a novel whose author has abandoned any thought of a coherent plot' (1991: 33). Like McLuhan, Anderson highlights the mosaic organization of stories within a newspaper. They are connected, he argues, not just by the coincidence of their all happening within the same approximate timeframe, but also by 'the relationship between the newspaper, as a form of book, and the market' (p. 33). The book, says Anderson, was the first commodity of mass-production, and from this commodity perspective, 'the newspaper is merely an "extreme form" of the book, a book sold on a colossal scale, but of ephemeral popularity. Might we say: one-day best-sellers?' (pp. 34–5). The significance of this ephemeral quality is that it focuses readers on particular stories at the same time, thus fostering the shared sense of specific commonality that Anderson terms *imagined community*; we'll return to this idea in Chapters 3, 5 and 6.

News and time

Among other things, the news is of course what's *new*. News gets its commercial value from being up-to-the-minute. From the telegraph onwards, news has been getting progressively faster, with financial news providers such as Bloomberg and Reuters competing to offer 'up-to-the-second' news (Hartley 2003). Can news be defined in terms of time? Philip Schlesinger has offered an important emphasis on the imperatives of *speed* in the production of news, labelling the production of news 'a stop-watch culture' (1987). The more quickly an event is reported, the more professional the performance is assumed to be (live, rolling news takes this to new levels, as will be discussed in Chapter 7). Getting a story to air as soon as possible after it breaks, beating the competition — these are measures of professionalism. At the same time, however, there is a tension between journalistic values of speed and immediacy and the institutional values that place a high premium on accuracy and reliability. Schlesinger's fieldwork inside the BBC drew him to conclude that speed and immediacy, the meeting of deadlines, were more than responses to market requirements for news. The journalistic emphasis on immediacy was 'a form of fetishism in which to be obsessional about time is to be professional' (1987: 105).

Why does this matter? Schlesinger argues that the emphasis on the ever-present *now* means that 'there is an inherent tendency for the news to be framed in a discontinuous and ahistorical way, and this implies a truncation of "context", and therefore a reduction of meaningfulness' (p. 105). The endless updating, the focus on the present, work against the audience's understanding of underlying processes. The result, as Pierre Bourdieu puts it, is: '... a series of apparently absurd stories that all end up looking the same [...] sequences of events that, having appeared with no explanation, will disappear with no solution' (1998: 7).

In a useful analysis of news and time, Bernard Roshco writes that: '*Timeliness* is inherent in the concept of news, which is distinguished from other kinds of information by the intimation that it is shared as soon as possible after it is learned' (1975: 10, emphasis in original). Roshco is right that timeliness is central to news presentation — think of how time is foregrounded within television news stories: *a short time ago... in news just in... we cross now live to...* More specifically, Roshco identifies three central aspects (1975: 11–13). News is characterized by:

- *recency* — the information has only recently been uncovered or publicized
- *immediacy* — it is published or broadcast as soon after its discovery as possible
- and *currency* — it has some relevance to current issues or concerns for its audiences

This is a useful approach in that it accommodates aspects of news production (recency), distribution (immediacy) and reception (currency). However, Roshco's definition does not have much to say about the specific forms that news takes — information, however timely, is not just relayed without mediation but is shaped into particular formats. Nor does Roshco's definition have much to say about the principles of selection involved: timeliness alone is not enough to ensure an event becomes news, although it is likely to increase the chances. What's more, an important temporal dimension of news is absent from Roshco's discussion — *regularity*. News is built around regular production, distribution and reception — the morning paper, the evening TV bulletin; even rolling news channels such as CNN have a daily programme schedule. This is important in a consideration of the *uses* of news: for example, in Carey's ritual model of communication (1989), in which the daily routines of news consumption can be seen as participation in, and maintenance of, a community (we'll return to this in Chapter 3).

This idea of including the uses — and users — offers an additional perspective in assessing the various definitions of news: for example, audiences (readers, listeners, viewers, Net users) are, at best, implied in Michael Schudson's otherwise very fine definition: 'News is what is publicly notable (within a framework of shared understanding that judges it to be both public and notable). It is also a machinery of notation' (2003: 6). Of notation, yes, but what about reading and discussion, or belief and rejection? These are processes that may be more awkward, uncertain or downright combative than is suggested by the comfortable 'shared understanding' here.

News versus journalism

Any mention of readerships or audiences is also generally missing from contemporary attempts to define journalism, although such attempts can offer much else that's useful to our present discussion. James Carey, for instance, again emphasizing a temporal quality, suggests journalism is 'the whole of the real defined under the category of the present' (2000: 22). John Hartley proposes journalism as the 'sense-making practice of modernity' (1996: 33). Martin Conboy captures a number of important features in this definition: 'Journalism is the working and revision of a combination of novelty, information and entertainment which has the topical, even the ephemeral, very much to the fore' (2004: 3). The idea of 'working and revision' here brings in an important emphasis on newswork as *processes* of production, while the inclusion of 'entertainment' points us towards one of the central tensions in many discussions of news — are news and entertainment compatible? This has implications in many areas, including the rise of tabloid media, broadcast news formats, and the narrative construction of news stories, all of which are considered in later chapters.

One spectacular contemporary definition comes from John Hartley: 'If journalism is a "profession" at all then it is the profession of violence' (2000: 40). Journalism, Hartley argues, is grounded in conflict:

> Journalism's heroic figures are the combative interviewer who won't take no for an answer, the war junkie following death around the world, the adversarial investigative reporter, the crusading paper or programme. The good journalistic watchdog fights for stories that someone doesn't want told; the best stories are those that expose violence and corruption concealed within seemingly respectable institutions, from tin-pot dictatorships to children's homes. Journalism is combat (2000: 40).

This argument does capture much of the mythology of the Fourth Estate ideal. But it perhaps concedes too much to one of the central tenets of that mythology, which conflates 'journalism' with 'investigative journalism'. The news media themselves often emphasize their crusading, investigative role, while downplaying the routine, the mundane, the pre-packaged, and the bureaucratic. The classic statement of this crusading view (and an interesting definition in its own right, if a limited one) is that attributed to the early UK press baron Lord Northcliffe — that news is whatever somebody somewhere wants to suppress. Of course, some journalism (and certainly much of the best journalism) is indeed investigative and premised on the revelation of significant hidden truths (many fine examples from figures such as Martha Gellhorn, Edward Murrow, James Cameron and Seymour Hersh can be found collected in Pilger 2004). But other journalism — other news — can be said to just happen (a train crashes, a shark attacks, a politician resigns, and the stories follow to order). And still more news is produced not *by* journalists, but *for* them, in the form of media releases, photo-opportunities or press conferences: examples of what Daniel Boorstin (1961) labelled 'pseudo-events', and which we'll discuss further in Chapter 5.

We should be clear that the distinction between news and journalism matters, and is worth maintaining. For one thing, not everything that journalists produce should be thought of as news (film reviews, celebrity profiles, and obituaries, to take just three examples). For another thing, the practices of journalism are, self-evidently, what *journalists* do; but the practices of news include things in which we *all* participate — story-telling and argument; reading, viewing, listening and discussing; gossiping and explaining; believing and, at times, scorning and dismissing. News, again, is too important to be left only to journalists.

Journalism is not perhaps a profession (Hartley 1996) but it is, among other things, a craft, a trade, and a body of literature or record which can be both ephemeral and of historical value and importance. News is an institutional product, shaped by the imperatives of news organizations. And news is also a cultural product — conditioned by our expectations (and in turn conditioning them) of character and event, of action and place; it is bound up in our cultural norms of inclusion and exclusion, of forming and sustaining community. But news is not just a product, it is also a complex of practices:

- practices of *production* — story-telling, writing, composing, editing, photographing, filming, recording, uploading; press release and news leak, gaffe and scandal, interview and photo-op
- practices of *distribution* — medium-specific packaging: the newspaper, the TV and radio broadcast, the website and blog; processes of distribution are also important — the schedules, formal properties, technical possibilities and constraints of, for example, a weekly news magazine and a live talkback radio session make possible different kinds of discussion
- and practices of *reception* — viewing, listening, reading and (crucially) talking. News is not just received, but is *used* by its audiences. It may be variously accepted, questioned, snorted at or half-ignored, but each of these is a use.

Conclusion

None of the definitions discussed so far captures the full complexity of the news. Each focuses on a particular aspect — time, narrative, organization — and so underemphasizes others. The definition of news that will be used in this book takes as its starting point Bantz's phrase the 'daily creation of nonfiction drama', introduced above. Bantz encapsulates some important aspects of news in an economical fashion: first, the word 'daily' points to the regularity, the scheduling, the timetabling of news — the news is not something that comes along only occasionally, when 'something happens', but is rather there day in, day out, come what may — if you live in Edinburgh, then Channel 4 news is on at 7pm on weekdays, no matter what; if you live in Manhattan, then the *New York Times* is available in time for your morning coffee, no matter what.

Some people might object to the word 'daily' here. Doesn't it sound a bit dated? What about the ways in which new(er) media technologies, from the VCR to podcasts and SMS, allow users to 'time-shift' the news, to customize the broadcast and print schedules? Can't news organizations distribute and update content more rapidly and more often than just 'daily'? All good points. And it's also true that news websites can be updated on an ongoing basis, and that bloggers keep to no schedule (Bruns & Jacobs 2006), all of which may seem to uncouple online news from the rhythms and constraints of the day (Sparks 2000a).

But 'daily' remains the most useful temporal element to understand the production, distribution and reception of news. Journalists may be on impossibly tight 15-minute deadlines at times, but these occur within their work day — and the word 'journalist' itself, as Hartley (2003) points out, is derived from the French word for 'day'. Live rolling news TV channels can drop everything to follow a developing story, but for most of the time they stick to a daily programme schedule. Much of what is discussed on talkback radio or in news blogs is directly related to the traditional news media's output of the day. And as audiences, too, we integrate the news into our daily routines — the morning paper, the evening news; perhaps some talkback radio in the car and a quick surf through a news website or our favourite blogs at lunchtime. So while there are indeed news outlets that organize themselves around weekly or fortnightly production (*Time* magazine) and those that organize themselves around instantaneous distribution (Bloomberg financial news), the *day* remains the news unit around which both faster and slower schedules can be seen to revolve. News is part of — to borrow a title from de Certeau (1984) — the practice of everyday life (and not just 'everyday' but 'every day' as well).

Second, Bantz's use of the word 'creation' points to the fact that news is constructed. This does not mean it is fantasized or imagined (although there are indeed some lurid instances of made-up news, such as the case of Jayson Blair of the *New York Times,* to which we'll return in Chapter 4), but rather that events and information are shaped to fit the requirements and expectations of both producers and audiences. And third, Bantz's juxtaposition of 'nonfiction' and 'drama' highlights the tensions between truth-telling and story-telling, between information presented as objective fact and simultaneously cast as a story. So 'the daily creation of nonfiction drama' is a good start. But some aspects of the news processes are still absent from this account and need to be added here.

So for the purposes of this book, news will be defined as *the organized daily production, distribution, and uses, of nonfiction drama.* This adds three dimensions to the original phrase. First, it recognizes and emphasizes the need to approach news as something that is *organized* (both by news institutions and for them). It focuses our attention on news as something that is *distributed* through a range of specific media (that is, something that is mediated). And it emphasizes news as something that is received and *used* by audiences (and for that matter something that is used for different purposes by other bodies as well, such as political parties, corporations, celebrities — and other news organizations).

The components of this definition — *organized, daily, production, distribution, uses, nonfiction, drama* — are the coordinates of news as symbolic power, and are the central terms around which the discussion in the rest of this book revolves. The following chapter, 'Know Your Product', turns first to the organization and production of news.

Chapter 2

Know Your Product

'Every newspaper when it reaches the reader is the result of a whole series of selections as to what items shall be printed, in what position they shall be printed, how much space each shall occupy, what emphasis each shall have. There are no objective standards here. There are conventions.' (Lippmann 1922: 223)

On Saturday 1 February 2003, NASA's oldest space shuttle *Columbia* disintegrated in flames at the end of its 16-day research mission. Sixteen minutes away from its scheduled landing, it entered the atmosphere 64 km above the Earth at more than 19,000 kilometres per hour and rained debris down on several US states. Some people found chunks of the shuttle on their roofs. All seven astronauts – four of them first-timers – were killed, including Michael Anderson, one of the few African-American astronauts, Kalpana Chawla, the first Indian-born woman space traveller, and Ilan Ramon, the first Israeli astronaut.

I watched this story develop in Sydney, Australia. By early evening in Sydney (where it was now Sunday 2 February), a mass of detail had been gathered for the early evening TV news report. Channel 7's bulletin included footage of Ilan Ramon's father, who had been watching events live in a TV studio just as the news was starting to look bad. They also showed Ramon's brother speaking immediately after he had heard the news. And then, the network went back to the studio for the newsreader Anne Fulwood to bring home the full horror of the event to Australians, to deliver the local angle with both barrels, as she announced with full gravity: 'Eight Australian spiders were also on board'.

What do we use news for? One snap answer is 'to find out what's happening.' But a moment's reflection suggests that much — perhaps most — of our news diet cannot be easily explained in this way. The space shuttle disaster was certainly 'what's happening.' But the matter of the Australian spiders lost in the crash would probably not meet many people's threshold of important or useful information. The real point of the Space Shuttle Spiders story was shown in the on-screen caption 'Aussie Link to Shuttle.' Other news outlets around the world highlighted different aspects of the event. My intention here is not to ridicule the particular way that this individual story was covered by Channel 7, but rather to note that the simple existence of different versions of the same event reveals the existence of *principles of selection.* To return to the epigraph of this chapter, these do not reflect objective standards, so much as conventions.

One fundamental mechanism through which news organizations exercise symbolic power is the *naming* of an event as news. Not all events qualify as news, and the capacity to make an event into news is a powerful example of symbolic power. This chapter discusses the central aspects of news organizations and their capacity to define reality by defining news. It first considers the concept of 'news values', the organizational influences on the selection and construction of news, and the concept of 'gatekeeping.' It then outlines some of the main arguments surrounding issues of news media ownership, before drawing these strands together in a discussion of Edward Herman and Noam Chomsky's 'propaganda model.'

Principles of selection

The concept of news values has been explored in a number of classic analyses of the principles of selection involved in shaping events into news. Some of these argue that news values are a mechanism for the operation of ideology. The first book authored by the Glasgow University Media Group (GUMG) opened with the claim that the news 'is a sequence of socially manufactured messages, which carry many of the culturally dominant assumptions of our society' (1976: 1). Other arguments around news values concentrate on the bureaucratic dimension. Richard Hoggart contributed a foreword to the same GUMG book, in which he argued that television news was not the result of a simple collection of the day's self-evident 'nuggets of each day's hard news', but rather a highly constructed product: 'There is simply too much possible material; there have to be filters, devices to select what shall be shown, in what order, at what length and with what stresses' (Hoggart 1976: ix–x).

These two positions, which are by no means mutually exclusive, are captured more fully in the following claims, each drawn from a book whose very title encapsulates the concept of news values. First, UK cultural studies pioneer Stuart Hall, from a contribution to the book *The Manufacture of News,* with a perspective that highlights the news as ideological:

> Journalists speak of 'the news' as if events select themselves. Further, they speak as if which is the 'most significant' news story, and which 'news angles' are most salient are divinely inspired. Yet of the millions of events which occur every day in the world, only a tiny proportion ever become visible as 'potential news stories': and of this proportion, only a small fraction are actually produced as the day's news in the news media. We appear to be dealing, then, with a 'deep structure' whose function as a selective device is untransparent even to those who professionally most know how to operate it (Hall 1981: 234–5).

Second, US sociologist Herbert Gans, from his book *Deciding What's News,* with a perspective that highlights the news as bureaucratic:

> In reporting the news about a nation [...] journalists could, in theory, choose from billions of potential activities. In fact, however, they can learn about only a tiny fraction of actors and activities; and having limited air time and magazine space, they must select an even tinier fraction. More important, they cannot decide anew every day or week how to select the fraction that will appear on the news; instead, they must routinize their task in order to make it manageable (Gans 1979: 78).

This emphasis on routines is summed up neatly in the title of a 1973 essay by Gaye Tuchman 'Making News by Doing Work: Routinizing the Unexpected' (see also Eliasoph 1997). People at work, Tuchman notes, tend to have too much work to do, and so develop coping strategies and routines to manage the flow of tasks. For news workers, this is especially complex as (like fire fighters or ambulance drivers) their work *routines* have to be based around the *unexpected.*

The title of Tuchman's essay is significant. Throughout the critical literature, analysts write about the *making* of news or the *construction* of news, rather than just the *reporting* of news. Schudson is surely right when he says that many journalists will find this 'offensive' (2000: 176). So it is important to emphasize that to talk about 'constructing' or 'making' the news is not the same thing as accusing journalists of making the news *up*. This discourse is not about inaccuracy or bias or sensationalism, and it is not about lying. Rather, it is about the simple fact that events and news are not the same thing. Events are turned into news by news organizations. News values are central to this process. News values are a manifestation of the symbolic power that accrues to recognized media organizations. They define a particular kind of world-view as *the* news, and in so doing make a claim on the definition of reality.

What does it mean to speak of news values? These, according to Golding and Elliott, 'are qualities of events or of their journalistic construction, whose relative absence or presence recommends them for inclusion in the news product. The more of such qualities a story exhibits, the greater its chances of inclusion' (1979: 114). But news values are not just selection criteria — they are also presentation guidelines, invoked in questions of sequencing, emphasizing or omitting stories from the final product. While Hall argues that these values are untransparent and mysterious even to those who use them the most expertly, Golding and Elliott discuss them as banal workplace procedures on questions of emphasis, inclusion or omission, and sequencing and prioritizing of items within the overall news structure.

A quick glance at the front pages of a tabloid and a broadsheet is generally sufficient to show that news values vary from institution to institution, and relate strongly to perceptions of the target audience. We should also note that news values vary across cultural contexts. For example, in November 2002, bush fires ravaged large areas of suburban Sydney, and dominated the headlines for a week. Local radio became virtually an information hotline for people in affected areas, with street-by-street updates in some cases. This was a disaster story on a local scale. In the UK, however, the fires were reported as an *entertainment* item. Here is how the *Guardian* had it:

> Sydney bushfires ravage *Home and Away* set. Bushfires have destroyed the set of Channel 5's Australian soap *Home and Away* as searing

summer temperatures wreak havoc around Sydney. The programme's storylines will not be affected because the show is filmed four months in advance of broadcast (5 December 2002).

The death of Princess Diana in 1997 offers another example: in the UK this was easily the biggest story of the year, perhaps of the decade; in Vietnam, on the other hand, it made only page three of one leading paper, two weeks after the event, under the headline 'Beautiful Woman Dies' (Thomas 1997).

News values

The key contribution to the study of news values remains Galtung and Ruge's 1965 essay on foreign news coverage, which identifies a list of factors that can influence an event's chances of becoming news. An interesting claim within Galtung and Ruge's article is that these news criteria lead to inevitable distortions: particular factors may influence selection, but once selected, those factors will be accentuated, leading to distortion. This essay is widely anthologized, widely cited, and widely taken as a starting point for further elaborations on the topic, although it has also been subject to serious criticism (Tunstall 1971: 21, Harcup & O'Neill 2001, Brighton & Foy 2007). What is not always noted is that Galtung and Ruge end their study by addressing the implications of their findings — this may be because one of the most cited versions of their text (Galtung & Ruge 1981) is an edited extract that omits this section. So in reading the following list of Galtung and Ruge's news values, note that those authors perceive them to represent problems.

Frequency. By frequency, Galtung and Ruge mean 'the time-span needed for the event to unfold itself and acquire meaning' (1965: 66). This refers to whether an event happens within a time-frame that enables it to be incorporated into the scheduled news-cycle. Does it fit the deadline?

Threshold. An event has to have a certain size, although what that size is depends on the kind of event.

Unambiguity. The more clear and unambiguous an event is, the easier it is to report (compare this with the over-riding criterion of 'frequency').

Meaningfulness. Is an event something that can be interpreted by the intended audience. Will they see it as relevant?

Consonance. This one can seem a little counter-intuitive: it suggests that the news is what we expect to happen, and in this sense, suggest Galtung and Ruge: '"news" are actually "olds", because they correspond to what one expects to happen' (1965: 67). They confirm our picture of how the world works.

Unexpectedness. This complements rather than contradicts the previous factor, because it is the unexpected event within the consonant that makes the news. For instance, a plane crash is always an unexpected event. But in an awful way it is also consonant with our expectations, with our perceptions of the dangers of flight.

Continuity. Once something becomes news, it can become a running story and maintain its position on the news agenda. The channel, as Galtung and Ruge have it, has been opened.

Composition. News stories are generally not presented as individual items, but within larger news objects or artefacts — a morning newspaper, the evening TV news broadcast, a website. Such artefacts are composed to meet certain ideas of variety and balance.

These factors, suggest Galtung and Ruge, exert a powerful influence on the selection of one story over another; they also list a further four factors that they suggest are culturally-specific to the 'north-western corner of the world' (1965: 68).

These are: *elite nations* and *elite people*. Events happening in and to certain high-status nations and to certain high-status people are more likely to become news than others. *Personalization*. Can the story be personalized? Can it be made to be a story about *someone* rather than about, say, complex and slowly-evolving social structures or economic processes? *Negativity*. Galtung and Ruge argue this is a culture-bound preference, but we should note that their own explanation for it is bound up with their earlier list of institutional factors: bad news will fit the timing demands of the news-cycle. It's likely to be unambiguous — if a bomb goes off in an orphanage, we're not likely to argue about whether or not it's a good thing. Bad news is also likely to be consonant with many of our expectations of the world, and at the same time is more likely to be unexpected.

Is this list useful? Let's again take the *Columbia* event as our example. How does this relate to Galtung and Ruge's news values? In terms of *frequency*, the event took only seconds to happen (although in this respect it couldn't compare with the 1986 *Challenger* shuttle explosion which was broadcast live on TV). In terms of *threshold* it represents a guaranteed story by many different measures: a spacecraft exploding with the loss of all on board — now *that's* a story. Moreover, it is an *unambiguous* event, with little in the way of scope for competing interpretations about the nature and meaning of what happened — it is an unambiguously unfortunate event, with seven people dead. It is both *consonant* with our deeper expectations of the space programme (a dangerous activity with a history of accidents) and at the same time *unexpected* — nobody expected this particular shuttle would blow up at this particular moment. It relates to *elite people* — who could be more elite than an astronaut? — and to an *elite nation*. It is a story that is easy to *personalize* — not only in narrating the deaths of particular astronauts, but in involving their families and colleagues for comment. And finally, of course, it is *negative*.

But by this point we might agree that simply going through Galtung and Ruge's list like that, ticking off each news value in turn, is not especially useful — measuring stories *that are already news* to see whether they *are* news is an exercise of little value. The usefulness of such models is more that they have a degree of predictive value in terms of what is likely to make the news (Tumber 1999: 4) and what is likely to be excluded (McQuail 2000: 343). They demonstrate one mechanism for the exercise of symbolic power — the definition of reality by deciding what counts as news.

On one level, the example of the *Columbia* disaster may seem like a no-brainer — is it *news? The space shuttle blew up!* Some British papers, including the *Sunday Telegraph* and the *Sunday Times*, gave over the entire front page to the story, withdrawing their usual masthead previews of features inside. The *Telegraph* gave more than half that page to a colour portrait of the crew, headed 'They Stood No Chance'. The *News of the World* ran more than ten pages on the shuttle. And yet not everyone agreed, and the event did in fact generate some debate about its value as news — a debate that hinged on concepts of news value and on the perceived exclusion of equally news-worthy stories. Three days after the accident (4 February 2003, p. 2), one *Guardian* journalist wrote a column attacking the hierarchy of values that led to so much coverage of the deaths of seven astronauts, but only a total of 350 words of UK newspaper coverage to the deaths of seven schoolchildren in an avalanche that same weekend. Various current and former editors were interviewed for that piece, all of whom offered defences or critiques of the coverage in terms that could have come straight from Galtung and Ruge's model: 'News value is equivalent to surprise' (Dominic Lawson, *Sunday Telegraph* editor); the *Columbia* story 'ticks a lot of boxes' (Roger Alton, *Observer* editor); 'There is a hierarchy of death' (Roy Greenslade, former *Daily Mirror* editor).

A number of other writers have built on Galtung and Ruge's discussion, which focused on foreign news coverage in newspapers. Golding and Elliott examined news values in TV production, producing a list which is to a large extent an elaboration of Galtung and Ruge's — so they follow them in discussing elites, personalization, negativity, frequency — but there are some important additions. One of these is *drama,* to which we'll turn in Chapter 3; another is news as *entertainment,* which we'll discuss in Chapter 6; still another is the importance of *visuality,* on which we'll focus in the next chapter — an event can become news purely because there is a good photo, and TV, obviously, depends to an even greater extent on the availability of images. A worthwhile experiment is watching a TV news item, counting the different visual images used, and then asking which of them were actually necessary to the audience's understanding of the story.

As already noted, Galtung and Ruge perceive their list of 12 news values to represent problems, and propose a list of solutions, including: greater emphasis in reporting on long-term processes rather than just short-term events; more stories about 'the trivial' to counter the image of the world as endless drama; increased emphasis on what they describe as 'complex and ambiguous events, not necessarily with any effort to interpret them'; more coverage of culturally remote and distinct material (perhaps by exchanging columns between newspapers from different cultures, for instance) (1965: 84–5). Galtung and Ruge also propose greater emphasis on the frequent and the predictable and more emphasis on continuity — not just on reporting discrete events, but on their follow-up and resolution. They also call for, among other things, more news about non-elite nations and non-elite people, and more positive news (1965: 85).

Some aspects of Galtung and Ruge's list of proposed reforms have been addressed in some ways since it was composed in the mid-1960s. Many newspapers, for example, now have weekend news review sections, where the week's main stories can be situated within a somewhat broader context and discussed at somewhat greater length. Moreover, developments in technology have meant that more news from culturally remote parts of the world is indeed now circulated globally, although often in ways that very much still conform to expectations, stereotypes and consonance.

Why does the concept of news values matter? I'll suggest two reasons here. First, while many people perhaps imagine news to be what individual journalists make it to be, news is arguably better thought of as an institutional product — as Golding and Elliott (1979: 207) have pointed out, the news does not change all that much when individual journalists come and go. We should probably not overstate the extent to which journalists' agency is subordinate to the structures of news organizations, and Cottle (2003a) is right to call for further research to be done which examines the extent to which journalists operate as knowing, conscious agents, rather than as replaceable cogs. Nevertheless, journalists — like all of us — do operate under significant constraints, and this poses problems for those who would like to blame all news of which they disapprove on the personal bias of reporters.

One interesting consequence of this emphasis on news as an institutional product is that it is in the interests of many social groups and actors to accommodate the demands of news organizations as best they can: Mark Fishman writes that '*the world is bureaucratically organized for journalists*' (1980: 51, original emphasis). He goes on:

> The news organization needs reliable, predictable, scheduled quantities of raw materials because it is set up to process these in reliable, predictable, scheduled ways in order to turn out a standard product (the newspaper) at the same time every day. [...] Whether one is turning lumber into toothpicks, people into clients, or court files into news stories, the flow of raw materials must be controlled or at least made predictable (Fishman 1980: 143).

Events that don't conform to this bureaucratic structure are likely to go unreported, left as though invisible. Moreover, this system works to the advantage of the *status quo*: 'Routine news', argues Fishman, 'leaves the existing political order intact, at the same time that it enumerates the flaws' (1980: 139).

The second reason why news values matter is that if there are principles of selection in use, then this suggests that the news could be selected and constructed differently. If the news is not a natural category of self-selecting events, then it is open to challenge and change. News values, Golding and Elliott argue, work to inhibit social change by obscuring social relationships; not in a deliberate way, but as part of the application of institutional news values. For instance, take the imperative of *frequency* — it means that news is about the present and the very immediate past. This can lead to, as Golding and Elliott put it: 'the loss of a sense of social process. News is about the present, or the immediate past. It is an account of today's events. The world of broadcast news is a display of single events, making history indeed "one damn thing after another"' (1979: 209). This absence of context, this focus on the event, is key to news. Todd Gitlin criticizes the routine journalistic approach as: 'cover the event, not the condition; the conflict, not the consensus; the fact that "advances the story", not the one that explains it' (1980: 122–3). And while acknowledging the proliferation of explanatory and contextualizing genres such as weekend news review sections, Gitlin's point still stands. Chambers, Steiner and Fleming (2004) emphasize how news values reflect male perspectives on what matters and how to present this, and that a greater representation of women in news industries and women's perspectives on the news generate a quite different form of news, including greater personalization of issues and more use of women sources.

Gatekeeping

This chapter emphasizes news as an institutional product: as something that is produced by and within news organizations (and, as we'll discuss in Chapter 5, in many cases *for* news organizations). It follows, then, that news organizations as work environments are important. They are organizations in which symbolic power is concentrated. Some of the most cited 'classic' news studies are concerned with the daily routines of reporters and their places of work. Much of the flavour of this kind of study can be inferred from the titles of the books — *Making The News, Manufacturing The News, Putting 'Reality' Together* (Tumber 1999: xvi). While important work in this area continues to be done (such as Küng-

Shankleman 2000, Tunstall 2001, Tuchman 2002, Cottle 2003b, Boczkowski 2004) we should note that some of these studies are now quite old, with the high-water mark of this kind of research being the 1970s (Tunstall 1971, Sigelman 1973, Tuchman 1978, Gans 1979, Golding & Elliott 1979, Fishman 1980, Schlesinger 1987 [1978]; see also Ericson, Baranek & Chan 1987). Much has changed since then, and so we should probably not read these studies today as up-to-date accounts of daily work practices, organizational structures or routines. However, where the classic studies most definitely do endure is in demonstrating the extent to which the news is shaped by organizational structures, by time and economic constraints, and by institutional imperatives.

One of the earliest significant contributions to this field was the concept — and metaphor — of gatekeeping. In Pamela Shoemaker's definition, 'gatekeeping is the process by which the billions of messages that are available in the world get cut down and transformed into the hundreds of messages that reach a given person on a given day' (1991: 1). From this definition it is clear that the concept shares much ground with that of news values, in its concern with the principles of selection and the variable criteria that affect the inclusion or exclusion of news items. However, it differs from news values in its emphasis on the agency of people in gatekeeping roles. As McQuail notes (2000: 296), the concept of gatekeeping has much purchase and applicability beyond the field of news, and can be applied to many other fields of cultural production (such as book publishing or the music industry, for example). Indeed, as Shoemaker suggests, 'all communication workers are gatekeepers to some degree, for gatekeeping is an integral part of the overall process of selecting and producing messages' (1991: 2).

The metaphor was first applied to news production in David Manning White's 1950 study of a lone wire service editor for an American regional newspaper, whom White dubbed 'Mr Gates'. White analysed the reasons Mr Gates gave for variously rejecting some 90% of the agency stories he received. White's analysis highlighted the subjective nature of the selection process, and its dependence upon the experience, preferences and values of the individual gatekeeper. But it does rather overstate the autonomy of that gatekeeper, something that White appears to acknowledge in remarks about the unexamined influence of other editors both within a given organization and working for its competitors.

Moreover, as Mr Gates dealt with pre-packaged stories from news agencies we should be wary about over-generalizing from his practices to those of news workers in other fields, where the news-creation process may be more complex than that suggested by the straightforward selection process in White's study. Several authors have also pointed out that Mr Gates's selections were strongly influenced by those of the gatekeepers at the wire services on whom he relied (McCombs & Shaw 1976, Whitney & Becker 1982).

The concept has been much elaborated and refined since White's day. Gieber (1999) [1964] argued that the individual gatekeeper was less important than the constraints of the organization for which that gatekeeper worked. The routines, the resources, and the institutional culture of the news organization were all factors that constrained the gatekeeper from exercising personal choice over stories. Breed (1999) [1955] discussed the institutional factors that socialized journalists into the mind-set of the organization. From this perspective, journalists learn the ropes of their organization's policy — the angle it takes on key issues — through the desire to be part of the group and the rewards of being part of that group (such as status). Bleske (1997) [1991] recreated White's original study with a female gatekeeper — Ms Gates — to assess whether gender played a role in story selection. The results of that particular question were inconclusive, but Bleske's study provided a useful historical comparison with White's, with his Ms Gates working in a larger organization and using different technology than did Mr Gates. Despite these differences, Bleske's research suggests that while individual gatekeepers retained a degree of subjective autonomy more than four decades after White's study, their selections were still strongly influenced by the emphases and categories of the wire services. Berkowitz (1999) [1990] adapted the approach for local TV news, looking for patterns in the selection and rejection of stories. He found that story selection was far more of a group activity than the individual decision-making usually assumed in gatekeeper studies, and that there were multiple gates a story had to pass through on its way to air (with, for example, breaking news likely to push planned stories off the broadcast, while lack of resources could in turn shut the gate on breaking news items).

Shoemaker (1991) offers both a comprehensive overview of this work and a revised model of her own. She notes that gatekeeping is a term that could in principle be applied to the activities of all news workers, given that it describes a fundamental aspect of the work of selecting, shaping and producing media content. Shoemaker's model retains White's focus on the subjectivity of the gatekeeper (their preferences, values and assumptions) but locates this firmly within a framework of constraints — routines, organizational culture, external forces and pressures, and the social contexts within which news is produced. Importantly, Shoemaker highlights not only the importance of contending types of news source, including governments, interest groups, advertisers and PR, but also the role of the audience in shaping the assumptions of the news organization and providing feedback. The usefulness of this model is that it widens the focus, seeing the gatekeeper not as an individual like Mr Gates but as the institution itself. Gatekeeping then becomes not just a daily work routine but a central mechanism by which news organizations exercise symbolic power.

The most important refinement to the concept of gatekeeping in recent years is Axel Bruns's term 'gatewatching', which he developed to discuss online participatory news projects such as Indymedia (see Chapter 8) and blogs (see Chapter 4). Bruns distinguishes between three different dimensions of gatekeeping: at the *input* stage (in what news organizations decide to cover), at the *output* stage (in what they decide to publish), and at the *response* stage (in the possibilities offered — or withheld — for audiences to add their voices) (2005: 11–12). Each of these moments of gatekeeping is about ruling things *out* — gatewatching, in contrast, is about ruling things *in*. Gatewatching projects monitor the outputs of other media organizations and point their users towards the particularly noteworthy. As it is built around the hyperlink, it's a practice distinctive to the Net. Many of the most popular blogs practice gatewatching in that they keep track of what's being published elsewhere, and link to what they think is worthwhile: annotating, elaborating, debating. Gatewatching is not just about *publishing*, but also about *publicising* (Bruns 2005: 19).

Bad company?

The one aspect of media organization and production that has attracted most attention is the question of who owns the media, and the complex questions of power, influence and control that follow from this. Does it matter who owns the media? Gillian Doyle identifies three groups to whom it matters a great deal (2002a: 171–3). It matters to the media owners themselves, who are tireless lobbyists with especially deep pockets, keen to carve out commercial and regulatory advantage. It matters to politicians, whose careers cannot be disentangled from the media, and who are often wary of offending a powerful news outlet: 'Outside the sphere of the media', as Manuel Castells observes, 'there is only political marginality' (2004: 370). And of course media ownership matters to audiences, in that the range of ideas to which we have access may be directly constrained by questions of profit: if the market is all, then only ideas that are *marketable* are likely to be marketed (Keane 1991: 90).

This book has already argued that news is bound up with questions of symbolic power (Bourdieu 1991, Thompson 1995). An important contribution to this concept is Couldry's insistence that symbolic power must be understood as something that is unequally distributed — large media organizations have enormous concentrations of symbolic power (2003: 38–9). One result of this is that questions of ownership are bound up with questions of diversity of opinion. As McChesney points out, there is an apparent contradiction between: 'a for-profit, highly concentrated, advertising-saturated, corporate media system and the communication requirements of a democratic society' (McChesney 1999: ix). News, perhaps more than any other media form, demands a plurality of voices and perspectives. It is important that we are exposed to as full a range of the contending positions on an important topic as is realistically possible. As Doyle suggests, this pluralist perspective can be understood as being about 'diversity within what is made available, rather than within what is actually consumed. It is about public access to a range of voices and a range of content, irrespective of patterns of demand' (Doyle 2002a: 12). This is a crucial argument in support of public service broadcasting (see Chapter 7) and alternative news organizations such as Indymedia (see Chapter 8).

Who owns the news media? Fewer people than before. One of the most striking features of the global communications environment is the ongoing concentration of ownership in an ever-smaller grouping of transnational corporations (Herman and McChesney 1997). In Graham Murdock's description, these are 'massive communications conglomerates with an unrivalled capacity to shape the symbolic environment which we all inhabit' (1990: 2). In 1983 Ben Bagdikian published *The Media Monopoly*, detailing how, in the United States, media production and distribution were effectively controlled by the 50 or so largest firms and conglomerates. With each revised edition of the book, this number has dwindled until the 2004 seventh edition (now re-titled *The New Media Monopoly*) surveyed a field dominated by just five major corporate entities: Time Warner, Disney, Bertelsmann, Viacom and News Corporation.

Of these five, only News Corporation has a figurehead who is well-known to the general public — Rupert Murdoch. So well-known is he that when the late playwright Dennis Potter revealed on television in 1994 that he had named his terminal cancer 'Rupert', no elaboration was necessary. Murdoch has attracted great academic, political and popular scrutiny around the world as he has moved into successive territories. This section will focus on Murdoch as an example, but it's important to note that he is only an example here, not the entire concept in himself. Media owners may increasingly be institutional investors rather than lone moguls, but Murdoch enables a personification of otherwise impersonal and abstract economic forces.

News Corporation

Murdoch's career began when he inherited an Adelaide newspaper in 1953. He built on this inheritance in Australia throughout the 1950s, expanding into the UK market in the late 1960s with *The Sun* and the *News of the World*. The 1970s and 1980s were marked by moves into the US, acquiring the *New York Post* in 1976, and TV stations, followed by Twentieth Century Fox in 1985 and the creation of the Fox network. The 1990s and first decade of the twenty-first century saw News become a genuinely global force, with the world's most extensive network of broadcast satellites, and a strong emphasis on expanding into China and India (Munster 1985, Shawcross 1992, Chenoweth 2001, Page 2003, Croteau & Hoynes 2005).

News Corporation's annual report for 2007 records revenues of over US$28 billion. The empire spans cinema (including Twentieth Century Fox); network, cable and satellite television in Europe and Australia, India and China, Latin America and the US (including the Fox News Channel); magazines (the *Weekly Standard*);

book publishing (HarperCollins); an expanding online presence (including MySpace.com); and of course newspapers: its newspaper interests the include the *Wall Street Journal* and the *New York Post*, and *The Sun* and the *Times* in the UK — *The Sun* alone regularly sells over three million copies a day. In Australia, News Corporation's annual report says it owns 'Approximately 145' newspapers (have they lost exact count?), including the country's biggest-selling daily, the Melbourne *Herald Sun*, and its only national broadsheet the *Australian*.

Does owning a media outlet mean complete control of its output? And what of the audience? Is a monopoly of the means of production the same thing as a monopoly of the production of meaning? While a full overview of media economics is beyond the scope of this book (see Murdock 1982, Doyle 2002b, Croteau & Hoynes 2005), the following section highlights some fundamental ways in which media owners can influence both the *content* and the *contexts* of news (cf. Murdock 1990: 7). It shows how economic power can become one kind of authority to exercise symbolic power. On the one hand, owners can intervene in the output of content, either directly (rewriting the editorial column) or by creating a workplace climate of shared understanding, in which the first form of intervention becomes less necessary. On the other hand, they can shape the wider media environment in which they do business, either through competition or through lobbying for favourable policy outcomes. Such powers are now deployed within an increasingly global and concentrated media environment (Murdock 1990). 'For the first time in media history', writes Murdoch in News Corporation's 2006 Annual Report, 'complete access to a truly global audience is within our grasp' (p. 5). Let's consider each of these powers in turn.

Influencing content

First, we need to examine the potential that an owner such as Rupert Murdoch has to directly intervene in the day-to-day coverage of stories and issues. This question is closely connected with his own political preferences and ideological convictions. Andrew Neil, who edited Murdoch's *Sunday Times* for over a decade, writes of Murdoch that he is 'much more right-wing than is generally thought' (1996: 166), and expects his papers to broadly support what he believes in, which Neil sums up as '... a radical-right dose of free-market economics, the social agenda of the Christian Moral Majority and hardline conservative views on subjects like drugs, abortion, law and order, and defence' (1996: 165).

However, it is clear that Murdoch's approach to politics is marked more by pragmatism than anything else, and that ideological conviction will always take a back-seat to whatever position is required to advance his commercial interests — as his biographer George Munster put it, 'The business of Rupert Murdoch was business' (1985: 135). Murdoch appears to like backing winners, and may be more motivated by business considerations than political principle. So in successive UK elections, for example, *The Sun* has veered from crucifying the Labour party to glorifying them. On the day of the 1992 poll, the front page displayed a picture of then-Labour leader Neil Kinnock with his head crammed inside a light bulb and the request that 'If Neil Kinnock wins today will the last person to leave Britain please turn out the lights.' *The Sun* later devoted its front page to the boast 'It's The Sun Wot Won It' (Greenslade 2003: 612). By the next election in 1997, the paper had switched its support to Labour and the headline was 'The Sun Backs Blair'. In 2005 the paper found a way to sustain this view while simultaneously cross-promoting Fox's latest *Star Wars* film, which was due for release a few days later: *The Sun*'s election day front cover was given over to an image of Tony Blair dressed as a Jedi and wielding a light sabre, with the headline 'May The Votes Be With You'.

Andrew Neil writes:

> There is a common myth among those who think Rupert Murdoch has too much power and influence that he controls every aspect of his newspapers on three continents, dictating an editorial before breakfast, writing headlines over lunch and deciding which politician to discredit over dinner. He has been known to do all three. But he does not generally work like that: his control is far more subtle (Neil 1996: 164).

There is no shortage of anecdotes about Murdoch taking an active or participatory role in the content of his newspapers. In the early 1970s Murdoch's support for the Australian Labor Party went as far as helping with the writing of a press release, which subsequently appeared in his newspapers as a news item (Tiffen 1989, Street 2001, Page 2003). Murdoch turned against Labor after they came to power and in the bitter election of 1975, after the dismissal of the Whitlam Labor government by the Governor-General, journalists at Murdoch's paper the *Australian* actually went on strike in protest at biased headlines and editorials in their own paper (printers also refused to handle some papers, and wharf labourers refused to process the newsprint). Murdoch told the journalists that if they wanted editorial input they could start their own papers (Munster 1985: 112).

An increasingly consistent pattern can be discerned in which Murdoch is seen to operate media outlets that are nakedly partisan, and bold in displaying and promoting particular points of view (Allan 2005). The aggressively right-wing Fox News was announced in 1996 in order to counter 'what Murdoch saw as CNN's "left-wing bias"' (Chenoweth 2001: 146). Fox News has startled some viewers and commentators with the stridency of its positions (Greenwald 2004). One example should give the flavour of the network: its host reporting a development in Iraq on 26 March 2003, with the words 'Don't look now, but the Shiites have hit the fan'. Yet Fox's coverage of the 2003 Iraq conflict was not inconsistent with the way that *The Sun* had presented the Falklands War 20 years earlier. The paper's infamous 'Gotcha' headline reported in a flippant style the sinking of the Argentinean ship the *General Belgrano* by the British Navy:

> The Navy had the Argies on their knees last night after a devastating double punch. WALLOP: They torpedoed the 14,000-ton Argentina cruiser *General Belgrano* and left it a useless wreck. WALLOP: Task Force helicopters sank one Argentine patrol boat and severely damaged another. The *Belgrano*, which survived the Pearl Harbour attack when it belonged to the U.S. Navy, had been asking for trouble all day [...] But the *Belgrano* and its 1,000 crew needn't worry about the war for some time now (4 May 1982, p. 1).

Three hundred and sixty-eight people had died. *The Sun*'s editor Kelvin MacKenzie was said to have been shocked by the combination of the 'Gotcha' headline and the death toll, and later editions of the day's paper ran with the revised headline 'Did 1200 Argies Drown?' (Greenslade 2003: 444–5.). Murdoch, however, was reported to have said it shouldn't have been changed, with one observer attributing to him the words 'Seemed like a bloody good headline to me' (Page 2003: 333).

A second important way in which owners can influence content is through the creation of a workplace culture in which direct intervention becomes unnecessary. Andrew Neil writes in his memoirs that Murdoch selects editors '...who are generally on the same wavelength as him' and who share 'a set of common assumptions about politics and society' (1996: 164). Making use of those assumptions and staying on that wavelength are part of the editor's role:

> Even when [Murdoch] has not expressed an interest or shown any desire to become involved, or you think his attention is absorbed in another part of his vast empire, such is his omnipresence that you strive to keep in mind whatever you think his wishes are (Neil 1996: 161).

Writing in the UK's *Guardian* newspaper (17 February 2003, p. 2), former tabloid editor Roy Greenslade pointed to one of the more remarkable coincidences of recent times. As head of News Corporation, Rupert Murdoch operates some 175 newspapers, publishing 40 million copies a week. Greenslade's survey of the leading Murdoch dailies in key territories showed them all to be staunchly behind the Iraq war, even though there was considerable variation in public opinion. 'What a guy!', wrote Greenslade. 'You have got to admit that Rupert Murdoch is one canny press tycoon because he has an unerring ability to choose editors across the world who think just like him. How else can we explain the extraordinary unity of thought in his newspaper empire about the need to make war on Iraq?'

Influencing contexts

Perhaps more significant than these potential influences on content are the ways in which media owners can shape and affect the *contexts* in which they work, both commercial (through competition) and regulatory (through lobbying).

Taking the UK newspaper industry as our example, there are many instances of Murdoch using his newspapers to radically re-shape the broader media landscape. One would be the relocation of his newspaper facilities to the purpose-built plant at Wapping in 1986, a move that led to an industrial dispute which dragged on for over a year, characterized by grim images of razor wire and sabotage (Neil 1996, Chenoweth 2001). In making the move,

Murdoch ditched the powerful printers' unions and replaced them with members of an electricians' union, slashing many jobs in the process and re-drawing the shape of the newspaper industry in the UK.

There is also a history of Murdoch initiating aggressive price wars. In the early 1980s he responded to the challenge to *The Sun* from *The Star,* by not only cutting *The Sun*'s price to match it but also by initiating the pricy gimmick of an expensive bingo game. (Page 2003: 331). In September 1993 *The Times* suddenly reduced its cover price from 45p to 30p. Over the next few years, the price would fall as low as 10p on Mondays (after newsagents established that they weren't prepared to give it away for free) and 20p on Tuesday–Fridays (Doyle 2002b: 131–4). During the eight years of this campaign the circulation of the paper doubled, and its share of the quality market (made up of *The Times, Daily Telegraph, Guardian* and *Independent*) increased from 17% at the start of the price campaign to 30% in August 2000. Murdoch's extensive resources made it possible to underwrite the heavy losses sustained by *The Times* throughout this period (and indeed to sell the paper at below cost-price, placing severe pressure on the *Independent* in particular).

Finally, media owners can affect the context of news production, distribution and reception by attempting to have the legal frameworks that constrain their activities adjusted in their favour. Murdoch's career is marked by an enormous capacity to lobby, and to have regulations crafted to his advantage or simply waived. He took US citizenship in 1985 but still needed waivers on the cross-media ownership laws to enable him to own newspapers and TV stations at the same time. While this was going ahead (and while he was setting up the Wapping coup), he simultaneously had to placate the Australian authorities and tax office, who had given him significant concessions on the grounds that he was still, despite all the evidence, an Australian resident (he was, for example, allowed to own TV stations, despite a ban on foreign ownership) (Chenoweth 2001). In 1995 he removed the BBC from the offerings on his Star Television satellite service, to placate Chinese authorities who found BBC news items too critical (McChesney 1999: 115, Bagdikian 2004: 39).

He is a frequent contributor of campaign donations, and has given lucrative book contracts with large advances to senior politicians such as Margaret Thatcher, despite political books rarely being big sellers (McChesney 1999). Major political figures such as Rudy Giuliani and Tony Blair have been implicated as lobbying on Murdoch's behalf (Chenoweth 2001). Blair generated particularly hostile press when he was seen to intervene for Murdoch with the Italian government in 1998 (a year after being elected, with Murdoch's strong endorsement in the UK papers). Chenoweth suggests that such dealings reveal that News Corporation, as a genuinely global operation, has corporate objectives that are not necessarily compatible with the national interest of any one country (2001: 288), which exposes politicians who support it to potential risks.

Manufacturing consent?

> 'See, in my line of work you got to keep repeating things over and over and over again for the truth to sink in, to kind of catapult the propaganda'.
> (George W. Bush, quoted, *inter alia*, in *Sydney Morning Herald* 31 December 2005, p. 12).

The question of concentrated ownership is central to Herman and Chomsky's propaganda model, to which we now turn. The propaganda model enables us to tie together the various perspectives canvassed in this chapter — news values, institutional constraints, gatekeeping and commercial ownership. It is presented in Herman and Chomsky's book *Manufacturing Consent* (1988), perhaps the only academic study for which there is not only a film-of-the-book (dir. Achbar and Wintonick 1992) but also a book-of-the-film-of-the-book (Achbar 1994). Somewhere between *Manufacturing Consent* and his book *9-11* (2001a), Chomsky crossed over from public intellectual to academic celebrity, and he has been the subject of a number of films. All of this tends to marginalize the contribution of Edward Herman somewhat, and so it is important to stress that the propaganda model is co-authored.

Herman and Chomsky's central argument is that the media 'serve to mobilize support for the special interests that dominate the state and private activity' (1988: xi). This strikes a discordant note with many popular views of the media, which have them as the classic Fourth Estate, as the questioning and independent watchdog of the people (see Chapter 4 below). Herman and Chomsky see the news media more as lapdog than watchdog, because the most powerful sectors of society are able to set the media agenda: 'to fix the premises of discourse, to decide what the general populace is allowed to see, hear, and think about, and to "manage" public opinion by regular propaganda campaigns' (1988: xi). The essence of the propaganda model, in Chomsky's words is that: 'you'd expect institutions to work in their own interests, because if they didn't they wouldn't be able to function for very long' (Chomsky quoted in Mitchell & Schoeffel 2002: 14–15).

Herman and Chomsky argue that information must pass through a series of five 'filters' in order to qualify as news. What remains — 'cleansed residue' (1988: 2) — represents a view of the world that is favourable to powerful corporate interests. Media debate inevitably reinforces a limited range of assumptions that reflect the interests of powerful institutions, so by representing only a limited range of debate, the basic premises of the debate are validated (Chomsky 2001b).

The five 'filters' identified by Herman and Chomsky are:

- the size and concentrated ownership of commercial news media
- their reliance on advertising as a source of revenue
- their reliance on official sources of information, for reasons of cost, shared interests, and credibility. These include government, business, the military, and 'experts' funded by each of these; see Chapter 5 below
- their vulnerability to organized criticism, or 'flak', ranging from letter-writing campaigns (such as that targeting veteran correspondent Peter Arnett in the lead-up to the 2003 Iraq invasion) to new laws, and
- an ideological position which presents 'anti-communism' as a central position. Clearly this is the filter that raises the most questions in the twenty-first century.

Herman and Chomsky argue that these five news 'filters' lead to a system that produces propaganda. In fact, in 1999 when NATO forces bombed a TV station in Serbia on the grounds that it was producing propaganda, Herman published an article called 'Bomb *The New York Times*?', arguing that the principle ought to be upheld all the way (Herman & Peterson 1999).

As well as being widely cited, the propaganda model has been widely criticized (Klaehn 2002). Schudson (1995) offers a good example of trenchant criticism of Herman and Chomsky. He describes their argument as 'misleading and mischievous' (1995: 4), rejecting their attempt to compare the *New York Times* with the Soviet-era state organ *Pravda.* First, Schudson says, western journalists believe in objective reporting, in professional ethics; they do not see their role as promoting a party line, as did *Pravda* staff. Second, he argues, the western news media try to represent the range of views within the limits of acceptable controversy, representing different viewpoints on social issues. Third, notes Schudson, the American news media offers a range of voices and are not uniform; moreover, they will pursue stories that are uncomfortable for government or other authorities, with Watergate and Iran-Contra standing as examples (here we should note that the bulk of *Manufacturing Consent* is taken up with detailed case studies which attempt to prove the opposite). Schudson also notes that the contemporary media environment is so complex and far-reaching (as is contemporary society) that the interests of audiences and media institutions can't 'line up neatly' (p. 5). *Sports Illustrated,* he notes, was among the first publications to write about acid rain, because of its many readers who fish or sail. Finally, Schudson observes that news media have to balance the making of profits with the maintenance of credibility in the eyes of their readers and viewers.

Writing in 2000, Herman acknowledges that the fifth filter, that of 'anti-communism' as a kind of secular religion, may seem to have lost its force. But he contends that while that specific enemy Other may have gone with the fall of the Berlin Wall in 1989 and the subsequent collapse of the Soviet Union, it's been replaced by another guiding ideology: 'the greater ideological force of the belief in the "miracle of the market"' (2000: 109). This is now so entrenched, at least among the elite groups who are the subject of the propaganda model, Herman suggests, that: 'regardless of evidence markets are assumed to be benevolent and non-market mechanisms are suspect' (2000: 109). It might also be argued that terrorism is now the evil Other, and that anti-terrorism is now the secular religion in whose name seemingly anything can be justified. It shares something very important in common with Communism: as Herman and Chomsky write, 'because the concept is fuzzy it can be used against anybody' (1988: 29).

Still another criticism of the propaganda model is that it has nothing to say about audiences. It addresses the production of news, but not its reception and seems to imply that audiences are hapless dupes (in the name 'propaganda model' for instance, or the phrase 'manufacturing consent'). Herman is quite unmoved by this criticism: the propaganda model, he wrote in 2000, 'is a model of media *behavior and performance,* not of media effects' (2000: 103). However, the fact that the authors rule out questions of the audience in this way does not mean that the audience do not pose a problem for the propaganda model. An entirely structural model of media performance like this can only be a partial account of the news.

The model is also somewhat monolithic, in that it can't account for moments when elite groups don't really know what their interests are (Wark 1992). And the model can't really account for cases when the media run counter to the interests they supposedly represent — the very existence of the various high-water marks of investigative journalism in the last 40 years or so, including the *Sunday Times*'s work on Thalidomide, the *Washington Post* on Watergate, and Seymour Hersh's more recent work on Abu Ghraib for the *New Yorker* would all appear to pose problems for the propaganda model.

Finally, for Herman, 'The political economy of the U.S. mass media is dominated by communication gatekeepers who are not media professionals so much as large profit-making organizations with close ties to government and business' (1995: 92). This leads to a final observation about the propaganda model, which is that it's very much an analysis rooted in the American context, and this needs to be taken into account in assessing its usefulness elsewhere. For example, it's worth noting the role of public service broadcasters in the British and Australian contexts as a corrective to this somewhat monolithic view of the media as commercial (see Chapter 7); it's also important to consider the role of alternative media organizations (see Chapter 8). Despite these caveats, the propaganda model stands as a powerful set of tools that can be used to examine the news media, and as a compelling — if very pessimistic — argument about news as symbolic power.

Conclusion

News organizations have great symbolic power resources. This chapter has outlined the key ways in which they exercise this power — defining reality by defining news, and shaping not just the content but the contexts of news. If at times this emphasis may have risked overstating the extent to which the agency of individual journalists is subordinate to the imperatives of the institutions for which they work, this will be balanced in later chapters. This analysis is complemented in the following chapter by a discussion of news as a *cultural* product: one that shapes and is in turn shaped by our cultural expectations — specifically our expectations of story-telling and of the visual.

Chapter 3

True Stories

> *'People seem to need news, any kind — bad news, sensationalistic news, overwhelming news. It seems to be that news is a narrative of our time. It has almost replaced the novel, replaced discourse between people. It replaced families. It replaced a slower, more carefully assembled way of communicating, a more personal way of communicating'* (Don DeLillo, interviewed in Remnick 2005: 143).

Shortly after the Indian Ocean tsunami of December 2004, Australia's ABC TV news introduced a new station promo, played each evening throughout early 2005. As Gary Jules's mournful version of 'Mad World' played in the background, a montage of news clips appeared and dissolved — the tsunami surging through the streets of Banda Aceh in Indonesia, troops running with a stretcher, a royal wedding, an injured Olympic athlete, a recently deceased World War I veteran, crowds demonstrating, fire fighters battling a bushfire, an old woman in despair, a child being carried through a flood, a group of refugees beside a small tent. A series of text captions accompanied these — 'News is more than just headlines. It's about who we are. Our strengths. Our emotions. Our passions. And most importantly, it's about our humanity. ABC News & Current Affairs — more than the headlines'.

It's about who we are. Is the news really about creating identity? News must be understood not simply as an organizational product, as discussed in the previous chapter, but also as a cultural form. It must be understood in terms of its dramatic qualities, its particular textual features and conventions. The most important thing about news stories is that they are *stories* that present themselves as *true*. Bird and Dardenne consider the wider cultural significance of news narratives. 'While news is not fiction', they write, 'it is a story about reality, not reality itself. Yet because of its privileged status as reality and truth, the seductive powers of its narratives are particularly significant' (1997: 346–7). They argue that news constitutes 'an enduring symbolic system' and that this system as a whole, '"teaches" audiences more than any of its component parts, no matter whether these parts are intended to inform, irritate or entertain' (1997: 343). News, as novelist Don DeLillo has it in this chapter's epigraph, is 'a narrative of our time'.

The previous chapter examined some of the institutional factors that influence the nature of news — so-called news values, or principles of selection, the operation of which constitute a part of the profession of journalism. Those factors, though, are only part of the story. Such an emphasis on the activities of news organizations needs to be anchored in a consideration of the cultural constraints in which they operate. The news has its own cultural requirements and traditions, which shape the work of anyone operating within them.

As Michael Schudson summarizes them, for instance, those cultural requirements include the following:

> ...how to know what is interesting or unusual, how to validate a claim, how to demonstrate one's own authorial legitimacy, how to write an arresting lead, how to win a journalistic prize, how to construct a news story as an acceptable moral tale (Schudson 1995: 13).

The professional perspective on such matters is that they constitute 'news sense', something you either have or you don't, or that you can only learn in years on the job (and certainly not, for instance, at university). But these can also be seen as cultural factors, themselves shaped and constrained by the wider culture and in turn shaping it. To explore this, this chapter first focuses on the importance of *narrative*. The cultural factors of news sense in Schudson's account — how to know what's unusual, how to grab the reader by the lapels, how to shape a story — are aspects of news as story-telling, of news as narrative.

James Carey argues that 'news is not information but drama' (1989: 21). Golding and Elliott point out that 'News stories are, as the term suggests, stories as well as news' (1979: 115). The news, notes Robert Stam, offers 'tonight's top *stories*, not tonight's top *facts*' (2000: 368, original emphasis). What are the implications of this? Telling stories, naming reality — the symbolic power of news is inseparable from questions of narrative and story-telling.

News, ritual, community

Carey distinguishes between two views of communication — a *transmission* model and a *ritual* model. The transmission model is the one that most of us probably think of *as* communication. Carey writes that: 'It is defined by terms such as "imparting," "sending," "transmitting," or "giving information to others"' (Carey 1989: 15). It is about communication across physical, geographical space. This view of communication, argues Carey, has at its centre the desire to control territory.

The ritual model, in contrast, is about time, and generates a very different list of key words, being linked to such concepts as participation, sharing and fellowship, and deriving from the common origins of the concepts of communication, community and communion: 'A ritual view of communication is directed not toward the extension of messages in space but toward the maintenance of society in time; not the act of imparting information but the representation of shared beliefs' (1989: 18). If the transmission view is about control, the ritual view is about participation in a shared ceremony; an act of 'fellowship and commonality' (Carey 1989: 18).

These perspectives offer two quite different ways of approaching news. If we think about news from a transmission perspective, then this points to a familiar range of issues and debates — questions of authenticity and effect, of truth and accuracy, of representation and bias, of influence and control. But if we think about news from a ritual perspective, then this suggests that getting the news isn't really about learning anything new — instead, it's about having our view of the world confirmed. From a ritual point of view, news is not simply about receiving information, but about participating in a depiction of all the world's 'contending forces' (Carey 1989: 20). It's about receiving an affirmation of our position in the world through the goodies and baddies arrayed for our entertainment every night — 'Under a ritual view, then, news is not information but drama. It does not describe the world but portrays an arena of dramatic forces and action [...] and it invites our participation on the basis of our assuming, often vicariously, social roles within it' (Carey 1989: 21).

News, then, is about community. This, of course, is a word with largely positive connotations, and if the media play a role in fostering and developing community, then this would be a good thing. But we also need to consider how processes of community formation through and in the mediascape can work by *exclusion* (the phenomenon of moral panic, for example, explored in Chapter 5). Ritual, as Couldry argues, may be understood as being concerned 'not with the affirmation of what we share, but with the management of conflict and the masking of social inequality' (2003: 4). As the previous chapter argued, symbolic power is not evenly distributed throughout the community but is concentrated in media organizations and institutions (Bourdieu 1991, Thompson 1995: 17, Couldry 2003: 38–41). The idea that the news is 'about who we are' should not blind us to the unequal power relationships through which this 'we' is created and maintained. Of course, audiences are not helpless or powerless and increasingly find new opportunities to participate in the news (blogs, for example, discussed in Chapter 4, or other uses of new media technologies, discussed in Chapter 8). But the concentration of symbolic power in large media operations is undeniable. It is not contradictory to observe that media power is simultaneously becoming more concentrated and more diffuse, through two separate kinds of process. On the one hand, media organizations grow ever larger, more integrated, manifest greater symbolic power resources; on the other hand, audiences blur into producers, and find new means of using the media to intervene in symbolic power relations.

What does it mean to think of the media from a ritual perspective? One example is Benedict Anderson's concept that the nation is an 'imagined political community' (1991) — 'It is *imagined* because the members of even the smallest nation will never know most of their fellow-members, meet them, or even hear of them, yet in the minds of each lives the image of their communion' (Anderson 1991: 6, original emphasis). All such communities — that is to say, nations — are limited by borders. All nations imagine themselves apart from others — the national community is most often defined in relation to others. The nation, Anderson writes, 'is always conceived as a deep, horizontal comradeship' (p. 7), and it is this comradeship for which people will fight and die. Anderson argues that nationalism emerged through a complex intersection of changing ideals: the declining centrality of particular script-languages (such as Latin in western Europe), the erosion of belief in divinely-appointed rulers, and pre-modern conceptions of cosmology and time, combined with the rise of what Anderson terms 'print-capitalism' — the rise, above all, of the novel and the newspaper, through which more people could think about themselves and each other in ways that weren't previously possible (Anderson 1991: 36).

How does this work? First, such imagined communities need symbols and they need to be put together into stories. In societies of our size and complexity, this process of putting symbols together happens through the media. It's in the media that we find the symbols we use to make our own contemporary sense of imagined community. It's in the media that we tell each other stories. Narrative and story-telling are central to news.

What do we mean by narrative? There's a rich tradition of narrative analysis in a wide number of disciplines: English Literature, Cultural Studies, Film Studies, Anthropology, Philosophy. However, not all of the debates in the literature are necessarily relevant to the study of news. A semiotic approach would see narrative as a particular kind of form for the creation of meanings. If a sign is something that produces meanings, and a text is a combination of signs, then we can think of a narrative as a particular kind of text: one which represents events in time and space (Thwaites, Davis & Mules 2002). Time is the key element here, as the order in which events are presented is a central emphasis in narrative. Narratives — unlike, say, recipes or train timetables — represent cause-and-effect relationships. All of these dimensions are captured in the useful definition from *Film Art* by Bordwell and Thompson, a standard introductory film studies textbook: 'We can consider a narrative to be *a chain of events in cause-effect relationship occurring in time and space*' (Bordwell & Thompson 1999: 90, original emphasis).

If we use the term 'narrative' this enables us to make a key distinction between 'story' and 'plot'. As Tzvetan Todorov makes this distinction: 'the story is what has happened in life, the plot is the way the author presents it to us' (1977: 45). Bordwell and Thompson illustrate this by offering the example of a classic whodunnit in which a detective solves a crime. The story is all the events which take place or can be inferred, in chronological order — so a crime is conceived, planned, carried out and then discovered; the detective then investigates and reveals the details of its conception, planning and execution (Bordwell & Thompson 1999: 95). This is a story which can be told and re-told again and again: what makes variety possible are the multiple ways in which the events can be arranged in time — each of these ways would be a different plot. The plot might, for example, begin with the discovery of the crime or with the execution of the crime or with the planning of the crime. Many combinations are possible — the story remains the same, but the plot can be told differently. In cinema, for instance, the plot is often the most important dimension of the narrative, and the ordering of events in films such as *Memento, Irreversible* or *Citizen Kane* renders otherwise unremarkable stories as compelling narratives (Murphet 2005). The following section explores some implications of this for the news.

Once upon a time

Let me tell you a story. How might it begin? We might as well take the best of all possible beginnings, so perhaps our story could begin like Gabriel García Márquez's 1970 novel *One Hundred Years Of Solitude:*

> 'Many years later, as he faced the firing squad, Colonel Aureliano Buendia was to remember that distant afternoon when his father took him to discover ice'.

Or perhaps our story could start like Donna Tartt's 1992 novel *The Secret History:*

> 'The snow in the mountains was melting and Bunny had been dead for several weeks before we came to understand the gravity of our situation.'

Or, better, like Hunter S. Thompson's *Fear And Loathing In Las Vegas:*

> 'We were somewhere around Barstow on the edge of the desert when the drugs began to take hold.'

Those three opening sentences, taken from books pulled from my shelf at random, share a powerful characteristic. Each hooks the reader immediately by withholding information. Each demands that we read on to find the answers to the questions posed by the opening. Consider the García Márquez, which lays a trail of questions for the reader — many years later than what? Who is this guy and why is he facing the firing squad? What does it mean to 'discover ice'? If, on any level, the reader desires an answer to even one of these questions, then they will read on, further into the story, finding some answers even as new mysteries are presented. The other examples offer the same kinds of enigma. In Donna Tartt's opening, who is this Bunny who has been dead for weeks? Who are the 'we'? And what is this grave situation? In Hunter Thompson's, again, who are the 'we' being introduced? What are they doing on the edge of the desert? And the drugs? What drugs?

Roland Barthes argued that a basic mechanism by which narratives function is through presenting enigmas like this. A narrative creates its energy and draws the reader in by posing questions, setting up little mysteries, little enigmas, which are resolved as the plot progresses. Barthes called this aspect of narrative the hermeneutic code, and argued that it incorporates all those parts of a story which work 'to articulate in various ways a question, its response, and the variety of chance events which can either formulate the question or delay its answer; or even, constitute an enigma and lead to its solution' (Barthes 1974: 17). Barthes outlined this idea in an extended analysis of a Balzac novella titled *Sarrasine*, noting that the title itself constitutes the first of many enigmas which drive the story: '*What is Sarrasine?* A noun? A name? A thing? A man? A woman? This question will not be answered until much later' (Barthes 1974: 17, original emphasis). In the meantime, the reader reads on in search of answers and resolution. From this perspective, the essence of narrative is the *withholding* of information from the reader.

But how does this relate to the news? Again, let me tell you a story. How might things be different if our story began like this one?

> 'At least 186 people were killed and more than 1000 injured when co-ordinated explosions ripped apart packed peak-hour trains in Madrid yesterday, the Spanish Interior Ministry said. The bombings came just four days before national elections and authorities immediately blamed the Basque separatist group ETA'
>
> (*Sydney Morning Herald*, 12 March 2004, p. 1).

This news story displays a very different approach to that of García Márquez. Rather than withholding information to hook the reader, it offers total revelation instantly. Rather than posing questions, the plot is structured so that the story is completely revealed at the beginning, within the first two sentences. All the rest that follows (several hundred more words) is elaboration and back-story — quotes from rescuers, quotes from witnesses, quotes from politicians. There's little in the way of enigma to engage our attention. In fact, we don't need to read on to find out what has happened. We already know. In arranging the plot in such a way that the information becomes steadily less important with each succeeding paragraph, the journalist not only assumes we'll stop reading before the end, but actually encourages us to do so. News stories like this one are the only stories deliberately written in such a way as to discourage us from reading to the end.

Upside-down pyramids

In saying that news stories discourage us from reading on, I have in mind the mechanics of a certain type of news narrative: the structure known as the inverted pyramid. A story structured in this way contains all the key information at the beginning. The inverted pyramid is 'a graphic representation of the journalistic principle that a story's most important elements should appear at the top. Other elements fall below, in descending order of importance' (Conley 1997: 155). The Madrid bombing example above includes the answers to the key news questions of *who, what, where, when, why* and *how* in just 45 words (although the *why* — ETA's response to the coming elections — turned out to be completely wrong). Subsequent paragraphs expanded on certain key details and introduced quotes from witnesses, emergency services, and political figures reacting to the atrocity. However, the actual story, the central events, had all been revealed in the first two lines.

We should note, though, that while individual news stories might not operate by presenting enigmas in the way that other narrative forms do, we can see the presence of such enigmas within the news as a whole. For example, many headlines operate in this way, such as the legendary one from the *New York Post* on 15 April 1983: 'Headless Body in Topless Bar', an enigma that simply demands the reader read on. Or this headline, 'Man Gives Birth to Baby Girl' (*Guardian,* 4 July 2008). Or this, from the *Sydney Morning Herald* (13 May 2004, p. 13): 'Washington

Braces For Deafening Six-Week Frenzy of Mating and Death' — a story which turned out to be about the peculiar life-cycle of the cicada (there is no guarantee that an intriguing narrative enigma will deliver on its promises). The enigma approach can also be seen with TV news, with trailers of what's coming up in the next bulletin, after the break, and so on. Other headlines trade in sheer ingenuity rather than enigmas — when the French Finance Minister suggested that her fellow citizens' tradition of philosophy encourages them to think too much, and that this hinders economic growth, the *Sydney Morning Herald* tagged its story with 'Don't Put Descartes Before The Bourse, French Told' (23 July 2007). The unbeatable example is likely to remain that from *The Sun* on 9 February 2000, leading a football report in which Inverness Caledonian Thistle (Caley) had tackled Celtic: 'Super Caley Go Ballistic, Celtic Are Atrocious'.

Why did this distinctive inverted-pyramid plot structure develop? Pöttker considers the most common explanations. The first of these is that it emerged for technological reasons (developing in the era of the early telegraph, with still-nascent and unreliable networks, which created an imperative to get the most important information through first). Or that it emerged for political reasons, during the US Civil War of the 1860s, masking official perspectives behind a veneer of objectivity. Or that the inverted pyramid developed in a context of greatly expanded literacy, and met the demands of a new kind of reading public, demanding a more concise, readable style. Or that the inverted pyramid emerged for economic reasons, again linked to the telegraph, where news organizations had to pay by the word in a context of increasing commercial competition. Pöttker finds all of these unpersuasive, arguing that the form developed because of deliberate attempts to improve the communicative qualities of news. In this view, the inverted pyramid developed and survived because it offered communicative advantages (Pöttker 2003).

What kinds of advantages? One evident advantage of the inverted pyramid form is that it provides reporters with a clear guide in how to organize complex material. The advantages of this are particularly clear in thinking about major breaking news events such as the Madrid train bombing — with updates flooding in from all kinds of sources, an inverted pyramid format provides a stable framework into which fresh information can be fitted, and provides a clear model within which to assemble and re-edit developing stories. It follows also that sub-editors can cut content from the bottom up, rather than extricating material from throughout the whole of a story. If a piece is too long, the inverted pyramid format ensures that the final paragraphs will be the least important and the easiest to cut out.

A more problematic kind of advantage is the claim that the inverted pyramid is an easy read. Readers can get the gist of a story from its first few lines and this is attractive to those of us who are busy or short of time. It isn't necessary to read a lengthy report in order to grasp the essential details of an event. 'By reading the first two or three paragraphs of every story,' suggests Conley, 'many readers will feel reasonably well-informed' (1997: 155). Yet how well-informed can we be on a diet of introductions? Cultural critic Neil Postman argued that the brevity, discontinuity and overall lack of seriousness of contemporary news (above all TV news) had created a situation in which audiences in America (and his analysis certainly travels) had become 'the best entertained and quite likely the least well-informed people in the Western world' (Postman 1985: 108). Postman argued that the views we hold about important issues are not based on sufficient information to qualify as *opinions* — rather, that our views on important issues are really *emotions* (1985: 109). We will explore Postman's argument in more detail in Chapter 6.

Bird and Dardenne argue that the inverted pyramid may well be a useful technique for the writer but that it is 'a disaster' for the reader. Readers, they say, ignore much of the news because the way in which it is written 'repels them' (1997: 342). In criticizing the inverted pyramid model as one which deters reading, then, what we're questioning is the *plot* structure, rather than the story elements.

More bad news

Why is there so much bad news? In the previous chapter, we saw how Galtung and Ruge identified *negativity* as a key news value. Consider, then, how narratives emphasize *disruption*: 'What is new', writes John Fiske, 'is what disrupts the normal. What is absent from the text of the news, but present as a powerful force in its reading, are the unspoken assumptions that life is ordinarily smooth-running, rule- and law-abiding, and harmonious' (Fiske 1987: 284). News constructs a sense of what is the normal, what is the *status quo*, what is the equilibrium. This means, as Fiske argues, that the solitary category of 'the abnormal' can encompass both a murder and an industrial dispute (p. 284). The clichéd complaint there is too much bad news misses the point that 'the bad' is set against an unspoken assumption that the normal, the *status quo*, is good.

Tzvetan Todorov offers an analysis of narrative that is useful in understanding why the news so often seems bad. Todorov argues that '*All narrative is a movement between two equilibriums which are similar but not identical.*' (Todorov 1975: 163, original emphasis). Any given story is a sequence in which a 'stable situation' is disrupted by something or someone, characters recognize this disruption and work to repair it, achieving a new stable situation at the end. 'The elementary narrative thus includes two types of episodes: those which describe a state of equilibrium or disequilibrium, and those which describe the transition from one to the other' (Todorov 1975: 163).

This concept of the 'minimum narrative' remains useful, although such approaches, which reduce the wild diversity of story-telling to a single formula, have fallen out of theoretical fashion (for a survey of more recent approaches to narrative see McQuillan 2000). One problem is that Todorov's model does zero in on a claim of what all narratives have in common, but it has to leave out all the vital things that are different about different narratives. But it is still possible to draw useful ideas from such a structural emphasis. For example, one implication of this model for news, is that deadlines (the news value of frequency) mean that there is often no resolution, no second equilibrium (or at least not on the day a story is initially reported). This goes a long way towards explaining why there is so much bad news. More importantly, as with the concept of news values, this model of narrative suggests that the news *could* be constructed differently, if stories were told in different ways. One thing to take from Todorov's model is that it's important to pay very close attention to what's presented as the equilibrium. What's presented as the stable situation? What is presented as the norm, and what as the disruption?

Fiske (1987) highlights the prevalence of combative metaphors in the news: for example, politics as war, politics as a game, politics as drama. A world in which politicians are forever under fire, fighting to stay relevant, shadow-boxing with opponents, coming under flak, launching attacks, and so on and on and on. This emphasis on conflict is key to thinking about news narratives, and fundamental to Todorov's model, with its focus on disruption. As John Langer (1980) has pointed out, even stories about the weather often depend on conflict. In news reports about bad weather, the weather is anthropomorphized, so that a hurricane, for example, is said to 'show mercy' or else to be 'a monster'. The weather is made an actor in the drama (thereby *creating* the drama); turned into a character in order to fill the role of 'cause' in a cause-effect chain of narrative events. More than this, it enables the weather to be set up as the 'them' in an 'us-and-them' narrative. News, as Walter Lippmann argued in the 1920s, 'is not a mirror of social conditions, but the report of an aspect that has obtruded itself' (1922: 216). As Stuart Hall (1984) argues, this emphasis on obtrusion, on deviance, exception and disruption, reinforces the 'normal' and the 'consensus' about what matters, and what constitutes the real world.

This book is not a how-to book for aspiring journalists. But some readers may well be aspiring journalists or be otherwise involved in aspects of news (through blogging, for example). It's to those readers in particular that I would suggest there is a challenge which follows from all this. That challenge is to create and develop new approaches to writing news. There is space for news which encourages discussion rather than sets up conflict; there is space for news which engages with solutions as well as with problems; there is space for news that can cope with complexity (cf Bennett & Edelman 1985). The media environment of the twenty-first century offers opportunities for such news to be developed, for new ways of writing which go beyond conflict. We will consider some of these opportunities in both the next chapter and Chapter 8.

Definitive gaze

'Modern life' suggests Nicholas Mirzoeff, 'takes place onscreen' (1999: 1). News is not just a matter of plot elements, but is experienced as visual imagery in photography and video, in graphics and film, on TV and online. Seeing, suggests Mirzoeff, is now more than believing. It is the stuff of everyday, media-saturated life. News websites offer video reports. TV news splits into multiple windows for two-way interviews, or is performed before giant walls of video screens, which conjure and dissolve images as the newsreader strides around before them. Newspapers make greater use of colour photographs and of graphics — they can devote an entire broadsheet front page or a two-page centre-spread to a single full-colour photograph. Images which would not have been possible until recently are now routine, whether created by satellite, by *paparazzi,* or by computer. This section considers some of the key issues that arise from news photography — defining reality by showing, as well as telling.

Here is a photograph which many readers will be able to call up in their minds (or if not, call up on their computer screens). It shows a man in a white shirt, falling backwards as his knees buckle, a rifle slipping from his outstretched right hand as he falls. This image, taken by Robert Capa, is one of the most famous of all war photographs, reproduced many times since its publication in *Life* magazine in July 1937. It is believed to show the moment of death of a Republican fighter in the Spanish Civil War. In this, it is an image of unusual power, and a tribute to Capa's commitment and skill as a war photographer. As an image of death taking place, it will evoke in many viewers what Barthes (1981) called the *punctum* — a piercing, unanticipated emotional response, as the viewers create their own connotations from the image.

But there is a degree of uncertainty and controversy about this picture. The controversy surrounds the question of whether the image was captured or posed. Did Capa, in a wild fluke, point the camera at the exact moment the soldier was shot? Or did he fake the image? There are claims on both sides (Mirzoeff 1999: 78, Knightley 2003: 227–30) and the exact circumstances of a single wartime photograph may not be recoverable after more than 70 years. Yet Capa's photograph retains not just its power but also its interest — interest created by the very uncertainty contained in the image. The next three short sections highlight three aspects of the 'moment of death' photograph that can be applied to other news images, including much more banal and mundane ones.

Seeing and believing?

First, there is the question of authenticity, as noted above. Does a photograph really show us what happened? Is seeing believing? And if so, are we right to believe? One central paradox here is that photographs, while in one sense showing us 'what really happened', are also themselves interpretations of reality (Sontag 1977: 7) — selected, posed, framed, timed, with every gradation of lighting or lens a choice that creates as much as it shows. Moreover, the presence of a camera can change the reality it captures: think, for example, of one common genre — the snatched tabloid photo of a celebrity caught off-guard (Becker 2003). It may appear to represent the celebrity 'as they really are': no make-up, street clothes, face contorted by the flash, arms thrown up to ward off the photographer. But the very presence of the camera has created the reaction being captured; it is an image whose content is dictated by the intrusive act of its own creation.

The question of interpretation has a renewed force in the digital era (Fetveit 1999). In August 2006 Reuters withdrew more than 900 photos from its database that had been taken by freelancer Adnan Hajj, who had altered images he had taken during the Israel-Lebanon conflict, using Photoshop to make his pictures more dramatic. Photo manipulation software is now bundled free with many computers and many readers will be very familiar with the capacity to touch-up or edit their own digital photos in a range of ways. Some celebrities have publicly objected to their pictures being digitally manipulated. In 2003 *GQ* magazine put a photo of Kate Winslet on its cover, altered to make her legs seem thinner, which provoked an angry public statement from the actress. Other celebrities — Jennifer Aniston, Martha Stewart, Jamie Lee Curtis, tennis star Andy Roddick — have voiced similar complaints. An infamous example was *Time* magazine's deliberate alteration of a cover photo of O. J. Simpson to make him appear darker-skinned, which some believe was intended to make him appear more 'threatening' to an assumed white readership (Mirzoeff 1999: 88).

What challenges does this pose to the news media? On the one hand, imperfect images can now be improved — indeed, perfect ones can be created from scratch. On the other hand, this can only increase scepticism and cynicism among readers and viewers; not only is a given image to be understood as true, but it appears within a larger news text (a newspaper, a TV bulletin, a website) which is also to be understood as true. So the digitally manipulated image undermines not only the credibility of the image itself, but also of the news more broadly. Or, perhaps worse, readers and viewers may not recognize the fakery at all. Some newspapers have adopted policies of stating when a photograph has been digitally manipulated. But does this reinforce readers' trust too much in non-digital images, images which, while not digitally altered, are still subject to selection, framing, cropping, and whose status as 'true' is open to challenge on a number of fronts? It is, then, possible to overstate the extent to which digital photographs are a decisive break: analogue photographs in the news are not only open to manipulation, but depend on context, on juxtaposition, on framing, and on the written stories of which they are a part (Manovich 2003). To doubt digital images while believing non-digital ones would be a mistake. The special problems of digital images in the news should instead encourage us to actively question *all* news images — not in the sense of a useless cynicism, but rather in the sense of being conscious, active participants in the creation of meaning from news.

Adding the missing voice

The second thing to take from Capa's photograph is that much of its power is not actually in the image itself. Rather, it is in the accompanying captions, titles, or other textual explanations which set out the claim that the image is indeed of the moment of a fighter's death. The original *Life* caption read 'Robert Capa's camera catches a Spanish soldier the instant he is dropped by a bullet through the head in front of Cordoba' (quoted in Knightley 2003: 227). Yet the image itself is rather unclear and ambiguous. There is nothing within the frame itself to indicate that it is in Spain at all, or to identify the figure as a soldier (he has a rifle, yes, but not a clearly identifiable uniform). It is not even clear from the picture that he has been shot, never mind whether this is the actual instant of this man's death. All of this must be conveyed in words. Words and image must be combined for this image to tell the story it is believed to offer. And, as Knightley points out, the *Life* caption tells a story about the photographer as well as about his subject. It celebrates the courage and skill of Capa, who is the actual subject of the caption. In noting this, I don't mean to take anything away from Capa's record of decades of physical courage as a war photographer; he was, in fact, killed by a land mine while on assignment. Rather, I want to focus on the importance of the caption to Capa's famous image. Walter Benjamin once observed that the caption would become 'the most important part of the shot' (quoted in Evans & Hall 1999: 7). Roland Barthes (1977) noted the ways in which words can 'anchor' the possible meanings of an image, bracketing off some possibilities and foregrounding others, pointing the viewer towards some potential meanings and away from others — and an image, as Gripsrud (2006) points out, can in turn anchor a written text. The caption, as Sontag put it, is 'the missing voice' of the photograph (1977: 108). More than tell us how an image reads, a caption may tell us how an image *ought* to be read (Hall 1981). Tirohl notes how this becomes even more essential with new developments in imaging technologies — more recent war photographs, from Kosovo, Afghanistan or Iraq, sometimes consist of low-resolution digital images released by the military, which may be screen grabs from targeting equipment complete with cross-hairs; in such cases, the caption strongly directs interpretation of the image, as many viewers lack the experience in interpreting such technically-specialized visuals (Tirohl 2000: 340).

What's outside the frame?

The third thing to take from Capa's photograph is how the picture works by standing in for the wider conflict (indeed, for conflicts more generally, as it has come to represent *war*, not just the Spanish Civil War). If news stories often work through metaphor (comparison) news photographs work through metonymy (association). We associate Capa's image with the wider conflict of which it is said to be a part. We don't see what is beyond the frame, but we make associations: the single image stands in for the wider picture. For instance, as former *Sunday Times* editor Harold Evans notes in his wonderful study *Pictures On A Page*, for many people the Vietnam War is captured in single images that, again, most readers will be able to visualize (or Google) — Saigon's police chief shooting a Vietcong prisoner in the head; a burned, naked child fleeing from napalm; a Buddhist priest sitting stock still as he deliberately burns himself to death. Each of these stands in for 'Vietnam', all the more so for those of us too young to remember. And all are, as Evans has it, decisive moments — 'moments when decisive content is indisputably synthesised with meaningful form' (1978: 107).

In the same way as these single pictures of Vietnam seem to capture many years of history, other major events or news stories may appear in our memories as single images. The 1990–91 Gulf War is fixed in my memory through Kenneth Jarecke's traumatizing image of a charred Iraqi soldier on the Basra road, with so many other details now lost to me. The London bombing of 7 July 2005 is fixed through Alexander Chadwick's mobile phone picture of survivors in a dimly-lit tunnel at King's Cross station, the one image that remains for me from days of non-stop coverage. The death of Kurt Cobain, and with it a certain era of rock music, is fixed for me in the single photo that shows the leg of his corpse, the banality of his jeans and trainers. All news photographs work through this process of using the part to represent the whole (a process called synecdoche, in rhetorical terminology). Any news photograph presents part of a much wider story, which must be inferred — or disregarded — by the viewer. We are presented, then, with a single aspect of an event to represent the complete story. So the most important question to ask of any news image, whether in print or on screen, is *what's outside the frame?*

Sound + Vision

TV is the most popular and the most maligned medium of news. Graeme Turner observes that for a long time the only respectable justification for studying TV was to enable students to protect themselves against it (Turner 2000). And while that is changing, TV and in particular the study of TV is still short on respectability — even for a thinker such as Pierre Bourdieu, TV poses 'a serious danger' (1998: 10). 'Television, the drug of a nation, breeding ignorance and feeding radiation', as the Disposable Heroes of Hiphoprisy had it. The paradox here is that despite all this scorn, TV is not only popular but also often the most trusted news medium (Castells 2004: 371–2). TV remains the most trusted source of news for UK adults (OFCOM 2006). In the US, similarly, TV news is routinely judged more credible than print (Pew Research Center for the People & the Press 2006: 50). For this reason alone, TV is central to an understanding of symbolic power and news.

What's distinctive about the nature of news as displayed through the medium of television?

- TV, including the news, is organized around *discrete programmes* which are themselves organized around discrete segments (Ellis 1982), even though these may be experienced as '*flow*' (Williams 1974).

- TV news is *repetitive* — key stories may be re-told several times in a half-hour broadcast; rolling news channels take this further. John Ellis has suggested that a TV news broadcast has much in common with other ongoing TV series, such as sitcoms or soaps: familiar characters recur in familiar situations — the doorstep of 10 Downing Street, the White House lawn, the film premiere red carpet, the football pitch; as Ellis puts it, 'the first true use of the open-ended series format would seem to be the news bulletin, endlessly updating events and never synthesising them' (1982: 145).
- Stories on TV news are *brief* — TV news, suggests Margaret Morse, is 'the antithesis of duration, a model of brevity and immediacy, focused on telling stories, and hearing from experts in the immediate present' (1998: 55).
- And this immediate present is bound up with another key fact of television — even when pre-recorded in the studio and taped at home to watch later, TV *seems live* (Bourdon 2000, Crisell 2006, Marriott 2007). This sense of liveness, of directness and immediacy, is, argues Scannell, central to the power of broadcasting: 'since it offers the real sense of access to an event in its moment-by-moment unfolding [...] what's happening? what's next?' (1996: 84) (Liveness is also central to the experience of the web, as McPherson, 2006, argues).
- TV is *domestic*, for the most part, although it can be both public and mobile. The presence of a TV set turns any space (dentist's, bus, shop window, pub) into a 'TV space' (Allen & Hill 2004). Hartley (1999: 40–1) argues that TV is 'transmodern', linking and blurring characteristics of the *pre-modern* (oral culture, storytelling, the centrality of the family and the domestic context), the *modern* (organized around industries and the production of commercial commodities), and the *post-modern* (in its particular textual forms and cultural position). The 'pre-modern' domestic quality of TV is central to the imagining of community, to the nation as mediated on television as a 'symbolic home' (Morley 2004).
- TV news works to establish a certain authority over both *time* and *space*. The opening sequence may use music or sounds (such as *News at Ten* with its use of the chimes of Big Ben to punctuate) or sound effects connoting drama, urgency, attention, with images of maps, globes, key national locations or landmarks (Allan 2004, Creeber 2004, Dunn 2005). The state-of-the-art set of ITN news, a spectacular arena of image with a semi-circular video wall three

> metres high and 20 metres wide, works to create the illusion of space, while simultaneously creating and recreating other, different spaces through video, graphics, onscreen texts and images and curiously mobile newsreaders. The 'theatre' itself is clearly a real place, but its workings create an incessantly mobile illusion, as images and contexts shift behind the presenter, and shots are combined from five different cameras (Lury 2005: 161–5).

Such news creates, as Joshua Meyrowitz has it, no sense of place (1985). Meyrowitz's analysis rests on two meanings of 'sense' and two meanings of 'place'. First, there's *sense* as in perception. but also *sense* as in logic (what we mean when we say something 'doesn't make sense'). Second, there's *place* as in physical location, but also *place* as in hierarchy and order. Television has altered all of these. It extends our senses, our perceptions, enabling us to see things far beyond our physical reach. It offers a different kind of logic, as audiovisual media operate through different grammars and conventions than does print, or other earlier communication media. At the same time, television has altered our experience of place — the home, for example, is no longer a bounded environment, isolating its members from the rest of society: now it's permeable and permeated by all kinds of communications. And television has contributed to enormous shifts in social orders — it is, writes Meyrowitz, 'a secret-exposing machine' (1995: 42). It contributed to the broader social and cultural context which made practical feminism possible, by bringing access to the public world into the private, domestic sphere of the home. It introduces children to aspects of the world that, in a book-dominated society, could be stepped-out and graded, introduced in a hierarchical sequence (Meyrowitz 1985, 1995). And it changes the public's perceptions of politicians, who must present themselves (and their opponents) in ways acceptable to the media. As Castells points out, for television, images take precedence over words, and people themselves are the simplest images. But an image needs to be effective as well as simple, which draws people to the use of *negative* personal images — the politics of scandal, smear and gaffe (Castells 2004, 2007, Thompson 2005).

Tele*vision* is of course a medium that depends on visual images — without them, a story cannot work on screen. This can often lead to some very banal and literal-minded juxtapositions of news script and available visuals. UK satirist Chris Morris drew attention to this in the 1994 BBC series *The Day Today*. In one brilliant sequence from episode two, an account of a fictional politician's resignation is accompanied by a very rapid montage of literal-minded images — so, for example, the italicized words in the phrase 'he *hopes* to *spend more time cultivating* his hobbies' are illustrated by shots of Bob Hope, a cash register, Sir Thomas More, a wristwatch, and a tractor. Both *The Day Today* and Morris's later Channel 4 series *Brass Eye* featured sophisticated graphics, made by the same company that produced ITN news's visual effects — one particularly impressive graph shows that 'crimes we know nothing about are also increasing'. This pointed to how, in the digital era, TV news has a new kind of relationship to visual images, using them as raw material to be re-worked in effects and sequences of graphic flair (Ellis 2000). Crisell captures the tone of the videographics now central to TV news: 'Moving diagrams and distinctive script may appear on the screen: the colour tones of the images may be altered and the images themselves twisted, stretched, rotated, shattered and peeled away like the pages of a book' (2006: 57). Both Ellis and Crisell suggest that such graphics — however busy they may look — are used to impose a sense of visual order on the otherwise chaotic range of images which TV news is now prepared to use (including images shot by mobile phone, for example). But there is a tension here that Bolter and Grusin (1999) argue is characteristic of digital media. On the one hand, new media are used to increase the sense of immediacy, the sense that we are actually *there* and witnessing an event in real time (as in the use of camera-phone video on TV) On the other hand, though, the look of the state-of-the-art TV news screen is flashy and cluttered, constantly drawing attention to itself (the logos, the clocks, the tickers, the windows, the invitations to push the red button), and this only reinforces the fact that we are *not* actually there.

Media events

To conclude this chapter, I want to discuss an argument which draws together specific kinds of television coverage, questions of media ritual and imagined community, and questions of narrative, in a concept that offers much to an analysis of symbolic power and news — Dayan and Katz's concept of media events (1992). Dayan and Katz analyse TV's capacity to create publics on a scale unprecedented in human history, and they analyse the particular kinds of events that create the largest kinds of publics:

> '... those historic occasions — mostly occasions of state — that are televised as they take place and transfix a nation or the world. They include epic contests of politics and sports, charismatic missions, and the rites of passage of the great — what we call Contests, Conquests and Coronations' (Dayan & Katz 1992: 1).

Dayan and Katz argue that such events integrate societies — if the nation is an imagined community, these media events are its moments of communion.

The three broad categories which comprise the genre are narrative patterns, story forms, which influence the ways in which an event will be mediated (Dayan & Katz 1992: 25). The category of Coronations includes televised weddings and funerals, with Princess Diana starring in the best examples of each. Such events dramatize cultural heritage and continuity (Dayan & Katz 1992: 37). The category of Contests inhabits politics and sport in particular: Contests are 'rule-governed battles of champions' (1992: 26) such as a major election debate or the World Cup final; the message of such events, the authors argue, is that the rules work. The category of Conquests describes one-off events in which improbable odds are overcome and limits heroically exceeded — the first Moon landing is the best example: 'The message of Conquest is that great men and women still reside among us, and that history is in their hands. Some people get up in the morning, decide to do or say something, and the world tomorrow is a different place' (1992: 37).

Dayan and Katz distinguish between news events, which are characterized by disruption, and media events, which are concerned with order — with the maintenance or restoration of society. Their media events are hegemonic. They invite endorsement of the established order. They call for participation in a media ritual which on some level involves what they call 'a *renewal of loyalty* to the society and its legitimate authority' (1992: 9, original emphasis).

Taken together, these media events are a broad category, including events as disparate as the Oscars, the Pope's funeral and an election debate. But they have several characteristics in common: for the purposes of Dayan and Katz's definition, they must be broadcast live and from a remote location (which is to say, not from a TV studio). They are not usually organized by a news institution, but *for* a news institution. So the 2005 Live8 concerts were not organized by the BBC, although they will have been organized with the needs and preferences of such news organizations in mind. On the one hand, these events are interruptions into the regular broadcasting schedule or routine, while on the other hand, they're preplanned and organized. Here, then, are the defining elements of the genre — live, organized outside the media, an interruption to the usual routine, and yet preplanned (1992: 5–7). A further characteristic that distinguishes media events from other news is, as Carey observes (1998: 66) the 'peculiar role of the audience; the audience's participation is central to the narrative of the rite'.

Dayan and Katz's concept is a strong statement of symbolic power. It sees media as the arena for social and cultural forces to bind a community together, through the presentation of authority, on TV, in a comforting narrative form. But Dayan and Katz impose too many limits on their own concept. Other perspectives on the 'media events' concept make it possible for us to open up its processes — to see them as more complex and volatile, and as something broader and more intrinsic to TV news, than just the special events that Dayan and Katz identify.

Couldry, for example, offers some challenges to these defining characteristics: why must they be broadcast live? Why must they be organized outside the media — isn't the broadcast of a climactic episode of a major drama series, or the finale of a show like *The Sopranos* or *Big Brother* a media event? Why must media events work towards reinforcing and celebrating hegemony — what of events which are not celebratory (such as September 11) or are not preplanned (such as the aftermath of Hurricane Katrina)? The restrictions imposed in Dayan and Katz's argument can be seen to place too much weight on events which reinforce value systems, and not enough on events which challenge them (Couldry 2003: 55–74).

Other commentators have argued that media events can indeed challenge established value systems and may catalyse change: the televised proceedings of the Senate investigations into the Watergate scandal, for example, or the broadcast of the beating of Rodney King by Los Angeles police, each led to the resignations of senior officials (Alexander & Jacobs 1998). A media event, then, can be seen as a particular kind of story, one that can force a rethinking as well as a reinforcement of consensus values. Carey (1998) argues that there is a further category of media events which Dayan and Katz do not address: events which express the shaming and ritual excommunication of an individual or group. Rather than 'high holidays' for the culture, media events can be low, business-as-usual for politics and politicians, even if the media coverage is anything but usual. The events surrounding the impeachment of Bill Clinton would fit this category. Such events do not work towards consensus but towards 'bitter discord and struggle' (Carey 1998: 67).

Dayan and Katz can usefully be read in conjunction with Wark (1994), whose *Virtual Geography* identifies and explores the terrain of 'weird global media events'. Like those of Dayan and Katz, Wark's concept addresses out-of-the-ordinary 'events' ('singular irruptions into the regular flow of media', p. vii), but extends this into a consideration of the 'global', or the ways in which telecommunications and television make possible new kinds of connections between new sites on the globe, and the 'weird', or the category of news stories that resist easy categorization within our conventional maps of the news and, indeed, of the world — events such as September 11, the public reaction to the death of Princess Diana, the O. J. Simpson trial, or the four events which are Wark's case studies: the fall of the Berlin Wall, Tiananmen Square, the Gulf War of 1990–91, and the stock market crash of 1987. A crucial dimension in such events is what Wark terms 'telesthesia' or perception at a distance — the reshaping of our experience of space and time through electronically mediated communication. We will return to this concept in greater detail in Chapter 7.

Conclusion

If symbolic power, in Bourdieu's phrase, is making people see and believe, then story-telling — through words, images, moving images and sound — is one central way of trying to exercise it. Newspaper narratives define reality through their plot structures. News images define reality by selecting and framing. TV news defines reality through its blurring of the public world out there and our own domestic domain, its sensation of liveness, its capacity to stage media events. The following chapter turns to those who shape such stories and events — to the journalists, the Fourth Estate.

Chapter 4

From Coffee-House to Cyber-Café

> *'In a country where the people — i.e. the great mass of the educated classes — govern, where they take that ceaseless and paramount interest in public affairs which is at once the inseparable symptom and the surest safeguard of political and civil liberty, where, in a word, they are participating citizens, not passive subjects, of the State, — it is of the most essential consequence that they should be furnished from day to day with the materials requisite for informing their minds and enlightening their judgment'* (Reeve 1855: 478).

The *New York Times* was in trouble, and knew it. One of the paper's rising stars, 27-year-old Jayson Blair, had been fabricating stories. He had invented quotes, misappropriated other writers' work, and described photographs in order to pretend he'd been at a scene when he'd really been at home. In his almost four years at the *Times* Blair had written over 600 stories, many of which now had question marks over them. He had reported on the Washington Sniper case, on the rescue of Private Jessica Lynch, and on the deaths of individual US soldiers in Iraq. Moreover, the *Times*'s stature and agenda-setting role, combined with its commercial agreements for syndication, meant that much of his work had been reprinted in other papers, and would also have been cited and drawn upon by still others. On 11 May 2003 the paper ran a 7,500 word story beginning on its front page, owning up and dissecting the case. The scandal was to cost not just Blair's own job but also those of managing editor Gerald Boyd and executive editor Howell Raines. CBS *Late Show* host David Letterman suggested that the famous masthead slogan of the paper — 'All The News That's Fit To Print' — should be changed to 'We Make It Up!'

The Jayson Blair scandal showed the extent to which the power of news is built on trust in journalists' integrity. Journalists are licenced agents of symbolic power — something we can see most clearly in the discourse of the Fourth Estate. This concept legitimizes the use of symbolic power by media organizations — it claims a central role for the media within a democratic political system. It operates in a fault-line between the news media as participants in democracy and as commercial enterprises.

To explore this, this chapter begins with a brief sketch of the rise of printed news. This frames the story of the newspaper as a story of the development of a particular kind of industry, as the evolution of a business and of business models (mass circulation, subscription, the bundling of editorial material with various combinations of classified and display advertising). A commercial perspective on news sets the context to explore some of the tensions between commerce and democracy, public and private, expression and censorship, editorial and advertising.

There is also a diametrically opposed perspective, which would frame the story of the newspaper as part of social and political histories — the newspaper form, in this kind of analysis, is part of a broader history of the emergence and development of representative democracy. Such stories find resonances in the revolutionary struggles for the franchise, for independence, for civil rights on the one hand, and for editorial independence, freedom to publish, and freedom from repressive censorship and unjust taxation on the other hand.

In practice, these two perspectives blur and intertwine. The commercial nature of the news media can't be separated from its political roles. The concept of the Fourth Estate, discussed later in this chapter, is an ideal role of the press, a democratic role of the press, but one which is made possible by the commercial nature of that press. Questions of democracy and questions of industry are both present — this is where models of democracy meet business models.

Of course, it's not possible to write a full history of printed news in only part of a single chapter, and readers in search of one are directed to Smith (1979), Conboy (2004), Chapman (2005) and Stephens (2007). What follows is very compressed — my intention is not to write a history of news, but to briefly outline the key stages in the historical development of news as an arena of symbolic power. The emphasis on the newspaper in most of this chapter is complemented by the focus on broadcasting and the Net in Chapters 7 and 8.

The chapter first sketches the commercial origins of news media. This leads to an analysis of the Fourth Estate, and its contemporary sense of the news media as watchdog; I include here a discussion of Watergate. To give a sense of the scope of the Fourth Estate discourse, I also include short contrastive discussions of the key issues surrounding two very different kinds of journalists — war correspondents and rock critics. The chapter finally discusses a more contemporary development that offers the potential to reinvigorate the Fourth Estate — blogging.

Commercial origins of news media

From its beginnings in the mid-fifteenth century, printing was organized around commercial operations (Febvre & Martin 1976, Eisenstein 1993). At the same time, it introduced new means of producing symbolic power, so placing publishers into often problematic relationships with existing powers — states and churches in particular (Thompson 1995: 53). Here, then, are two of the central forces that shape the development of the news media — the commercial and the political.

Smith (1979: 10–11) traces four stages in the development of news publishing, each of which appeared in the form of a book. First, the publication of single stories (the 'relation'). Second, the publication of a series of such 'relations', in the form called a 'coranto'. The oldest surviving coranto in English was published in Amsterdam in December 1620 and opens — brilliantly — with an apology for not actually containing the news: 'The new tydings out of Italie are not yet com' (Stephens 2007: 139). Third, a weekly publication called a 'diurnall' which offered a day-by-day account of the week's events. Fourth, the 'mercury' and the 'intelligencer' which brought the idea of a writer using their own voice to try and build an audience. The basis for the newspaper as we know it today was in place by the seventeenth century in Britain and North America. By the eighteenth century these forms had developed into the publication of the daily newspaper with a distinct voice covering a diverse range of topics, and establishing an ongoing relationship between the reader and the publication (Smith 1979: 9–12).

The first issue of the first North American newspaper, *Publick Occurrences,* was published in Boston on 25 September 1690, promising to appear monthly — 'or if any Glut of Occurrences happen, oftener'. It never appeared again. *Publick Occurrences* makes for a fascinating read. It records that 'The Small-pox which has been raging in Boston, after a manner very Extraordinary is now very much abated', and also reports that some of the indigenous peoples who had been converted to Christianity had introduced a day of Thanksgiving — 'Their Example may be worth Mentioning'. The first newspaper in Britain, the *Daily Courant,* appeared in 1702. The first edition compiled paragraphs from publications from Haarlem, Amsterdam, Paris, most of which were concerned with the mobilizing of various bodies of troops. 'Sold by E. Mallet, next Door to the King's Arms Tavern at Fleet-Bridge', it read.

Commercial imperatives have always been central to the newspaper business, and the importance of advertising was already clear in the 1730s, as more and more papers incorporated the word 'advertiser' in their name (Harris 1978: 92). Advertisements were so important that newspapers had been printed in the 1660s containing no political news — nothing except advertisements and trade news (Conboy 2004: 80). In the eighteenth century newspapers became increasingly important economically, as ownership shifted from printers to booksellers, and advertising became more central to the news (Smith 1979: 61–2). In the late eighteenth and early nineteenth centuries, newspapers began to appear in every small community in the US and Britain (Smith 1979: 81). By 1820 Britain was filled with newspaper reading-rooms which may have had as many as 80 newspapers each (Smith 1979: 95). Of great importance in this period were the unstamped radical papers which succeeded in surviving through circulation sales alone (Curran and Seaton 2003). This meant they could concentrate on their core working-class audience, without the need for advertisers (Curran 1978).

Throughout the nineteenth century a whole series of developments combined to make possible the mass circulation popular newspapers of the twentieth century. The repeal of the Stamp Act in Britain in 1855, and of other taxes in the same period, enabled a huge explosion of new publications. The end of the stamp taxes meant that paper was no longer taxed by the sheet, and so publishers were no longer tempted to cram many stories and many lines of text onto a visually dull and cramped page to save money. Newspapers became more visually striking, with bigger headlines and more display ads (Smith 1979: 152).

In order to attract wide audiences, some papers began to focus on the popular, the crusade, the accessible. W. T. Stead, the figure most closely associated with the so-called New Journalism of the nineteenth century, introduced such features as scoops, illustrations, interviews (one of a number of American imports), investigative reporting, campaigns and crusades, and colourful, emotive writing (Conboy 2004: 168). The late nineteenth century saw increased use of such popular innovations as sports news, visuals, gossip, human interest stories, summary leads and front page leads (Conboy 2004: 171).

New forms of newspapers emerged (Smith 1979: 106–8). Sunday or evening editions were introduced and new genres and techniques were developed, including serialized fiction and syndication. Education reform created a greater pool of literate potential readers, and the invention of the kerosene lamp and the electric light made it possible for reading time to be increased into the night. There were more post offices which could facilitate distribution. With electoral reform there came more voters in search of political information on which to base their decisions. Industrialization created a market economy running on the consumption decisions of consumers who found suggestions and recommendations in both newspaper advertising and in criticism and reviews. Paper became cheaper and printing became dramatically faster through mechanization. (Smith 1979: 106–8, Gorman & McLean 2002: 6–7). Moreover, the telegraph made possible a huge increase in the amount of material available to newspapers, and created a new kind of commercial competition — the race to be first with the story (Carey 1989); we'll discuss the telegraph in more detail in Chapter 7.

The major development in newspaper publishing in the second half of the nineteenth century was the introduction of the first cheap (penny) papers which aimed to gather a mass circulation. Stephens writes that 'Two truths have governed the economics of the newspaper business: one is that well-to-do readers are more attractive to advertisers; the second is that poorer readers, because they are much more numerous, build higher circulations' (2007: 183). The key British example here was the *Daily Mail* which was launched by Alfred Harmsworth (later to become Lord Northcliffe) in 1896 with a price of one halfpenny; within 20 years its circulation had reached a million (Smith 1979: 154).

By the end of the nineteenth century the news industry was one that other industries depended upon — most obviously advertising, but also those other industries that needed successful advertising to market their products. As a result of these developments, by the early twentieth century the press had become a major industry, focused upon advertising and seeing its readers as consumer demographics (Smith 1979: 147). Today's blizzard of free CDs and DVDs given away free with newspapers has its antecedents. The publisher of *Tit-Bits* launched a brilliant scheme in 1885 — a life insurance scheme which covered anyone killed in a train accident who was found to have a copy of the paper with them (Conboy 2004: 167). In the 1930s subscribers might even be offered a free piano (Conboy 2004: 178). By the early twentieth century, because of their dependence on advertising and their availability to advertisers, newspapers had become a particularly central part of the modern industrial economy (Gorman & McLean 2002: 8).

For Murdock and Golding, the central trend of the twentieth century is that of 'an industry which has become increasingly concentrated in fewer and richer hands' (1978: 146–7). Early in the twentieth century the first major press barons began to consolidate their empires and their power — Northcliffe, Rothermere and Beaverbrook in Britain, Scripps and Hearst in the US. The latter two were particularly significant for their development of what became known as 'chains' of papers in common ownership, with Hearst adding newsreel and feature film production companies and wire services to his portfolio (Stephens 2007: 197). The phenomenon of concentrated media ownership discussed in Chapter 2 is not such a recent development. It's in this context — the rise of a commercial industry — that we'll consider the ideal of the Fourth Estate.

The Fourth Estate

Journalism's heroic figures are the combative interviewer who won't take no for an answer, the war junkie following death around the world, the adversarial investigative reporter, the crusading paper or programme. The good journalistic watchdog fights for stories that

> *someone doesn't want told; the best stories are those that expose violence and corruption concealed within seemingly respectable institutions, from tin-pot dictatorships to children's homes. Journalism is combat* (Hartley 2000: 40).

This provocative argument from John Hartley captures a good deal of the mythology of the Fourth Estate. However, the idea of journalism-as-combat concedes too much to one of the central tenets of that mythology, which conflates 'journalism' with 'investigative journalism' — *adversarial, investigative, crusading, watchdog, expose.* Such terms emphasize one particular dimension of the news — the ideal of the Fourth Estate: that the news media have a central role within a democratic system (Schultz 2002). But such terms also play down the routine, bureaucratic, mundane aspects of news. Not all news results from investigation. Some news is routine (quarterly trade figures are released). Other news is produced for journalists, rather than by them (in the form of media releases). And sometimes news just happens (a plane crashes). As Conboy observes, journalism has in large part built its social and cultural credibility by focusing on its Fourth Estate role and understating its others (2004: 110). Yet actual investigative reporting is a very small part of what goes on, and much of the rhetorical power of the news media's claim to independent political status comes from disproportionately over-stating this component of the news.

At the heart of the concept of the Fourth Estate is the idea that the news media are 'entitled to claim independent standing in the political system' (Schultz 2002: 102). The news media carved out a role for themselves: 'to act on behalf of the people and report on and give voice to those in positions of political, corporate, economic and social power' (Schultz 1998: 1). By the twenty-first century, though, the media themselves fit that definition well — they are among the pre-eminent institutions that can exercise symbolic power; and the largest of them have significant economic power as well. This is a central paradox of contemporary thinking on the Fourth Estate. Two hundred years ago, when a lot of people could read but only a few people could vote, the press was an important check and balance, a central political institution representing its readers. But now the news media are part of major global industries, and their interests are by no means necessarily identical with those of national audiences (Thompson 1995, Curran & Seaton 2003).

Freedom of speech (just watch what you say)

The Fourth Estate discourse is grounded in a history of debates about freedom of speech. The poet John Milton's pamphlet *Areopagitica* made the case for press freedom from government interference as early as 1644. Writing in a context not only of censorship but also of an explosion of printed material, opinion, argument and news, Milton wrote:

> '... as good almost kill a man as kill a good book: who kills a man kills a reasonable creature, God's image; but he who destroys a good book, kills reason itself, kills the image of God, as it were in the eye' (1990: 578).

Responding to the Licencing Order of 1643 which required all publications to obtain prior official approval, Milton's challenge was that publishing should be free from any such requirement of licencing, arguing that readers should be allowed — and could be trusted — to discern for themselves: 'Let [Truth] and Falsehood grapple; who ever knew Truth put to the worse, in a free and open encounter?' (Milton 1990: 613).

Journalism was not just commercial but political. In the eighteenth century, political essays of writers like Jonathan Swift and Daniel Defoe became important political weapons, establishing journalism as 'a direct form of political power' (Smith 1979: 62). By the end of the eighteenth century the press gained a further degree of consolidation into political life when they won the right to report on Parliament (Smith 1979: 63).

In the US, Congress ratified the First Amendment to the Constitution as part of the Bill of Rights in 1791. The First Amendment enshrined legal protection for the press with the words: 'Congress shall make no law [...] abridging the freedom of speech, or of the press'. Here too we can see how both political and commercial forces are intertwined in the development of news — on the one hand, the First Amendment is a political victory for press freedom, a guarantee that US publishers can put out the material which, ideally, the public needs to function as active citizens; on the other hand, the Amendment can also be seen as conferring unique privileges upon one particular industry.

In the nineteenth century, James Mill restated the argument for press freedom:

> The very foundation of a good choice is knowledge. The fuller and more perfect the knowledge, the better the chance, where all sinister interest is absent, of a good choice. How can the people receive the most perfect knowledge relative to the characters of those who present themselves to their choice, but by information conveyed freely, and without reserve, from one to another? (Mill 1992 [1823]: 118).

In this view, any attempt by the state to restrict the flows of information would be contrary to the nature of democracy. A free press was essential to the creation of informed public opinion and to restraining any potentially despotic or corrupt governments. John Stuart Mill, writing in 1859, suggested that the case for freedom of the press no longer had to be made: 'The time, it is to be hoped, is gone by, when any defence would be necessary of the "liberty of the press" as one of the securities against corrupt or tyrannical government' (1991 [1859]: 20).

It's in this context that the classic statement of the Fourth Estate was made in an 1855 *Edinburgh Review* piece by Henry Reeve:

> Journalism is now truly an estate of the realm; more powerful than any of the other estates; more powerful than all of them combined if it could ever be brought to act as a united and concentrated whole. Nor need we wonder at its sway. It furnishes the daily reading of millions. It furnishes the exclusive reading of hundreds of thousands. Not only does it supply the nation with nearly all the information on public topics which it possesses, but it supplies it with its notions and opinions in addition. [...] For five pence or a penny (as the case may be) it *does all the thinking* of the nation; saves us the trouble of weighing and perpending, of comparing and deliberating; and presents us with ready-made opinions clearly and forcibly expressed (Reeve 1855: 477–8, original emphasis).

Such views echoed throughout the nineteenth century. W. T. Stead, one of the major figures of the nineteenth-century New Journalism (not to be confused with the 1960s New Journalism) saw the Fourth Estate as dominant over the other branches of the political system: 'Parliament will continue to meet in the midst of a newspaper age, but it will be subordinate. The wielders of real power will be those who are nearest the people' (Stead 1886: 657). Stead argued that commercial interests gave the press more democratic interests than Parliament. Politicians restricted their attention to voters, whereas newspapers had a broader constituency:

> Everything that is of human interest is of interest to the Press. A newspaper, to put it brutally, must have good copy, and good copy is oftener found among the outcast and the disinherited of the earth than among the fat and well-fed citizens. Hence selfishness makes the editor more concerned about the vagabond, the landless man, and the deserted child, than the member (Stead 1886: 669–70).

Is this kind of argument sustainable in the twenty-first century? The media environment is now global, not just local. The biggest media firms are enormous transnational enterprises. Entertainment is now a central part of the news, not just information. Politicians have learned to manage the media. And the news media have no claim to express *representative* public opinion: indeed, they may be, Curran and Seaton suggest, more right-wing than the public in whose name they profess to speak (Thompson 1995: 237–40, Curran & Seaton 2003: 346–7).

To gain for themselves greater legitimacy, Boyce suggests, the press 'invented a political myth' (1978: 21). The myth was that: 'the press would act as an indispensable link between public opinion and the governing institutions of the country' (1978: 21). In this way, the press could claim for itself a privileged role of its own invention at the heart of the political system of the nation. The Fourth Estate expressed a relationship between the press and the state that was questionable, and a relationship between the press and the public which was equally idealized. It also depended upon an elitist view of the public. The extension of the franchise would also gradually erode the idea that the press was needed as a watchdog on behalf of those who could not vote (Boyce 1978: 39). And, moreover, there was the question of the increasingly commercial nature of the press and whether this was amenable to the Fourth Estate role:

> The paradox of the Fourth Estate, with its head in politics and its feet in commerce, can, however, only be understood if it is appreciated that the whole idea of the Fourth Estate was a myth (Boyce 1978: 27).

Yet this idea of the press as an unelected — indeed, self-appointed — branch of government has proved one of the most enduring and influential of all the debates surrounding the media. This is true despite (or perhaps because of) some central paradoxes: for one, the paradox of an unelected bulwark to democracy; for another, the paradox of a democratic agency whose success is judged commercially. Schultz cites an advertising slogan for the *New York Times*, which captures this exactly: 'From Fourth Estate to Real Estate' (1998: 5). Some commentators see the fact that the news media are for the most part commercial enterprises as a serious impediment to carrying out a Fourth Estate role (Schultz 1998). Others argue that dependence on advertising paradoxically enables independence in reporting and commentary, that advertising ensured independence from financial support from politicians (Boyce 1978: 34–5). Others have argued that commercial imperatives actually underwrite investigative journalism, that performing a Fourth Estate role makes good business sense (Sparks 2000a: 275–6).

Who let the dogs out?

The term Fourth Estate has changed and evolved over time, from denoting a *place*, a physical space in the British parliament, to denoting the *people* of the press, and on to indicating an *idea*: today it is most useful to think of it as an *ideal* — as a kind of shorthand for not just the news media, but for their 'idealized role' (Schultz 1998: 48). That idealized role is most commonly expressed today through the metaphor of the watchdog. 'The duty of a journalist is the duty of a watchman' (Stead 1886: 667). But the obvious question about watchmen, is who watches them (which, in the case of the media, is where Media Studies comes in). What does it mean to suggest the media are a watchdog? US scholar John Merrill has been particularly scathing on this:

> To whom does the watchdog belong? Whom is it watching, and for what reasons? If the press is a 'watchdog', presumably it is protecting something. Just what is that? Is it the people's watchdog, watching the government, and keeping the government from doing harm, or violence to the people? This must be the core of the concept. But the question arises: Who gave the watchdog this mission? Did the 'people' buy the dog for this purpose? [...] The 'people' do not own the press; it cannot, therefore, be their watchdog. It has no specific duties — except

those which the press people themselves want to accept (Merrill 1974: 117–18)

The watchdog dimension has expanded from the original demand to be able to report on the UK House of Commons to the scrutiny of all in power (although 'power' is rather loosely used here, and in practice this might come down to scrutinizing a dodgy vacuum cleaner repair shop rather than, say, the board of directors of Union Carbide). One dimension of the watchdog brief is the idea of the press as adversarial. The role of the writer, said playwright Arthur Miller, is to be the party of the opposition — not supporting whoever was the opposition party, but taking on the role of critical opposition, regardless of who was in power. Australian writer David Marr has suggested that arguments over the supposed personal biases of journalists are the wrong way to approach what is, genuinely, an important question. 'The much more interesting division', Marr told one interviewer, 'is those that are comfortable with authority and those who are skeptical of authority... For journalists, what matters is are you comfortable or skeptical with the authority that those political parties and those governments represent?' (*Sydney Morning Herald,* 'Guide', 1 April 2002, pp. 4–5). The same idea was expressed less elegantly but with rather more force by *Sun* columnist Richard Littlejohn, who has described his job as 'to sit at the back and throw bottles' (quoted in Franklin 2004: 14). The classic example of journalists-as-watchdogs is the Watergate case, in which the news media effected the resignation of the US President in one of the most spectacular demonstrations of their capacity for symbolic power.

Watergate

In the 1970s *Washington Post* reporters Bob Woodward and Carl Bernstein made history with their pursuit of the Watergate affair. The story led from a small burglary at the Democratic National Committee's offices in Washington D.C.'s Watergate building on 17 June 1972 to the forced resignation of US President Richard Nixon on 9 August 1974. Among many other cultural impacts, Watergate stands as an exemplar of a modern version of the Fourth Estate. Woodward and Bernstein wrote a best-selling book about it called *All The President's Men*, which was made into a hit film with Dustin Hoffman and Robert Redford. Bob Woodward in particular remains one of America's most influential reporters, with a string of books in which he manages to get access to the most elite sources (some of them seem to have been written inside the Oval Office).

Schudson points out that Watergate, and the subsequent best-selling book and film, gave investigative journalism a certain glamour (1978: 191). They also created an enduring symbol for the crusading reporter — *Watergate!* — which acted to entrench the importance of investigative journalism, not least in the popular imagination. Woodward and Bernstein became the celebrity faces of investigative reporting, and the eventual resignation of US President Richard Nixon as a result of the scandal was extraordinary evidence of the power and impact of an investigative press.

Yet as James Carey argues, while the *Washington Post* was right to follow the Watergate story to the end, it wasn't entirely a triumph of a high-minded Fourth Estate. Carey highlights a single episode in Woodward and Bernstein's best-selling account of their investigation, *All The President's Men,* in which Woodward studied a list of potential grand jurors, memorized names, and then went so far as to visit some possible members of the grand jury in order to quiz them for leads for the *Post*'s investigation; at least one juror reported this, and Woodward and Bernstein came close to being held in contempt of court. The striking thing about this episode, Carey suggests, is not just what it revealed about how far the news media would go in pursuit of their own interests, but also that it showed 'the extent to which they unquestioningly identified the interests of journalists with the interests of democracy' (Carey 2002: 84).

Reading *All The President's Men* shows that the grand jury example is part of a larger pattern. Again and again, Woodward and Bernstein would do whatever it took to get further with the story — they used contacts at phone and credit card companies to obtain confidential records (1974: 35, 121); on one occasion Bernstein 'bent the rules a bit' and misrepresented himself on the phone by not mentioning he was a reporter (p. 120). Some rules, of course, and some laws, are best broken — what counts is justice — and the ends did seem to justify the means in the Watergate case. Nixon, speaking from Disneyworld, told a national TV audience: 'I am not a crook' (Woodward & Bernstein 1974: 334), but the evidence was against him, and it's to the reporters' great credit that they followed the trail that helped expose this. But, while justifiable, the means they took to reach this end also put Fourth Estate rhetoric in a stark context — in this most celebrated of examples, they reveal a certain arrogance and disdain for the law and for other democratic institutions. The Fourth Estate might be at best an important component of a democratic system — but it does not constitute one by itself.

The myth of Watergate, of two young journalists toppling a corrupt presidency, is irresistible. It's a myth that both book and film of *All The President's Men* did much to create: the book opens from Woodward's point-of-view and leads to descriptions of Bernstein and Woodward that fit Tom Wolfe's features of the 1960s and 70s New Journalism — scene-by-scene construction; use of dialogue to establish character; shifts in point-of-view; and description of Woodward and Bernstein's 'status life' (gestures, habits, clothes, hairstyles and so on) (Wolfe 1973: 47). *All The President's Men,* it is clear from the first few pages, is not a book about the presidency, about government, or about democracy — it's a book about journalists.

But as Schudson argues, the central tenets of the Watergate myth are all open to challenge. For one thing, the press did not accomplish all this alone: the courts, Congress, and the FBI all played crucial parts, as did various individuals involved in the saga, although none of these offers the romance of the idea of underdog reporters taking on the President. Moreover, the news media as a whole did not pursue Watergate. It is, then, an anomaly rather than proof of the success of a system, of the Fourth Estate (Schudson 1995: 142–65).

War correspondents

In 2005, Kevin Sites set out to report from every war zone on Earth in a single year as a special correspondent for Yahoo!, producing the 'Kevin Sites in the Hot Zone' website <http://hotzone.yahoo.com>. A former CNN and NBC reporter, Sites reported from Afghanistan, Cambodia, Colombia, and a dozen other countries in 12 months, equipped with two cameras, two phones, a satellite modem and a laptop. This is war reporting as an extreme sport, as a backpacking spectacular, an opportunity to set a world record. Even the slogan sounds like a movie poster — 'One Man. One Year. A World Of Conflict'.

War reporting is one extreme of the Fourth Estate ideal. It's also news at its most gendered. Women war correspondents such as the BBC's Kate Adie or CNN's Christiane Amanpour are becoming more visible, but still face different kinds of scrutiny and criticism than their male counterparts (Chambers, Steiner & Fleming 2004). Senior Associated Press correspondent Edie Lederer had to get a letter from the Saudi authorities confirming that she was not a prostitute in order to be able to travel and report on the first Gulf War (Sebba 1994: 255). Yvonne Ridley of the *Sunday Express*, captured by the Taliban in Afghanistan, was criticized by other reporters for taking such risks when she was a single mother — women war correspondents are vulnerable to a charge of irresponsibility, which male journalists are not. They are also far more likely to be judged (and employed) on their looks. Kate Adie of the BBC complains that people always ask why she's not married, and that she is persistently judged on her appearance (Chambers, Steiner & Fleming 2004). Male war reporters don't attract this kind of attention, even though the risks they face are the same.

Those risks are, of course, very real. The Reporters Without Borders website records that 64 journalists and their media assistants were killed in Iraq alone in 2006 <http://www.rsf.org>. In 2003 ITN's Terry Lloyd was killed along with members of his crew while reporting in Iraq. The BBC's John Simpson was injured by a US bomb — this incident was not only broadcast, complete with the indelible image of blood smearing the camera lens, but has also been used to promote BBC World News, which ran a promo in 2005 in which Simpson held his damaged flak jacket up for the camera: 'This is where the bits of shrapnel hit me'. Journalism, after Hartley (2000), as combat.

But the history of the war correspondent is not just a history of courageous reporters determined to bring back the truth from dangerous places. It's also a history of media management, censorship and propaganda (Knightley 2003, Taylor 2003). On one occasion in the US conflict against the Taliban in Afghanistan, American forces came under 'friendly fire'. Knightley writes that 'journalists stationed in a nearby marine base were locked in a warehouse so that they could not report it' (2003: 530). An official press release, created in Florida, was later distributed instead.

Such media management was at its most sophisticated in the 'embedding' of reporters with Coalition forces in Iraq in 2003. This allowed the military to manage the press, while giving the illusion of openness and access, and also nudging the media towards identifying with the troops. Part of the intention was to deflect attention away from civilian casualties, by focusing it on the roles played by individual military personnel. Embedded reporters received some basic training and were assigned with an honorary officer's rank to a particular unit, which provided them with food, transport, accommodation and security. As Knightley notes, one of the immediate consequences of this was reporting which came in the first person plural — reporters spoke not of troops in the third person, but of what 'we' were doing. One BBC correspondent said he even felt under pressure to help out with military activities rather than observe (p. 532). The result? Knightley's research turned up only two examples of embedded reporters taking a critical perspective on their unit and diverging from the official account of an event.

Reporting from a war is the Fourth Estate at its most extreme — journalists risking their lives for a story. But it also highlights the limitations of this, as censorship, propaganda and media management combine to make war news a hot zone of struggles over and through symbolic power. For contrast, a very different form of journalism — rock writing — is discussed in the next section.

Rock critics

The Fourth Estate ideal, and in particular its contemporary emphasis on investigative journalism, covers only a part of the wider journalistic field. While it may be convenient for the news media to highlight investigative journalism and a Fourth Estate ethos in their own self-promotions or in arguments and lobbying around press freedom and regulation, it's worth noting that the term 'journalism' stretches to cover a very broad terrain, much of which is far removed from the tenacious exposure of, say, Thalidomide, Watergate or Abu Ghraib.

Take music journalism, of the kind practiced in dedicated mass-market publications such as *NME, Q, Spin* or *Rolling Stone*. In what ways is this different from the 'hard' news journalism of the Fourth Estate ideal? Where news reporting deals in facts, music journalism deals in interpretation. Where news values objectivity, music journalism trades in subjectivity. Where news describes, music journalism evaluates. Above all, the concerns of music journalism are led by the release of new products — music journalism is a type of consumer advice (Forde 2003: 114).

Back in the 1960s and 70s, popular music journalism had a certain counter-cultural weight and credibility, and the best writing of its star practitioners — such as Lester Bangs (1987) and Nick Kent (1994) — still stands up as strong examples of the kind of personality-driven, immersive, subjective New Journalism identified by Tom Wolfe. Other writers, such as Greil Marcus (1975), Jon Savage (1991) or Simon Reynolds (2005) used the music press to develop ideas, experience and reputations which informed books combining authoritative music history, criticism and serious cultural analysis (Savage & Kureishi 1995).

But by the end of the 1990s, much rock writing had become little more than promotional product-placement. In the UK context, Forde (2001) points to a confluence of factors here, including the rise of PR and news-management strategies within the music industry, the saturation of the market with niche titles, and a bureaucratic restructuring of some music media around corporate house styles. In some publications, as Forde observes, 'it is becoming progressively harder to distinguish the voice of the individual from the voice of the magazine' (2001: 40). In many ways, music writing is at the opposite end of the spectrum from war reporting. But in other ways — in its vulnerability to media management and manipulation — it's very similar. The reliance on advertising, the concentrated ownership of the industry, and the dependence on official sources to provide access to performers, make it an exemplar of Herman and Chomsky's propaganda model (1988).

Blogging

In a 2005 speech to the American Society of Newspaper Editors, Rupert Murdoch cited statistics that claimed people between 18–34 were more than twice as likely to use the web for news than a printed newspaper. Fewer than 10% of respondents in the study in question found newspapers to be either trustworthy or useful; only 4% found them entertaining. Murdoch concluded from this that young people 'want their news on demand, when it works for them. They want control over their media, instead of being controlled by it' (Murdoch 2005). Of particular interest was Murdoch's suggestion that young people 'want to be able to use the information in a larger community — to talk about, to debate, to question, and even to meet the people who think about the world in similar or different ways'. (Murdoch 2005).

Community. Talk. Debate. Question. Meet. These are words that characterize the blog phenomenon, and offer the possibility of rethinking the Fourth Estate for the twenty-first century. What exactly are blogs? There are as many points of difference as of commonality, and definitions are almost always contested (boyd 2006). Some have tried to find a metaphor that defines blogs. Halavais suggests that blogging can be understood by comparing it with earlier forms and forums for the exchange of ideas — the notebook, the coffee-house and the newspaper opinion page. Like a notebook, a blog is useful for 'externalizing thought' (Halavais 2006: 119). Like the eighteenth century coffee-houses in which Habermas locates the ideal public sphere (see Chapter 6), blogs thrive on conversation and debate, and on the creation of 'loose communities' of comment (2006: 120). And like the opinion page, blogs are the natural home of the pundit, the analyst, the commentator.

Such comparisons recall Marshall McLuhan's observation that 'When faced with a totally new situation, we tend always to attach ourselves to the objects, to the flavor of the most recent past. We look at the present through a rear-view mirror' (McLuhan & Fiore 1967: 74–5). Much media commentary about blogs sees them through McLuhan's rear-view mirror — looking at the future, but seeing the past. So we have a debate from the BBC's *Newsnight* programme, which sees blogs as journalism, but finds them wanting (28 March 2007). Or we have a piece from the *Guardian*, which sees blogs as discussion forums, but finds them wanting (11 April 2007, p. 31). Or one from the *Sydney Morning Herald,* which sees blogs as diaries, but finds them wanting (14 April 2007, p. 27). Those are analogies — and all analogies are imperfect. Blogs are a new form, one which is not journalism, not a discussion, and not a diary.

If we want to understand and evaluate them, rather than see them as dodgy updates of the past, then we need to see blogs for what they are — automated, personalized, participatory online publishing, built around hyperlinks. The importance of the link is where the comparison with diaries breaks down — diaries point inwards towards their author, but blogs most often point outwards, towards other blogs, other resources, other writers. The currency of blogs, as Rebecca Blood (2002: xi) points out, is the link, an emphasis which is shared by Jill Walker's definition:

> A weblog, or blog, is a frequently updated website consisting of dated entries arranged in reverse chronological order so the most recent post appears first [...] Typically, weblogs are published by individuals and their style is personal and informal [...] Examples of the genre exist on a continuum from confessional, online diaries to logs tracking specific topics or activities through links and commentary. Though weblogs are primarily textual, experimentation with sound, images, and videos has resulted in related genres such as photoblogs, videoblogs, and audioblogs. Most weblogs use links generously [...] (Walker 2003).

Part of the importance of links here is that they can create networks. Bruns and Jacobs (2006) argue that the 'social networking' made possible by blog practices is the important aspect of weblogging, bringing as it does a subjective and personal dimension to public debate, as well as a collaborative one (cf. Kahn & Kellner 2004). Blogger, journalist and author Dan Gillmor suggests that blogs point to a sea-change in the news: 'from journalism as lecture to journalism as a conversation or seminar' (2004: xiii; see also Rushkoff 2002, Jenkins 2004, Rosen 2005).

It's important to note that many — no doubt most — blogs are not concerned with news or current affairs. And of those that are, many — no doubt most — bloggers are not engaged in journalism as such: that is, they are not reporting. One 2006 survey calculated that 8% of US Net users maintain blogs (equivalent to some 12 million adults), while almost 40% read blogs (equivalent to some 60 million adults) (Pew Internet & American Life Project 2006a). Of those bloggers, only 34% think of their blog as a kind of journalism, and relatively few report taking the time to verify the facts they cite, to source direct quotes, or to post corrections. Instead, for the most part, bloggers engage in commentary and analysis. Blogging is open-access punditry, and it is in a certain sense parasitical on the news agenda of the established media. But we should also note that this parallels industrial developments within the established news world too. As Bruns and Jacobs point out, many news outlets rely on agency copy and on media releases, and so: 'It would therefore be disingenuous to single out bloggers as regurgitators of second-hand news when in reality this practice is far more widespread' (2006: 15). Bruns's concept of 'gatewatching', introduced in Chapter 2, is useful here: much blogging is about keeping tabs on what the established media have published, and pointing the blog's readers towards anything important. Blogging is often about gatewatching — about linking to items published elsewhere, and about discussing, commenting on, annotating or elaborating on those items. Blogging is about publicizing as well as publishing (Bruns 2005: 19).

So is blogging journalism? Matheson has argued that as blogs are extremely heterogeneous, it is inappropriate (as well as perhaps impractical) to try to isolate the blog as a news genre (2004: 50). Blogging, he suggests, might not be best thought of as journalism at all — not because it fails to meet some criterion or other, but rather because to call blogging journalism may be too narrow and reductive to do justice to the form. Blogging blurs lines, it amplifies and extends (and it can be boring and puerile too, of course, as can older news forms). To call blogging journalism may be another rear-view mirror moment.

Chris Atton suggests that one reason why blogs have captured so much of the established media's imagination and attention (compared to the modest coverage of such projects as Indymedia, Wikinews or OhmyNews) is that the personal nature of much blogging lends itself to discussion as a form of human-interest story (2004: 55). This was the case with the so-called 'Baghdad Blogger', who offered one of the most intriguing voices in the 2003 Iraq conflict. Using the pseudonym 'Salam Pax' (words meaning peace in both Arabic and Latin), this young Iraqi maintained a blog from inside Baghdad, during the build-up to the conflict and as it actually occurred <http://dear_raed.blogspot.com>. Salam Pax became a web sensation, with huge numbers of people reading his postings, linking to them, and reprinting and reporting on them. One *Guardian* writer found Salam Pax's success the war's major irony:

> While the world's leading newspapers and television networks poured millions of pounds into their coverage of the war in Iraq, it was the internet musings of a witty young Iraqi living in a two-storey house in a Baghdad suburb that scooped them all to deliver the most compelling description of life during the war (*Guardian* 30 May 2003).

Some suggest Salam Pax's status was due to the novelty of his situation (Redden 2003: 162). But as a writer, Salam Pax has an eye for detail that many professional journalists should envy. To read his descriptions of daily life in Baghdad in February and March 2003, is to be struck again and again by the sheer surrealism of people trying to go about their daily lives while they wait for their city to be destroyed. He wrote of shopping for CDs and then going home to tape the windows up (the latter described as 'actually a very relaxing exercise, if you forget why you are doing it in the first place'). He wrote of grocery shopping in the knowledge that nine B52 bombers were in the air and on their way to Iraq. He wrote of the difficulty of washing the dishes when you know the kitchen window could be blown in any minute by tons of explosives. And he recorded indelible details, such as that Iraqi radio DJs were allowed to play the latest record by UK rock band Bush, but were not allowed to say their inappropriate name, only to spell it out.

Conclusion

What challenges does such blogging pose to the established nature of news? One answer to that question might focus on the news institutions and the reporters who work for them. News, writes Michael Schudson, surveying the literature on news professionals, can be characterized as 'negative, detached, technical, and official' (1995: 9). These characteristics have been shaped by — and in turn shape — institutional demands and expectations of news. Yet news is not just an institutional, but also a cultural product:

> A news story is an announcement of special interest and importance. It is a declaration by a familiar private (or sometimes public) and usually professional (but occasionally political) entity in a public place that an event is noteworthy (Schudson 1995: 20–1).

It is this public nature that gives news its moral authority, and its cultural hold on audiences. It is not just that something noteworthy has happened, but that it has been endorsed as noteworthy by the guardians of this status. The example of Salam Pax points to the developing tensions that the Net makes possible around the question of who is endorsed as such a guardian, and of what licences an individual to participate in the public story-telling that is news. Salam Pax's writing, related to Schudson's description of news, was certainly often negative — but it was neither detached, nor technical, nor official. Instead it was highly personal and subjective, while at the same time deeply engaged with the central issue on the world's news agenda at that moment. His blog highlights the possibilities of the new media environment for rethinking the Fourth Estate — an emphasis on access and participation; an emphasis on new avenues and methods for new people to create news; an emphasis on shifting the boundary of who gets to speak. We will return to this argument in the final chapter. The next chapter turns to news sources — high-status or otherwise established groups and individuals who are able to exercise symbolic power through the news media by having their concerns presented as news.

Chapter 5

'Pay No Attention To That Man Behind The Curtain'

> *'If you wonder how the people in charge of giving us information get their own information, it appears that, in general, they get it from other informers'* (Bourdieu 1998: 26).

In November 2003, eight months after the Iraq invasion began, US President George W. Bush made a quick visit to Baghdad to share Thanksgiving dinner with American troops. It was of course, among other things, a photo opportunity, and pictures of the President holding a traditional Thanksgiving turkey on a platter duly appeared around the world. But there was one problem with the pictures — the turkey wasn't real. It was a stunt turkey, a display turkey, a prop turkey — a model. One might imagine that it would have been simpler for everyone involved to simply cook a real turkey, rather than go to the trouble of obtaining a simulated one, but no. If there was a real turkey involved, it wasn't the one on the platter.

This small, strange flake of world news recalls Jean Baudrillard's infamous commentary on the first US-Iraq conflict of 1990–91, *The Gulf War Did Not Take Place* (1995). This was not a great book, but has nevertheless been dreadfully misrepresented by many commentators who took its title at face-value, falsely casting Baudrillard as a denier of the many deaths that took place in that conflict. Baudrillard used hyperbole to call attention to what might otherwise pass without comment. In this case, he exaggerated and distorted in order to highlight, among other things, the media-management strategies of the military, the restrictions on reporters' movements and access, the meaningless briefings staged for the cameras — and the gulf between what took place and what was represented on TV. A televised, simulated turkey for Thanksgiving dinner is an image straight from Baudrillard's repertoire. It introduces our focus in this chapter — events and images created not by, but for the news media, and manipulations of the news by sources and spin.

News is about defining reality. While previous chapters have concentrated on the symbolic power of media organizations, their employees, and on the cultural context in which they work, this chapter focuses on other major actors in the creation of news — sources. This opens up the news as an arena in which contending forces attempt to influence perceptions and define reality. It also provides a stark context in which to think about the news media's doctrine of objectivity. The chapter also explores the phenomenon of the pseudo-event (Boorstin 1992), and the use of 'spin' in political communication. The final section of the chapter addresses the concept of 'moral panic', and the roles that high-status sources can play in the generation of such media events.

Take us to your leader

Much news is the product of behind-the-scenes attempts to manipulate or guide the news agenda and through it public opinion. Public relations and publicity work shape the news as much as journalism does (Cottle 2003c, Davis 2003, Turner 2005). Our informers, as Bourdieu says in the epigraph of this chapter, get their information from other informers. A major study published in 2008 demonstrated the enormous extent to which news items are generated by PR material and the extent to which they rely on the verbatim replication of copy produced by agencies such as the Press Association. A team of researchers from Cardiff University analysed more than 2,200 domestic news items in the *Guardian, Times, Independent, Daily Telegraph* and *Daily Mail*, and more than 400 broadcast items from BBC, ITV, and Sky services (Lewis, Williams & Franklin 2008a, 2008b; see also Davies 2008).

The major news agencies were found to provide a very large proportion of stories, many of which were simply reproduced verbatim: 30% of the newspaper stories analysed in this study reproduced agency copy more or less unchanged (2008a: 5), with another 19% 'largely dependent' on agency material, and another 21% drawing elements from press agency copy (for more on news agencies, see Chapter 7)

Moreover, the quantities of stories directly derived from PR materials were even more striking: more than 40% of newspaper stories and more than 50% of broadcast news stories were found to 'contain PR materials which play an agenda-setting role or where PR material makes up the bulk of the story' (2008a: 10). Almost 20% of the newspaper stories and 17% of the broadcast items were 'verifiably derived *mainly* or *wholly* from PR material or activity' (2008a: 7, original emphasis). And almost 60% of broadcast news stories which were presented only by the anchor, without the on-air participation of another reporter, were entirely or mainly PR material.

The authors conclude that the routine practices of the UK's major news organizations would be considered plagiarism in any other context. Their findings suggest that 'any meaningful independent journalistic activity by the media is the exception rather than the rule' (Lewis, Williams & Franklin 2008a: 17).

In the classic movie version of *The Wizard of Oz*, Dorothy's little dog Toto breaks the illusion of the wizard's power by pulling back a curtain to reveal an ordinary man pulling levers and spinning dials as he roars into a microphone: 'Pay no attention to that man behind the curtain!' For this chapter, the men and women behind the curtain are sources — not just PR operatives, but those high-status officials who have the capacity to place their interests and concerns in the news. Symbolic power is highly concentrated in media organizations, but it's not restricted to them. Political power also generates symbolic power resources. A Prime Minister or a President can set the day's news agenda just by getting out of bed. And those with lesser concentrations of political power can also find a formidable capacity to affect the news, in particular those with some kind of claim to 'official' status. As Bell puts it, 'News is what an authoritative source tells a journalist' (1991: 191). Or in Sigal's view, 'News is not what happens, but what someone says has happened or will happen' (1986: 15).

How easy is it to make the news if you have 'official' status? Too easy. In Australia in the 1990s, young Newcastle writer Matthew Thompson heard a talkback radio host frothing about the name of the band The Hard-Ons. In response, as a joke, Thompson wrote a letter to the Sydney tabloid the *Daily Telegraph Mirror,* claiming to be the 'head of a growing movement called Young People Against Heavy Metal T-Shirts'. His letter urged teenagers to give up anti-social behaviour such as 'smoking, drinking, taking drugs, easy sex and in particular, wearing heavy metal T-shirts' (Thompson 1997). The paper printed his letter, with a caption reading 'Stamp out T-shirt terror'.

What happened next was revealing. Lots of other media outlets got in touch asking for interviews — national TV and radio, other newspapers. Thompson later wrote that no one ever checked his claims about the size, activities or in fact existence of the non-existent group, even when he began to talk about organizing youth training camps in the desert — the only thing they *did* all check was whether their competitors had also called. Having got onto the media agenda, Thompson found it was very easy to stay there. One paper ran a feature story on heavy metal T-shirts in which they invented a conflict between him and outraged metal fans — 'a storm is brewing among rival youth factions', it said. One TV current affairs show manufactured a conflict by setting up a showdown between Thompson and the owner of a heavy metal record shop. Letters came in from around the country from people wanting to start local chapters of the group. Thompson was able to sustain this hoax until he grew bored with it because as 'head' of a 'national organization' he had official status. As 'leader', he was a legitimate, credible source of news.

Primary definers?

An earlier chapter discussed the concept of news values — that news is the product of selection and construction, that events are cut and shaped to fit the news. Who can influence this selection, construction and shaping? Obviously, news organizations and their employees do this on a daily basis, both in their selection of this story over that, and in the structuring of their news output around certain kinds of topic. For example, many papers now have specialist higher education correspondents, which both reflects the importance the paper is placing on higher education for its assumed readership, and also guarantees that stories on higher education will be generated. The assumed audience has a further influence, as events are interpreted and presented in ways which the news organization thinks will fit with their imagined audience. The media, then, as Stuart Hall and his colleagues at the Birmingham Centre for Contemporary Cultural Studies argued in their 1978 book *Policing The Crisis*, not only report to their audiences what has happened, but they also offer interpretations — they tell us what has happened *and* suggest how to understand it. From this perspective, such interpretations are skewed towards certain kinds of high-status authorities who are able to gather and create news coverage. Government departments and agencies, the police, the law courts — such institutions generate, and make available to the news media, enormous amounts of information. Hall and his colleagues label such groups *primary definers* of news topics (1978: 57–60).

The news media's reliance on 'primary definers' is partly bureaucratic — there are deadlines, for example, and resources need to be allocated (Sigal 1986, 1999). So it is in the interests of many social groups and actors to accommodate the demands of news organizations as best they can — as Mark Fishman puts it, 'the world is bureaucratically organized for journalists' (1980: 51). Hall and his colleagues argue that the reliance on primary definers is also partly ideological, in the sense that the media's use of such concepts as 'impartiality' and 'objectivity' inevitably leads them to privilege certain kinds of sources. For news to be 'objective', it needs to draw on the statements of individuals and organizations who have a certain kind of legitimacy, a certain kind of credibility, a certain kind of official status. News, as three leading scholars put it, is 'a representation of authority. In the contemporary knowledge society news represents *who* are the authorized knowers and *what* are their authoritative versions of reality' (Ericson, Baranek & Chan 1989: 3, original emphasis).

The importance of this is that it allows 'primary definers' to set the terms of a given topic or debate: 'the primary definition *sets the limit* for all subsequent discussion by *framing what the problem is*' (Hall *et al* 1978: 59, original emphasis). In this sense, the news media don't so much make the news as have it made for them. From this perspective, the media's role is that of *secondary definers*, distributing and amplifying the definitions set by their high-status, official sources; some scholars argue this gives too little weight to the media, who are able to act as primary definers themselves as in, for example, cases of investigative journalism (Schlesinger & Tumber 1994: 19).

Reliable sources are essential to the news. Some are monitored on an ongoing or regular basis (courts, police). Other organizations create their own media releases and supply these in the hope that they will run as news. Some research organizations of various kinds, including pollsters, exist to generate news stories, and may be owned by media organizations in turn — Rupert Murdoch's Newspoll provides a dependable stream of front-page stories to his national daily the *Australian.* There are also elite individuals, such as celebrities, who can generate pseudo-events in their own right. And there are regular events, such as sports matches, that can be managed in advance (Fulton 2005: 219–20).

Why does this matter? For one thing it means that many news stories are framed before they even reach the news media. Frames, writes Gitlin, guide selection, guide emphasis, guide presentation. They are, he says, 'little tacit theories about what exists, what happens, and what matters' (Gitlin 1980: 6). They make it possible for journalists to make sense of complexity for their audiences. The point, then, is not to complain that frames exist, but rather to be alert to their existence. Gitlin argues that the analyst of news (and we might add the audience) must ask what the frame is in a given story, must ask why this frame and not that one, and must ask how important framing is for the world beyond the story. What lies outside the frame? What's not in this picture? To what extent does this story reflect the world-view of those who gave it to the media?

Primary definers don't get it all their own way all the time. They may have to struggle to set the news agenda in competition with other primary definers. Their status may change and decline (as has happened to trade unions). There are opportunities for other kinds of group or actor to intervene in the news agenda. And the media themselves are hardly passive — the media can influence primary definers as well as be influenced by them (Schlesinger 1990, Schlesinger & Tumber 1994, Manning 2001). The relationships between sources and news organizations should be recognized as working both ways (Gans suggests that it 'resembles a dance', 1979: 116). News organizations have the capacity to exercise symbolic power in ways that demand accommodation by other bureaucracies:

> the power to deny a source any access; the power to sustain coverage that contextualizes the source negatively; the power of the last word;

> and, the power of translation of specialized and particular knowledge into common sense (Ericson, Baranek & Chan 1989: 378).

But established institutions, and people with demonstrable 'official' status, have significant opportunities and potential to access the news — or, indeed, to create the news: the *New York Times* reported in March 2005 that more than 20 US federal bodies, including the military, were creating, filming and providing news stories to TV stations that were then broadcasting them without attribution (13 March, p. 1). More than 160 articles were published with the by-line 'Tony Blair' in his first two years as Prime Minister, although most would have been written by his communications staffers, including Alastair Campbell (Franklin 2003: 52). As Chancellor of the Exchequer, Gordon Brown followed up his 1998 budget by publishing articles in 120 local newspapers, addressing local issues in every one — a feat that can only have been accomplished by having his staff write the articles (Jones 1999: 132). In October 2007, the US Federal Emergency Management Agency (FEMA) held a media conference that showed how much they had learned the need for good publicity after the scandal of their botched response to Hurricane Katrina — all the questions were asked by FEMA staff pretending to be reporters (*Washington Post,* 26 October 2007, p. A19).

One reason that primary definers are able to set parts of the news agenda is that reporters favour official or otherwise credentialed sources, in part in order to avoid seeming partisan. Robert McChesney points to the problem with this:

> Reporters report what people in power say, and what they debate. This tends to give the news an establishment bias. When a journalist reports what official sources are saying, or debating, she is professional. When she steps outside this range of official debate to provide alternative perspectives or to raise issues those in power prefer not to discuss, she is no longer being professional (McChesney 2002: 95).

McChesney describes this as not journalism but stenography, as taking dictation, and contends that many reporters have come to accommodate this stenographic role so that they see it as both normal and desirable. Edward Herman, similarly, highlights this characteristic of news reporting:

> If a highly placed person makes some statement, this is newsworthy in itself. The more authoritative and credible the source, the easier it is to

> accept statements without checking, and the less expensive is news making. Hence the paradox that even if untrue, such statements may be broadcast without commentary, as 'objective' news (Herman 1995: 81).

Objectivity, neutrality, impartiality, bias — these words orbit any discussion of the news. Objectivity serves as a kind of guiding doctrine for some news outlets (such as major American newspapers or the BBC, discussed further in Chapter 7), while others are openly partisan (such as Fox News or the UK tabloids, discussed further in Chapter 6). The next section sets objectivity in the context of the exercise of symbolic power. Objectivity is not a black-and-white category, but is a line that can be moved in struggles to define reality.

Objectivity

> 'Inextricably intertwined with truth, fairness, balance, neutrality, the absence of value judgements — in short, with the most fundamental journalistic values — objectivity is a cornerstone of the professional ideology of journalists in liberal democracies' (Lichtenberg 2000: 238).

The dependence on official sources of information is intrinsic to the doctrine of objectivity: Yet as Michael Schudson points out, objectivity is in some ways a weird demand to make of news organizations — for the most part, these are commercial enterprises, and yet we demand of them that they adhere to a set of standards that are by no means necessarily compatible with profit-making (1978: 3). This is part of the cultural bargain by which news media claim their political status as Fourth Estate.

But the terms of this bargain aren't always clear. One major survey of Australian journalists found that 88% identified objectivity as 'very important' (Schultz 1998: 133). Yet the same study found that there wasn't much agreement about what the term actually meant. Respondents variously identified 'objectivity' with the fair presentation of both sides of an issue, or with making it clear which side has the stronger case in a dispute, or with keeping the reporter's own views out of the story.

So in news terms, what is objectivity? Hallin (1986: 68–75) identifies an ideology of 'objective journalism' that draws together different ideals:

- *independence* — journalistic autonomy from political, commercial or other sources of pressure, including the news organization
- *objectivity* — presentation of 'the facts' untainted by opinion or judgement
- *balance* — impartial coverage of controversy

One *New York Times* reporter told Hallin (1986: 71): 'No interpretation of any kind. If the president says, "Black is white," you write, "The president said black is white."' The conventions of this kind of journalism, Hallin suggests, 'make the *New York Times* essentially an instrument of the state' (1986: 71). How does this play out when the news is presented to its audience? In McNair's phrase, the doctrine of objectivity is 'essentially an appeal for trust' (1998: 65). But this trust isn't always earned.

The ideal of the Fourth Estate, as discussed in the previous chapter, assumes that the news media stand at a certain distance from other institutions of democracy. But the growing professionalization of journalism throughout the twentieth century brought political reporters closer to those they wrote about — officials would brief, confide in or leak to journalists, and those journalists came to rely upon those same officials as their principal sources of information (Hallin 1986: 69). Indeed, the very professionalization of journalism, as expressed in the doctrine of objectivity, *demands* that reporters rely on official sources. The authority of their official status in itself ensures that their announcements and statements will be covered by the media (Hallin 1986: 70).

As Lichtenberg observes above (2000: 238), objectivity is central to the professional ideology of journalists and to the roles they claim within our culture (cf Tuchman 1972). So it's important to note that there are occasions when they are deliberately not objective. As syndicated columnist Ellen Goodman wrote of the September 11 attacks: 'No editor demanded a quote from someone saying it was fine to fly airplanes into buildings. No one expected reporters to take an "objective" view of the terrorists' (quoted in Schudson 2002: 39). So how movable is the line around objectivity?

In his study of the media coverage of the Vietnam war, Daniel Hallin puts forward a useful framework for thinking about this movable boundary around the concept of objectivity-as-neutrality. Hallin proposes that journalists' commitment to objectivity shifts, depending on the material they're covering. This can be expressed through imagining the world of the news media as consisting of three concentric circles. Certain topics fall within the middle of these circles, what Hallin calls 'the sphere of legitimate controversy'. This contains most political debates, and journalists generally try to be balanced in reporting these, seeking both sides of an issue, looking for balancing quotes, and so forth. However, other issues fall within the innermost circle, what Hallin calls 'the sphere of consensus' — the domain of issues on which there is little controversy. This is where journalists speak for 'us' and take for granted a national, cultural consensus on the meaning and significance of an event; they may feel no obligation to present a balancing viewpoint, and may instead serve as cheerleaders or advocates. Third, there is the outermost region — Hallin points to this as a 'sphere of deviance', the domain of those whose views are felt to be unworthy by both the political establishment and the news media; reporters will gleefully sneer at and trash those caught within this sphere of deviance (1986: 116–18). The operation of the 'sphere of deviance' is discussed more fully in the final section of this chapter, on moral panics.

Michael Schudson argues that with the events of September 11, 'journalists felt thrust into the sphere of consensus' (2002: 40). Schudson proposes three kinds of occasion on which journalists drop the doctrine of objectivity and where the 'sphere of consensus' dominates. One is in moments of tragedy, when a solemn air obtains. A second is in moments of danger to the population, when practical guidance and reassurance become important. A third is when national security is threatened (2002: 41). What this points to is that objectivity and neutrality are something less than binding and immutable. But the news media need their claim to objectivity. And so their dependence on official sources to sustain this claim makes them vulnerable to manipulation through *spin*.

Sexing up dodgy dossiers

'It used to be, everyone was entitled to their own opinion, but not their own facts. But that's not the case anymore. Facts matter not at all.

Perception is everything.' Stephen Colbert, interviewed in The Onion's A/V Club 25 January 2006 <http://www.avclub.com/content/node/44705>.

On 29 May 2003, journalist Andrew Gilligan made a live contribution to BBC Radio 4's *Today* show. When he was asked by host John Humphrys about the dossier of information used to support the Blair government's claims about Iraqi weapons of mass destruction, Gilligan's reply included the claim that the dossier had been 'sexed up, to be made more exciting'. Gilligan's suggestion that the government 'probably' knew certain claims were false, and his indelible phrase 'sexed up', would ultimately lead to the resignations of the BBC's two most senior figures, director-general Greg Dyke and chairman Gavyn Davies. But what was most striking about Gilligan's comment was its casual — and, it transpired, accurate — assumption that the government might 'sex up' information for presentation purposes.

Every government gets the satire it deserves — Jon Stewart of *The Daily Show* looks positively presidential compared to George W. Bush. Former Australian Prime Minister John Howard, who pledged to make Australians 'relaxed and comfortable', got *The Chaser's War On Everything*, in which five youngish men lounge around on couches, mocking other TV shows. And in the UK, the defining satire of the Blair era was Armando Iannucci's *The Thick Of It* — a *Yes, Minister* for the twenty-first century, in which the manipulative civil servants of that earlier series have been replaced by party spin doctors. Peter Capaldi plays Malcolm Tucker, a thinly disguised version of Alastair Campbell, Tony Blair's former press secretary, and Tucker offers a masterclass in media manipulation and control freakery.

The word 'spin' became firmly associated with the Blair government (Jones 1995, 1999, 2001, 2006). Alastair Campbell became as famous in the UK as any politician, perhaps more famous — by one count, in 1998 he received more press mentions than 29 cabinet ministers put together (Stanyer 2007: 76). One commentator suggests why: 'Campbell did in government what he had done in opposition — seduced, cajoled, harried and intimidated the media from behind the scenes into giving his leader the best possible coverage in any given circumstances' (McNair 2003: 146–7; see also Franklin 2003). Campbell's published diaries record that by March

2000, Blair felt Campbell's profile made it hard for him to brief the media, that Campbell himself was becoming too implicated in stories (2007: 445). By July 2000, Labour pollster Philip Gould write in a leaked memo that the 'New Labour brand' was 'badly contaminated', with the reliance on spin exposing the government to 'ridicule' (quoted in Jones 2001: 1). The index to Campbell's own published diaries (2007) contains no entry for 'spin'.

One US pollster went so far in 2007 as to write: '"Spin" has become the cancer at the heart of British politics' (*Guardian*, 16 March 2007, p. 39) — a claim that was all the more remarkable because the person making it, Frank Luntz, was himself a pre-eminent spin doctor. In a now-famous memo, Luntz advised US Republican politicians to use the phrase 'climate change' rather than 'global warming', as 'climate change' sounded 'less frightening' and was therefore more suitable in arguing against environmentally-friendly policies. The kind of euphemism used by Luntz here is a basic technique of spin, as we'll discuss below.

Shortly before stepping down as Prime Minister in June 2007, Blair described the media as 'a feral beast' — this revealing image suggests a world-view in which control of perceptions and media management are perhaps too important. It is, of course, essential and desirable that governments effectively communicate with the public. Governments use increasingly sophisticated techniques to coordinate their complex information flows. In 1997 Campbell introduced Downing Street's 'grid', in which the various speeches, announcements, statistics and interviews of the coming week are mapped against other upcoming events (sports matches, scheduled international news, cultural events) that might overshadow them (Moore 2006: 213, Campbell 2007: 430). A leaked copy of the grid in June 2000 revealed the complex ways in which speeches and announcements were sequenced to complement and reinforce each other (Jones 2001: 145).

But the central criticism of spin is that it goes beyond communicating information. Spin involves government manipulation of the media — and, through them, of the public. Spin is not about communicating government information to the public, for the public's advantage. Spin is about communicating perceptions and imagery to the public, for the government's advantage. So it's important to distinguish between, on the one hand, necessary attempts to manage the flows of information from complex bureaucracies, and, on the other hand, attempts to manipulate or distort the public's understanding.

Politicians have always had to adapt to the communication environment of their time. Periods of transition, when newer media forms are rising in prominence and importance, can cause difficulties for politicians used to dealing with older media. In the Australian Federal Election of 2007, then-Prime Minister John Howard was persuaded to post special campaign messages on video-sharing website YouTube; that his first began with the words 'good morning', as though he were addressing a simultaneous TV audience, revealed immediately how little he or his team understood the new platform or how to exploit its specific characteristics. Winston Churchill declined to give TV interviews as UK Prime Minister in the 1950s, uncertain that he could use the newer medium as effectively as he had radio (Jones 1995: 9). Successive US Presidents have developed and reworked their media management strategies, from the introduction of regular interviews by President Andrew Johnson through the use of the press conference by Woodrow Wilson (Smith 1979: 168–9) and on to Franklin Roosevelt's radio 'fireside chats' (Meyrowitz 1985). John F. Kennedy used television to connect directly with the public. Contemporary media management practices can be set in the context of the televising of politics, from Kennedy through the difficulties Richard Nixon initially faced in adapting to a TV environment, and on to the media strategies of the Reagan administration, which sought to simultaneously get the president 'close' to the public in the sense of using TV to exploit his personal qualities while keeping him 'distant' from reporters' questions (Thompson 1995: 138–40). Bill Clinton appeared on the *Arsenio Hall Show*, wearing shades and playing Elvis tunes on his saxophone. Bush and Gore appeared on late-night comedy shows. In a powerful spin strategy, Nixon and later Reagan both used a 'line of the day' approach; in the UK, the Blair government introduced a 'line for the following day's news agenda' in 2001 (Stanyer 2007: 47).

The term 'spin' itself dates back, appropriately, to 1984 (Schudson 2003: 147), although the practice of managing perceptions is obviously far older than that. Spin represents the convergence of news and public relations. Edward Bernays, a hugely influential figure in US public relations, is often cited for his success in marketing cigarettes to women by persuading 1920s marchers for women's rights to brandish cigarettes as 'torches of freedom' (Ewen 1996: 4; on the extreme ends of PR see Stauber & Rampton 1995). Bernays saw that public relations is not just about the creation of images — rather, it is about the exercise of symbolic power, of defining reality, 'of making people see and believe', in Bourdieu's phrase (1991: 170). As Bernays told one interviewer: 'we don't deal in images... We deal in reality' (Ewen 1996: 6).

George Orwell (1961 [1946]) warned about the potential of language as a means of concealment, rather than of communication. Political speech, Orwell wrote, was 'largely the defence of the indefensible' (p. 363). So euphemisms are used to political ends — 'friendly fire', 'ethnic cleansing', 'final solution', 'illegals', 'non-core promise', 'extraordinary rendition', 'comfort women' (and while writing that list I was interrupted by a 'courtesy call' from a telemarketer). When three detainees at Guantanamo Bay hanged themselves in June 2006, the camp's commanding official described the suicides as 'an act of asymmetrical warfare waged against us' (*Guardian*, 12 June 2006). The US deputy assistant secretary of state for public diplomacy (a job title which itself speaks to a spin world-view), told the BBC that 'Taking their own lives was not necessary, but it certainly is a good PR move'. Tactical media activists the Yes Men have a long history of using such euphemisms in satirical interventions against the extremes of corporate culture. In November 2006, they impersonated the World Trade Organization at a Philadelphia conference on business in Africa and proposed the reintroduction of slavery under the title of 'full private stewardry of labour' or 'compassionate slavery' <http://www.theyesmen.org>. As the Yes Men show, such euphemisms have political objectives. At worst, as Orwell saw, the debased stock of euphemistic expressions become taken up as standard usage. Every time a journalist uses the term 'ethnic cleansing', something important has been lost. The debate has been framed by its primary definers, and a premise that should have been questioned has instead been assumed.

What are the tactics of spin? Gaber (2000) proposes a distinction between 'above the line' and 'below the line' activities performed by media advisers. By 'above the line' he refers to the kinds of activity traditionally performed by 'old-fashioned' press officers — distributing media releases and announcements; reacting to announcements by the other side; promoting and publicizing interviews, speeches and articles and reacting to those made by one's opponents; and reacting to news events as they break. Such activities, in Gaber's analysis, are about managing the necessary flows of information from politicians to the public. In contrast, by 'below the line', Gaber is identifying the often covert strategies and tactics of spin that are intended to manage perceptions, to frame an issue favourably, even when the facts are not favourable, to secure support and consent regardless of the merits of the situation.

The tactics of this kind of approach include the relentless 'staying on message' now characteristic of the political interview, in which any question will receive the pre-programmed reply that is the line-of-the-day. One legendary interview that illuminates politicians' tenacity in not answering direct questions involved the BBC's Jeremy Paxman repeating the same yes-or-no question to Conservative MP Michael Howard more than a dozen times without ever getting anything resembling a yes-or-no answer — watch the encounter and count for yourself at <http://news.bbc.co.uk/1/hi/programmes/newsnight>. Other 'below the line' spin tactics include creating diversions from embarrassing stories, and raising or lowering expectations about, say, a Budget in order to manage public perceptions. One very blunt example of a 'below the line' tactic is the story of then-UK Chancellor Gordon Brown's one-time spin doctor Charlie Whelan deliberately unplugging a BBC reporter's microphone to prevent him from asking an unwanted question (Jones 1999: 164).

One particularly unattractive tactic involves taking advantage of major news events by releasing bad news at the same time, in the hope that the latter will pass unnoticed. This tactic became starkly visible in an incident on September 11 2001 — within half an hour of the second plane striking the World Trade Centre, Jo Moore, adviser to the then-UK Transport Secretary Stephen Byers, had emailed her colleagues with the advice that 'It's now a very good day to get out anything we want to bury.' As Franklin notes, what was significant here was not the poor judgement or taste of Ms Moore, but rather what it revealed about how far politicians and their staffers will go in using the media to manipulate public debate (2004: 3).

So what? It seems clear that such manipulation of politics contributes to the electoral disillusionment that makes people stay at home on polling day (Castells 2004: 367–418). Elections, as Stanyer puts it, are becoming a 'niche interest' (2007: 116). The 2001 UK election drew five million fewer voters than the 1997 one (Franklin 2004: 13). In the 2005 UK general election, Tony Blair's Labour Party got 35% of the vote — but 39% of eligible voters didn't bother to show up. In the US, in 2006, Taylor Hicks won the fifth season of *American Idol* in a finale that drew almost 64 million votes — more than the 62 million George W. Bush managed in the 2004 US election. But between hanging chads and hackable voting machines, perhaps *American Idol* just has the better technology.

Public image

Let's go back for a moment to the image of the fake turkey photo opportunity. The photo-op, the interview, the media release — these are examples of what Boorstin (1992) calls pseudo-events. Boorstin's essay on the pseudo-event dates from the early 1960s, yet appears extremely contemporary. More and more, he writes, journalists do not make the news, so much as they have it made for them by others. Much of what we see and read and hear as news concerns not unexpected events or the revelations of investigative journalism, but rather the products of PR and spin.

How much of what you see on today's TV news fits with the characteristics of the pseudo-event? That is, how much of today's news takes the form of photo opportunities or scheduled press briefings? How much of it is planned, not spontaneous? How much consists of prepared announcements, written in advance to be reported in hindsight? Indeed, how much of today's news is in the future tense ('... *the Prime Minister will today announce*...')? How many events that appear in today's news were organized in order to be reported, to be filmed? How many take place for *no other reason* than to be reported?

The creation of pseudo-events is the business of what Molotch and Lester (1981) call *promoters*, those who are in a position to push an event as noteworthy — politicians and their staffs, corporations, police, and the apparatus of PR everywhere. And while such promoters have considerable resources of symbolic power, they are also vulnerable to its use by others, in the politics of scandal, smear, leak and gaffe (Castells 2004, 2007, Thompson 2005). Pseudo-events are so common as to be taken for granted. They have become the natural stuff of the daily news. In war, because the stakes are so high, pseudo-events can become more visible and can overlap with propaganda. And yet pseudo-events, argues Boorstin, are not propaganda. Propaganda appeals to the emotions, while pseudo-events appeal to our reason. Propaganda is 'an appealing falsehood', but a pseudo-event is 'an ambiguous truth' (1992: 34). Propaganda works through 'our willingness to be inflamed [...] our desire to be aroused', while pseudo-events 'thrive on our honest desire to be informed' [and] appeal 'to our duty to be educated' (Boorstin 1992: 34).

A clear example is Bush's arrival on the aircraft carrier *USS Abraham Lincoln* on 1 May 2003, dressed in a green flight suit and carrying a white pilot's helmet, to stand beneath a banner reading 'mission accomplished'. Or the toppling of Saddam Hussein's statue in Baghdad, and the moment when US marine corporal Ed Chin briefly decorated it with a US flag. Or the televised briefings at the US military's official media centre at Doha in Qatar, such as the one in which General Vincent Brooks announced that troops in Iraq were being issued with decks of playing cards that featured the faces and ID details of the 55 most-wanted members of the Iraqi regime (with Saddam as the Ace of Spades, and so on) — cards he was unable to actually produce when journalists pressed for a pack. With the conflict underway, Australian TV viewers were treated to night-vision footage of Australian commandos on desert patrol in Iraq — which turned out to have been filmed in advance in Australia, for the mutual convenience of the military and the media. A particularly revealing example came when the Australian naval vessel *HMAS Sydney* left for the Gulf. Its departure, and its official farewell by Prime Minister John Howard, was filmed — the ship's departure was a real event, but the televised farewelling was a pseudo-event. The ship had not yet left Sydney Harbour before it was intercepted by two Greenpeace activists in dinghies, who attached themselves to the ship and unfurled a 'no war' banner for the cameras — one pseudo-event was absorbed into another, in competing versions of political theatre.

Panic on the streets of [*your town here*]

The news, writes John Hartley, 'is organized around strategies of inclusion and exclusion from "our" community' (1992a: 207). The news tells us what's ours and what's theirs — people, values, behaviour. In this sense, the news media work to generate and sustain that sense of collective identity. They do this through stories that represent people or events or values as being 'ours' or 'theirs'. This might be at the level of one nation versus another. But it can also happen within our imagined national community. Because, as Hartley puts it, 'there are people and actions which cannot be rendered in the news as "we" and "ours", but which instead are only intelligible as "they"' (1992a: 207). Such people and actions are subjected to a certain kind treatment in the media — they'll be stereotyped and simplified so that they are all seen to be like each other (and hence different from 'us'). As McKenzie Wark writes:

> 'When an enemy is identified by a series of contradictory excesses but no-one is actually named, then we are probably dealing with an irrational expression of fear and resentment — a fantasy. An expression of the passions, mediated by rhetoric, untouched by reason. "They" are doing bad things. "They" are responsible for it all. But "they" never seem to get to speak.' (Wark 1997: 180).

The moral panic is where these processes of inclusion and exclusion come to the surface, as the media become the forum for a specific debate about the nature of 'us' and the nature of 'them'.

An earlier chapter introduced James Carey's distinction between ritual and transmission perspectives on communication. That chapter offered Benedict Anderson's concept of the nation as 'imagined community' as one idea that builds upon a ritual view of media use. This section explores the concept of moral panic, as one phenomenon in which a source-centred view of the news can be explored. The moral panic is one mechanism by which our imagined community actually gets imagined. In particular, the moral panic is one way we police the boundaries of our imagined community — it's how the fences get put up.

What is a moral panic? A moral panic is a media event about the boundaries of culture and social behaviour. A moral panic is about negotiating values, about negotiating cultural norms and boundaries. This cultural dimension is what separates the moral panic from other media controversies over what McNair calls 'problematic reality' (1998: 51), such as food scares (salmonella in eggs, foot-and-mouth disease, Mad Cow Disease). The key thing to a moral panic is that it presents 'us' as being under some kind of threat from 'them'. But who 'they' are tends to be different each time — and who 'we' are can be problematic as well. Moral panics are an expression, in the media, of cultural negotiation. Culture is not something static or fixed, but rather something that is constantly being worked out — moral panics are moments or events when this process bubbles up to the surface of the media.

One way this process of cultural negotiation works is by *inclusion* and *exclusion*. What, for example, does it mean to be 'British' or 'American' or 'Australian' today? Particularly, what does it mean to be that peculiar creature that politicians love to talk about, the *mainstream* member of society? We could try and offer a positive definition of this, but we can also do this negatively — we can define ourselves by reference to others. 'We' are different from 'them', and this becomes part of the explanation of who 'we' are. We argue over who's in the gang and who's not. And by excluding those who're not in our big cultural gang, we define ourselves negatively — by exclusion.

Naming and shaming

'Unspeakably Sick', rasped the *Daily Mail,* the 'sickest TV programme ever shown'. The show, it said, would not have been broadcast 'in a civilised society'. Its creator, the *Mail* went on to suggest, could be prosecuted for 'the ancient crime of outraging public decency', an offence that the paper noted carries a potential life sentence, although it conceded — perhaps with a certain reluctance — that this would be unlikely in the case of a network TV programme (*Daily Mail*, 30 July 2001, pp. 4–5). What show was this? A one-off 2001 special of Chris Morris's Channel 4 series *Brass Eye.*

Brass Eye (the original series of which ran in 1997) remains some of the most insightful — and vicious — commentary on news formulas and current affairs ever produced. Each episode presents a fictitious news magazine programme — new drugs, new threats, and new kinds of crime are breathlessly announced (such as 'bursting shops', in which gangs of kids fill shops with rice and then add water). The 2001 *Brass Eye* special that so exercised the *Daily Mail* explored media exploitations of public anxiety over paedophilia, a topic that was much in the UK news at the time. In 2000, the best-selling Sunday paper the *News of the World* had begun a campaign of printing the names and photos of convicted sex offenders. On 23 July 2000, the paper led with the front-page headline 'Named Shamed'. Inside on page three were 49 passport-sized photos of convicted sex offenders. The facing page ('what to do if there's a pervert on your doorstep') listed the names, ages and towns of dozens of further offenders, and promised more online ('our website maps beasts'). Such coverage was guaranteed to inflame tempers and, despite the editorial cautioning against vigilantism ('that would be counter-productive', p. 6), there were indeed outbreaks of mob violence against suspected paedophiles, including nights of rioting and a surreal incident in which a paediatrician was driven from her home by a gang of vigilantes with very real spelling problems (*Times,* 30 August 2000, p. 4).

In response to this climate, the *Brass Eye* episode was framed as a live crisis special, with parents urged to herd their kids into major stadiums around the country, where they'd be fitted with 'anti-paedophile canisters'. The programme featured CCTV footage of a paedophile who had 'disguised himself as a school', and reported that over 80% of people have sex with children 'if you define a child as anyone under thirty'. A range of British celebrities and public figures were exposed as prepared to lend their vocal support to causes that they clearly didn't understand: 'I'm talking nonce sense' said singer Phil Collins, pointing at the latter two words on a T-shirt with which the programme's makers had supplied him, while one Labour MP was persuaded to announce that child sex offenders were 'using an area of the Internet the size of Ireland'.

The programme was not laughing at paedophilia, but was rather satirizing the representation of this issue in news and current affairs, in particular identifying a blurred line between reporting and prurience — a point that the *Daily Mail* was to prove neatly in its subsequent attack on *Brass Eye.* In the same issue as the 'Unspeakably Sick' piece (in fact, on the preceding page, which was — appropriately enough — page three) the *Mail* printed a voyeuristic paparazzi photo of the then-11 and 13-year-old princesses Eugenie and Beatrice wearing bikinis. *Brass Eye* set out to satirize one moral panic and in turn became the subject of a new one.

Problem people

Moral panics usually focus on *problem people* or *problem technologies* (and the problem with problem technologies often turns out to be that problem people have access to them — terrorists exchanging anonymous emails, paedophiles in online chat rooms, anyone at all with violent movies, and so on and on). In his analysis of inclusion and exclusion, Hartley offers examples of problem people such as criminals, drug traffickers and paedophiles. But these processes can operate at a much more mundane level than that — young people, in general, for instance, are frequently the subject of public anxiety about their behaviour. In May 2005 the Bluewater shopping centre in Kent banned hooded tops and baseball caps from its premises ('to drive out young thugs', as *The Sun* explained on 12 May, p. 21). The hoodie became a metonym for discussion of anxieties surrounding 'respect' and 'anti-social behaviour'. The *Express* suggested that: 'Anyone caught wearing what has become the uniform of the yob should be treated in the same way as a person carrying an offensive weapon' (13 May 2005, p. 12). Then-Deputy Prime Minister John Prescott told of being harassed by a hooded gang. Tony Blair made noises about the need to bring back 'respect', and *The Sun* quickly found a five-year-old photo of Cherie Blair in a hooded top — 'Cherie Blair has given hubby Tony a hood-ache' (14 May 2005, p. 31). As the hoodie debate shows, the news is one arena in which the relations between generations get worked out. For the news, young people, almost by definition, are problem people. Youth subcultures can *always* be represented as being other to the mainstream — that's the whole point of having them.

Why does this matter? The moral panic is a useful concept for interpreting many news events. It draws together aspects of the news process from all points canvassed in this book. First and foremost, a moral panic is a struggle over and through symbolic power — it is an event which works around defining a particular aspect of reality, around fixing and framing a certain view of a certain cultural boundary. A moral panic generates certain kinds of text — stories with certain characteristics and genre features, of the kinds discussed in Chapter 3. A moral panic is unimaginable without the participation of media institutions — indeed, the institutional imperatives and commercial strategies of news organizations can be identified as the driving force behind the generation of many moral panics.

The concept also enables a consideration of the roles of different kinds of actors involved in the news:

- *Journalists* — and the questions of public good and public interest that come to the fore in any discussion of any media event which foregrounds sensationalism or the drawing of them-and-us boundaries.

- *Audiences* — whose concern and anxiety may be variously reflected, assumed, manipulated or fantasized in a given moral panic.
- *Sources* — in particular organized interest groups and social institutions whose high status gives them the capacity to place their concerns on the news agenda.

As Critcher observes (2006: 3), to call something a moral panic to make a judgement — it's to claim that the event is driven by hype and distortion, and that the response is disproportionate to the actual threat. Catharine Lumby imputes a certain paternalism to the moral panics thesis: 'To claim someone else is panicking is to make a claim to the high rational ground... To state: "They're panicking. I'm *concerned*"' (1997a: 40, original emphasis). These are strong points. But concepts of moral panic remain useful in identifying and analysing media events in which questions of ideology as a particular subset of symbolic power relations can be seen.

Models of moral panic

Critcher argues that there are five types of actors who have the capacity to define social problems, and that this capacity is increased when two or more of these groups act together. He calls these 'the five powerful Ps of moral panic' (2006: 4). These are the press and other media, pressure groups, politicians, police, and public opinion. We might go further and add a sixth P to this list — producers. This would be to draw upon McRobbie and Thornton's analysis of the panic around Acid House in UK in the late 1980s. This fed upon controversy driven in part by the marketers of the earliest records in the genre — 'Moral panics', they write, 'are one of the few marketing strategies open to relatively anonymous instrumental dance music' (2006: 269). They note that for popular cultural products such as videogames, films, clubs, or new musical sub-genres, the risk of censorship and scandal, and the suggestion that the product is subversive or alternative in some way, can attract both media controversy (useful as free publicity) and consumers prepared to pay for rebellious individuality.

There are several useful major approaches to the study of moral panic (Cohen 2002 [1972], Hall *et al* 1978, Goode & Ben-Yehuda 1994). Both Kenneth Thompson (1998) and Critcher (2003) offer careful comparisons and syntheses of these approaches. But the term 'moral panic' is most commonly associated with Stanley Cohen. He writes that the moral panic is about establishing 'the gallery of types that society erects to show its members which roles should be avoided and which should be emulated' (Cohen 2002 [1972]: 1–2). No discussion of moral panics is complete without quoting Cohen's full definition, the opening paragraph to his book *Folk Devils and Moral Panics*:

> Societies appear to be subject, every now and then, to periods of moral panic. A condition, episode, person or group of persons emerges to become defined as a threat to societal values and interests; its nature is presented in a stylized and stereotypical fashion by the mass media; the moral barricades are manned by editors, bishops, politicians and other right-thinking people; socially accredited experts pronounce their diagnoses and solutions; ways of coping are evolved or (more often) resorted to; the condition then disappears, submerges or deteriorates and becomes more visible. Sometimes the object of the panic is quite novel and at other times it is something which has been in existence long enough, but suddenly appears in the limelight. Sometimes the panic passes over and is forgotten, except in folklore and collective memory; at other times it has more serious and long-lasting repercussions and might produce such changes as those in legal and social policy or even in the way the society conceives itself (Cohen 2002 [1972]: 1).

In Cohen's model, then, a moral panic is a cycle of events — a small group or individual commits an act that can be represented as in some way different from what 'we' would do. The news media report this, identifying the people involved as 'them' — as 'problem people'. If the initial story creates interest, then similar stories will be looked for, found (or created) and reported. These stories will be sensationalized and any underlying social causes will be downplayed or ignored in favour of scapegoating and blame. There will be public pressure for 'something to be done', as both the general public and the news media start to call for the authorities to exercise some measure of control. The final stage is where there is a change to the law or to regulation or sentencing in order to clamp down on 'them'.

In a different analysis from that of Cohen's cycle, Goode and Ben-Yehuda (1994) argue that moral panics are characterized by certain attributes. They specify five criteria:

- an increased level of public *concern* about the behaviour of a particular social group, demonstrated in media attention, lobbying, proposed new laws, and so on
- a degree of *hostility* towards the group in question, creating an 'us' and 'them' division
- widespread agreement or *consensus* that the group pose a significant threat to society
- *volatility* — moral panics flare up and fade away; some recur periodically, others become routine
- above all, moral panics are *disproportionate*. The scale and intensity of public concern is out of proportion to the actual nature of the 'threat' posed (1994: 33–41).

The most useful part of Goode and Ben-Yehuda's analysis is their discussion of where moral panics come from (1994: 124–43). Different panics have different causes, so we need to unpack each specific instance on a case-by-case basis. The key to doing that is to ask the question *who benefits?* Goode and Ben-Yehuda analyse three broad types of explanation of where moral panics come from.

First, the '*grassroots model*' — in this view, an issue becomes a moral panic as a result of widespread anxiety about a particular issue. When the media pick up on this, they're then just reflecting a wider concern which is already out there. They can sense a story.

The second broad category of explanation, '*interest-group theory*' argues that moral panics are produced by social institutions with the necessary influence to have their concerns taken seriously by the media, and later by politicians. Groups like religious or educational organizations, professional associations, the police, lobby groups and non-governmental organizations — and, of course, the media themselves.

The third type of explanation, the '*elite-engineered model*', argues that political elites consciously and deliberately stage campaigns to create moral panic and social concern, in order to deflect attention away from problems that are harder to deal with. Moral panics are, then, about creating a symbolic threat, which can then be neutralized with tough action from the same people who're making us anxious about the symbolic threat. The thing to note here is that this is about imposing a simple solution on a complex set of problems — problems that might need a whole set of complex solutions which are instead ignored.

Taking over the asylum seekers

To conclude, we can look at just one of the major contemporary categories of people who can provoke moral panic — asylum seekers. What's at stake here? As Cohen argues, the demonization of asylum seekers as 'folk devils', the labelling of anonymous individuals as a deceitful, threatening group, has made it possible for harsh and punitive measures such as indefinite detention in privately-run camps to seem like normal, indeed conventional, responses (2002: xxxiv). Some of the media panic surrounding asylum seekers can also be seen as evidence of Goode and Ben-Yehuda's 'elite-engineered' model.

Asylum seekers have been both symbolically and literally excluded through the media:

> 'ASYLUM SEEKERS EAT OUR DONKEYS' (*Star,* 21 August 2003, p. 1).
> 'Callous asylum seekers are barbecuing the Queen's swans, *The Sun* can reveal' (4 July 2003, p. 1).
> 'BOMBERS ARE ALL SPONGEING ASYLUM SEEKERS' (*Express,* 27 July 2005, p. 1).

In Australia, for example, the 2001 Federal Election was fought almost entirely around the theme of 'border protection'. This theme emerged when the Howard government attempted to deny entry to a Norwegian freighter, the *Tampa,* which was carrying 433 asylum seekers it had rescued after their ferry had sunk on route to Australia. The *Tampa* proved to be only the first of a series of such controversies, with the subsequent introduction of the so-called 'Pacific Solution' (the exporting of asylum seekers to small island states such as Nauru for processing); the drowning off Indonesia of more than 350 other asylum seekers bound for Australia on 19 October 2001; and what became known as the 'children overboard' affair, in which government ministers falsely claimed that asylum seekers at sea had flung their own children into the ocean in order to force Australian officials to rescue them and take them to the Australian mainland.

Here's how Sydney's Murdoch tabloid the *Daily Telegraph* introduced the 'children overboard' saga:

> Desperate parents yesterday threw their children overboard from an Indonesian people-smuggling boat which had its passage to Christmas Island intercepted by the Royal Australian Navy. Several adults also catapulted themselves into the heavy seas, in what Immigration Minister Philip Ruddock described as a 'clearly planned and premeditated' bid to reach the Australian territory (8 October 2001, p. 11).

Some other front pages from the day the story broke — 'Boat People Toss Young In Sea' (Townsville Bulletin). 'Iraqis Go Overboard in Asylum Bid' (Cairns Post). 'Illegals Throw Kids Into Sea' (Gold Coast Bulletin). The country's biggest-selling daily, the Melbourne *Herald Sun*, led with 'Overboard: Boat People Throw Children Into The Ocean', and ran a poll on its front page: 'Should boat people who throw children into the sea be accepted into Australia as refugees?' Then-Prime Minister John Howard called it 'an attempt to morally blackmail Australia'.

But the problem with all of this was that the story was completely untrue. No children were ever thrown into the sea. There were no attempts to 'morally blackmail' Australia. Instead, a subsequent Senate Committee inquiry found 'deliberate deception motivated by political expedience' (Parliament of Australia 2002: p. xxii) and concluded that the then-Defence Minister Peter Reith had 'deceived the Australian people during the 2001 Federal Election campaign' (p. xxiv). The children overboard affair offers a clear example of a moral panic directed and sustained by politicians (Marr & Wilkinson 2003). Government ministers vilified vulnerable refugees and deliberately offered photos of a separate event to bolster the false claim that children had been used as weapons of intimidation.

Conclusion

The 'children overboard' events, in which government sources ran a deliberately misdirected media agenda throughout an election campaign, is an example that draws together the themes of this chapter — the capacity of officials to drive the news agenda; the movable boundary around objectivity; the creation and manipulation of pseudo-events; the tactics of spin; and the creation of 'us' and 'them', the drawing of cultural boundaries, the erection of a fence around the imagined community. It's a vivid illustration of political authority being expressed as symbolic power, the defining of reality in a certain group's interests.

The next chapter focuses on the fourth crucial set of actors in the processes of news — audiences. It discusses the most important perspectives on users, readers and viewers of news, and it canvasses debates around celebrity culture and tabloid media, and around news as entertainment.

Chapter 6

Here We Are, Now Entertain Us

> *'we are presented not only with fragmented news but news without context, without consequences, without value, and therefore without essential seriousness; that is to say, news as pure entertainment'* (Postman 1985: 102)

Mika Brzezinski was as mad as hell and not going to take it any more. The MSNBC newsreader couldn't face leading her bulletin with an update on Paris Hilton's release from jail. 'Do you have a lighter?' she said, grabbing one from a colleague and trying to set fire to her script, 'I'm going to make a point. We're not covering this, alright? I'm *done* with the Paris Hilton story.' As her two male co-hosts squabbled and teased her about it, Brzezinski fed the script into a shredder. Over her protests, her colleagues then screened footage of Paris Hilton walking from jail to her car, before the camera cut back to the studio with Brzezinski slumped, head in hands. The video clip of the newsreader's June 2007 stand against celebrity culture quickly became an online favourite, with hundreds of thousands of downloads turning Mika Brzezinski herself — of course — into a celebrity.

Mika Brzezinski's Paris Hilton moment opens up some of the central debates in contemporary news and current affairs — to what extent is entertainment an important part of the news experience? Are news and entertainment compatible? Why so much coverage of celebrities? Such questions are often asked within the context of debates about *infotainment* (Hartley 2001) or *tabloidization*

— debates which some commentators suggest verge on moral panic (Gripsrud 2000, Sparks 2000b).

This chapter introduces the fourth crucial set of actors in the processes of news — audiences. It discusses celebrity culture and tabloid media, news as information and news as entertainment. It sets these debates against the concept of the public sphere. And it surveys the most important perspectives on media audiences.

Are we having fun yet?

Tabloid media blur the line between news-as-information and news-as-entertainment. They blur the lines between the public and the private. They create their own audience by affecting a unique kind of voice. What kind of voice? For example, in the UK *The Sun* gave its full front page to a colour photo of Saddam Hussein wearing only a pair of white y-fronts: 'TYRANT'S IN HIS PANTS' (20 May 2005). The next day, as the Pentagon announced it would search for who had leaked the pictures to the Murdoch press, *The Sun* splashed again with 'BUSH PROBES SADDAM'S PANTS. President Vows: I'll get to bottom of it' (21 May 2005, p. 1). Some scholars, such as Neil Postman (1985), argue that the line between entertainment and information is one that should be policed more vigilantly. Others such as Hartley (1996) or Lumby (1997b, 1999) argue a contrasting viewpoint — that contemporary popular media, the realm of the tabloid, enact a new, more democratic public sphere.

The word 'tabloid' originates in the pharmaceutical industry of the late nineteenth century, meaning 'compressed, easy-to-digest medicine' (Stephens 2007: 198) — a meaning which survives in Bourdieu's description of the tabloid approach: 'the focus is on those things which are apt to arouse curiosity but require no analysis' (1998: 51). The term 'tabloid media' covers a range of material (Sparks & Tulloch 2000). It could refer to the full spectrum of content which mixes information with entertainment. It could include the now-retired News Bunny — for several years, someone in a rabbit costume sat behind the newsreader of UK satellite channel Live TV, reacting to each story with a cheery thumbs-up or a downcast thumbs-down. It could include the Canadian website 'Naked News' <http://www.nakednews.com>, in which a team of ten female anchors, or a smaller team of male ones, strip while reading the news — 'Iran's supreme leader has warned his country will strike against US interests around the globe if it is attacked' announced its newsreader on 8 February 2007, smiling into the camera as she removed her blouse (*Time* magazine's issue of 23 April 2001 declared that 'Naked News' 'offers best international coverage this side of the BBC'). And tabloid media could include MSNBC's online 'Newsbreaker' game <http://www.newsbreakergame.com>. This is a version of 'Breakout', in which the player uses a paddle and ball to break down a wall of coloured bricks, only with the addition of up-to-the-minute headlines, scrolling down the screen — 'Collect 25 stories for an extra life!' (I missed the high score, distracted by the headline '74 Slain at Oil Field in Ethiopia' floating gently past my paddle).

Mapping tabloid media

In the US, the tabloids are the supermarket weeklies, such as the *Weekly World News* (now no longer available in actual supermarkets, but only online at http://www.weeklyworldnews.com) or the *National Enquirer*. Some of these, such as the *Weekly World News,* may seem to operate in a largely different universe from the rest of us ('I WENT TO HEAVEN, MET ELVIS, AND TOOK HIS PHOTO AS PROOF'). But the *Enquirer* for one, will cover serious news stories and has broken significant news in the past, giving it something of an agenda-setting role (Bird 2002, Turner 2004). Bird concludes that the supermarket tabloids are popular with their readers for the same reasons they are unpopular with their critics:

> they are exciting yet predictable, formulaic yet titillating; they celebrate excess and ordinariness at the same time. They value gossip and speculation; they are nosy and fascinated with people and the way they cope, or might cope, with what life throws at them (1992: 201).

The US also pioneered the daytime talk shows, such as those hosted by Oprah or Jerry Springer or Sally Jesse Raphael ('today — women who eat in their sleep'), in which the private, the personal and the domestic are placed firmly in the public domain. And there are the current affairs TV programmes such as *60 Minutes*, which changed the TV industry's view of the genre by making a profit.

In Australia, the term connects most clearly with the early evening TV current affairs shows *Today Tonight* and *A Current*

Affair, partly modelled on these US counterparts, the flavour of which is caught in Catharine Lumby's synopsis, from her book *Bad Girls*:

> Breast implant addicts. On-camera liposuction. Charles and Camilla's secret love-tapes. Teenage lesbian vampires. Date rape. Miracle cancer cures. Bisexual kindergarten teachers. Surfing rabbits. Cellulite. Latex. Gutter journalism. Mass crass. Trash TV. Or as one Australian tabloid dubbed it — 'the news without underpants' (1997b: 117).

Today Tonight once chained an elderly woman to her wardrobe to create a news story. In February 2007, the programme ran a story about bad conditions in nursing homes for the elderly — 'As we go to air tonight, this 84-year-old grandmother remains locked up in her nursing home room, chained to a cupboard' announced host Anna Coren. But it transpired that the show's reporter, Nicholas Boot, had himself chained the woman up to manufacture some visual interest, taking his chains home with him after filming. Graeme Turner argues that such shows should not be able to use the discourses of journalism or 'the public's right to know' in justifying what they do, describing *A Current Affair* as 'a highly inventive game show, producing spectacle and performance around people's actual lives' (1996: 89). The problem with such programming, for Turner, is in the ways its practitioners justify what they do. On the one hand, they trade on a Fourth Estate discourse of journalistic rights, and of the public's right to know. On the other hand, they also trade on a discourse of what-the-public wants, of commercial considerations, in which anyone who complains about their risible output just doesn't understand the way the business works. Journalism, in this analysis, 'simply supplies the rhetoric to defend the tactics' (1996: 88). As Turner argues, this is unsustainable, not least because these practices have very real consequences for real individuals (2005: 20).

In the UK, the tabloids are the 'red-top' newspapers (with or without actual red tops), including *The Sun, The Star,* and the *Mirror*. If, by chance, you've never read one, their tactics, tone, themes and concerns are all displayed in this sample entry from the published diaries of one of their leading practitioners, Piers

Morgan, a former editor of both the *News of the World* and the *Mirror*:

> We've exposed a Tory MP called Richard Spring for having a three-in-a-bed sex romp with a Sunday school teacher and a business friend. The reason we're so sure of our facts is that she took a tape recorder into the bedroom for us (Morgan 2005: 73).

For Conboy, such news represents 'the refinement of a commercialized journalism which prioritizes the desires of advertisers to reach large audiences above all other concerns' (2006: 207). As Sparks (2000b) points out, one of the distinctive features of the UK newspaper industry is the unusual degree of competition between national daily papers, with many more national dailies available in a city like London or Glasgow than is true of a city like New York or Sydney. One consequence of this competition is that while much of the 'quality' press may fret about tabloidization, they are complicit — they have moved from reporting what the tabloids are saying to covering the same stories.

Defining the tabloid

How can we distinguish the tabloid newspapers from the rest of the market? Size is not an adequate way to categorize the tabloids, as former broadsheets such as the *Independent* have migrated to smaller formats — when it comes to the tabloids, size doesn't matter. And subject matter is not an adequate way to define the tabloid either — *The Sun* does cover political stories (even if it often trivializes them) and the *Times* does cover celebrities (even if it often trivializes them). The *Observer* will run a colour photo of Britney Spears having her hair coloured, under the caption 'Oops, I dyed it again' (1 May 2005, p. 26) and the *Guardian* will run a large front-page picture of extras dressed as Imperial stormtroopers at the Cannes premiere of a *Star Wars* movie (16 May 2005, p. 1).

To clarify the debates, Sparks (2000b) offers three overlapping main ways in which the term 'tabloid' is used by critics. First, a content-specific usage, mainly concerned with newspapers and broadcasting, in which news focused on entertainment, celebrity, scandal and sport increase at the expense of news focused on economics, politics and society. Second, a shift in broadcasters' priorities, especially those of public service broadcasters such as the BBC, which have traditionally placed news and information programming at the centre of their schedules. Third, changing patterns of taste, as seen in the example of Jerry Springer. The problem with Springer's show, for critics of such 'tabloid TV' is not that it's a talk show as such, but with the kinds of people talking and the kinds of things they talk about: 'What is distinctive about the *Jerry Springer Show* is that the wrong kinds of people (who are not accredited experts) talk about the wrong kinds of topics (their deeply private dilemmas and experiences) in the wrong atmosphere (that of the game show)' (Sparks 2000b: 11).

Sparks distinguishes between five different kinds of newspapers on a continuum from, at one extreme, a high concentration on public life, and on economics, politics and society, and at the other extreme, a high concentration on private life, and on scandal, entertainment and sport. The first group, The Serious Press, includes the *Wall Street Journal* and the *Financial Times*. The second group, The Semiserious Press, includes papers like the *Times* and the *Guardian* — papers which, while very much concerned with public life and social issues, also emphasize feature articles, visual presentation, and all branches of the arts, including TV. The third group, The Serious-Popular Press, includes such middle-market papers as the *Daily Mail* or *USA Today* — each of which could be said to emphasize visuals, to focus on scandal and sport, while adhering to largely the same news values as the first two types of paper. Fourth, there is The Newsstand Tabloid Press, such as *The Sun*, for whom the scandal, sport and entertainment agenda is paramount, and fifth, The Supermarket Tabloid Press, such as the *National Enquirer*, who blend the same scandal/sport/entertainment agenda with 'a strong element of the fantastic' (Sparks 2000b: 15).

Sparks concludes from this exercise that the lines between 'quality' and 'tabloid' are far from clear-cut, with similar topics appearing across the continuum. One example shows this. On 31 May 2005, Bob Geldof and Midge Ure called for a million people to gather in Edinburgh to lobby the nearby heads of the G8 countries, gathered at Gleneagles, for change in Africa. The UK newspapers' responses the next day spread across most of Sparks's continuum (with the exception of the Supermarket Tabloid perspective). The *Guardian* led with investigations into corruption in western companies' dealings with African-aid money. The *Independent* offered an entire special Africa issue, with 16 pages devoted to the continent and its troubles. The *Daily Record* worried about the prospect of a million marchers descending on Edinburgh, as did the *Scotsman*, the *Mirror*, and the *Express*. 'GELDOF'S POP ARMY CONQUERS THE WORLD' decided the *Mail*, while 'WE'RE GONNA ROCK THE WORLD' said *The Star*, next to a half-page picture of Abi Titmuss. The emphases varied, but Geldof and Africa were on every front page.

Talking tabloid

Conboy (2006, 2007) focuses on the peculiar style of the UK tabloids, arguing that it is the weird demotic voice of these papers, rather than the physical size, format or content of the paper itself, that truly characterizes the 'tabloid' (2006: 14). *The Sun*, the *Mirror*, *The Star* — for Conboy, these papers 'provide a view of a community with a strong sense of nation. They do this to a large extent through the deployment of a range of language appropriate to that sense of national belonging' (2006: 213). The tabloid press, then, represent a commercial exploitation of deep-rooted forces in popular culture that operate through inclusion and exclusion, through creating and demonizing outsiders in a particular voice (p. 213). Tabloid language is not just some dumbed-down, minimalist vocabulary for slow readers, as some might suggest, but is rather a sophisticated, highly-developed style, designed to both create and appeal to a certain type of reader and to that reader's sense of community. Conboy (2006: 14–45) identifies its key features as including the following (the examples are my own):

- a reliance on puns and word-play — 'From Hitler Youth To Papa Ratzi', as *The Sun* announced the papacy of Joseph Ratzinger on 20 April 2005.
- appeals to interaction with readers, including phone-in polls, letters pages, and vox pops — 'Is there a sneaky benefit cheat living — and working — in your street? Call us on 0141 420 5254 and help us expose the rats' (*News of the World*, 3 April 2005, p. 15).
- the use of familiar names for figures in the news (Posh and Becks)

- informality and slang — 'FOOTIE WIVES ARE ALL SLAPPERS says Footie Wife' (*Star*, 7 April 2005, p. 1).
- intertextual references to popular culture ('MAY THE VOTES BE WITH YOU', as *The Sun* endorsed Tony Blair on election day, 5 May 2005)
- a fondness for innuendo and salacious topics ('Bisexual Boffin: I'm a Slut', *The Sun*, 4 April 2005, p. 12).
- and a self-referential, self-congratulatory emphasis on tabloids themselves as forces in British culture — most famously, in *The Sun*'s front-page boast that it had swung the 1992 UK General Election — 'IT'S THE SUN WOT WON IT!', 11 April 1992).

All of these features can be seen in the ways the tabloids tried to sex-up the UK General Election in 2005. *The Sun* marked the launch of the campaign with 'THEY'RE OFF! Page 3 Girls Keep You Abreast of Election Swings' (6 April 2005, p. 1), in which four topless models were each assigned to a political party for the campaign: 'As a leader, Michael Howard is a powerful speaker and isn't afraid to expose the puff and PR that Tony Blair continues to peddle', said Keeley, holding her blue bra up for the camera, while the designated Labour model Nicola said 'We mustn't let apathy ruin Labour's chances. So, like my boobs, let's concentrate on the feelgood factor' (pp. 28–9). Headline? 'THE SUN IS NO 1 FOR POLITITS'. The Murdoch paper's swing behind Labour for the 1997 election was maintained for 2005 — the day after the papal conclave in Rome announced the new Pope with its traditional puff of smoke from a Vatican rooftop, *The Sun* endorsed Blair's New Labour with a puff of red smoke from its Wapping chimney:

> at 7pm the world held its breath as the smoke turned WHITE to indicate The Sun had reached its decision. Finally, a few minutes later, the smoke turned RED to reveal that The Sun is endorsing Labour's bid for a historic third term. The gripping scene was transmitted live to our army of readers via webcam and The Sun's internet site (21 April 2005, p. 5).

The day before the election, *The Sun* went with 'WHY SIZE MATTERS Cherie says Tony needs a BIG one... a big majority!' (4 May 2005, p. 1). Inside, a page-five piece headed 'MY TONY IS FIT... AND UP FOR IT' ('Mr Blair joked he was a "five times a night" man', revealed a photographer) was placed next to the full text of Shakespeare's 116th sonnet ('Let me not to the marriage of true minds/Admit impediments'). On polling day, *The Star* judged that the election wasn't actually the biggest story of the day, leading with the headline 'LOIN KING: NOISY BRAD 'N ANGELINA'S WILD AFRICAN LOVE ROMPS' (5 May 2005, p. 1). But inside they did also try to spark interest in the night's TV coverage of the poll results with a two-page spread — 'SEX MARKS THE SPOT. TV girls to keep you up all night', which suggested that 'News rivals Natasha Kaplinsky, Katie Derham and Julie Etchingham are turning telly's election night into the battle of the babes' (p. 6). The *Mirror* gave over its front page to an image of Tory leader Michael Howard as Dracula ('VOTE LABOUR: THERE'S TOO MUCH AT STAKE'), while *The Sun* found a cross-promotional tie-in with the new *Star Wars* movie and mocked up a photo of Blair as a Jedi with a red light sabre: 'MAY THE VOTES BE WITH YOU'.

The puns, the slang, the informality, the intertextuality, the self-referential congratulations, and the inexhaustible capacity to find a sex angle in anything at all (Holland 1998), are all clearly to be seen. For some critics, such news cheats the public:

> Entertainment has superseded the provision of information; human interest has supplanted the public interest; measured judgment has succumbed to sensationalism; the trivial has triumphed over the weighty; the intimate relationships of celebrities from soap operas, the world of sport or the royal family are judged more 'newsworthy' than the reporting of significant issues and events of international consequence. Traditional news values have been undermined by new values; 'infotainment' is rampant (Franklin 1997: 4).

Franklin sees these trends are the result of increased competition, of a lack of government regulation on the outputs of tabloid media, of technological developments which made greater casualization possible, and of changes to the structure of the journalism profession itself (more freelancers, more PR, less in-house training).

That's entertainment

The same kinds of complaints are made not just against particular newspapers but also against TV news in general. In his book *Amusing Ourselves To Death*, Postman offers a large number of arguments about what he sees as the negative impacts of TV on news, culture and the status of knowledge (Postman 1985, Postman & Powers 1992). He neatly encapsulates these impacts in the phrase 'now... this', an image of the organizing principle of TV news; and a phrase, moreover, which doesn't connect two items so much as underline their separateness (1985: 101–15). In the phrase 'now... this' Postman tries to capture a number of features of news-as-entertainment: the casting of credible-seeming newsreaders, the use of music, the brevity, the discontinuity.

There is no event, Postman argues, so important that it can't be followed by something unconnected to it — 'There is no murder so brutal, no earthquake so devastating, no political blunder so costly [...] that it cannot be erased from our minds by a newscaster saying, "Now... this"' (1985: 101). *That's that. Now this...* What's at stake here? The effect, he argues, is to flatten out events into a meaningless plane. The world of broadcast news is one without meaning or structure or order and is one that cannot be taken seriously. This argument, which served as the epigraph to this chapter, is that TV news is not only a montage of discontinuous fragments, each related to the other by a 'now... this' link: it is also 'news without context, without consequences, without value, and therefore without essential seriousness; that is to say, news as pure entertainment' (1985: 102).

Postman describes the news as 'a stylized dramatic performance whose content has been staged largely to entertain' (p. 105). He points, for instance, to the phenomenon of attractive newsreaders, selected for their ability to perform the role, to inhabit a persona of reliability. He points to the brevity of most TV news items ('It is simply not possible to convey a sense of seriousness about any event if its implications are exhausted in less than one minute's time' p. 105). He points to discontinuity, to the way in which one story does not really relate to the next. Postman even finds it odd that the news has theme music. The fact that most of us *don't* find it odd he sees as evidence that the lines between serious public discourse and entertainment have become blurred. Why is there music, he asks? His conclusion is that it frames the programme in a reassuring fashion, reminding us that there's nothing really to worry about. TV, then, doesn't just provide entertaining content, but presents *all* content as entertainment. For Postman, the news gives us information that creates the *illusion* of knowledge in place of actual knowledge.

Switching on the actual TV news after reading Postman, you'd expect to hear a laugh-track. His argument is a sophisticated and persuasive version of what John Langer has called the 'lament' for television news (1998). Langer argues that critics such as Postman place too much emphasis on complaining about how TV fails to live up to idealized criteria for the role of news media in a democracy. Proponents of this 'lament' see TV news as dumbed-down, narcotizing, celebrity-crazed fluff, which actively works against the Fourth Estate role of the news media. If democracy needs well-informed citizens, TV news instead produces viewers who are among 'the best entertained and quite likely the least well-informed people in the Western world' (Postman 1985: 108). Postman devotes the first half of the book to establishing 'typographic America' as a golden age of discourse. But the problem with golden ages, of course, is that we've always somehow managed to miss them. Lumby points out that newspapers of the seventeenth century featured stories about sea monsters and 'at least one report of a cow giving birth to human twins' (2002: 321), while Bird draws the history of the US supermarket tabloids back to seventeenth-century printed ballads (1992: 8–12), suggesting the golden age thesis is less than secure.

The public sphere

This kind of lament for lost standards is an important component of debates about the public sphere. What is the public sphere? It is, writes Jürgen Habermas, 'a realm of our social life in which something approaching public opinion can be formed' (1974: 49). The public sphere is a kind of conceptual arena in which citizens participate whenever they discuss ideas freely. Whenever private individuals come together to form a public body, and opinions can be formed, discussed and developed, then the public sphere is in operation. In societies of our size and complexity, the media become a necessary part of this: 'Today newspapers and magazines, radio and television are the media of the public sphere' (Habermas 1974: 49) (we would also need to add the Internet to this list). However, for Habermas, the major media are a problem: 'The world fashioned by the mass media is a public sphere in appearance only' (1989: 171). Habermas's book *The Structural Transformation of the Public Sphere* was published in German in the early 1960s, but wasn't translated into English until 1989. It became influential very quickly, and has been applied in various ways to contemporary media; of particular interest today are the ways in which it has been discussed in relation to the Internet.

Habermas's ideal public sphere was the coffee-house culture of seventeenth- and eighteenth-century London, where reasoning individuals would discuss events, and where this discussion would influence the political culture of the time. Habermas emphasizes the role of the periodical press in the development of his public sphere. The public sphere was closely linked to the development of liberal democracy. He argues that the critical discussion made possible or stimulated by the press (in such cases as the essays of Addison, Steele, Swift and Defoe) came to affect the nature of public institutions in emerging modern nation states (Thompson 1993: 177). The British Parliament allowed reporters to publish accounts of its sessions by the end of the eighteenth century, and the rights of freedom of expression and speech became guaranteed in, for example, the US through the First Amendment. There was a mutual dependence between, on the one hand, a public that can read and discuss issues; and on the other hand, a state which is representative and non-oppressive (Habermas 1989: 57–67).

The public sphere concept makes much use of such examples as coffee-houses or the ancient Athenian *agora* — physical spaces. But it's important not to confuse the public sphere with a physical space: the public sphere is not the same as a marketplace or a coffee-house. The public sphere is perhaps not so much a physical space as a headspace — that headspace is one in which we're free from coercion, manipulation, or other influences. One in which we come together as rational individuals to make rational choices through reasoned discussion. To *form* opinions. Such public opinion is a crucial part of the democratic process — informed discussion leading to public opinion is central to the relationships between the citizens and our representatives in government (Habermas 1974: 49).

However, according to Habermas, the contemporary political mediascape is a long way from this ideal public sphere. Public opinion is no longer produced *by* the public — instead, public opinion is now something produced *for* the public. Discussion, writes Habermas, 'assumes the form of a consumer item' (1989: 164). In the past, discussion was separate from commodity forms such as books or theatre tickets — books were commodities, but discussing them was free. Now, argues Habermas, such discussion has itself become a cultural commodity. Moreover, public opinion is no longer simply about discussion, but about persuasion. Debates are framed by the media from the start, and industries such as advertising, opinion polling, market research and PR, mean that the media are more and more the site of private interests working to persuade the public to support their positions. Ideas are now held up for endorsement rather than offered for discussion.

Some commentators have seen Habermas's account of the supposed decline of the public sphere as too pessimistic (such as Calhoun 1992, Garnham 1992). Oliver Boyd-Barrett, for example, writes:

> Newspapers, radio and television — some media, some of the time — clearly do still serve as a forum for discussion of issues of public interest among people who are knowledgeable, interested, able to speak on behalf of broader social interests, and whose discussions have the potential of being of political influence (1995: 230–1).

Habermas has acknowledged that his presentation of the public sphere was somewhat idealized (1992).

One response to Habermas which is useful in thinking of the public sphere as an arena of symbolic power is to see it as a gendered concept. Not only were the participants in the coffee-house culture primarily male, but the concept itself is underpinned by a distinction between public and private which places women in the domestic sphere, in turn contrasted to the rational arena of the public sphere. Not only does the model privilege an era in which women were essentially excluded, but it depends for its conceptual framework on such an exclusion (Thompson 1993). In response to this, Fraser argues for the importance of what she calls 'subaltern counterpublics' (1992: 123). By this she means that people from socially subordinated groups find it useful to form alternative public spheres. In a strong example, Fraser points to feminism in the US as an alternative public sphere of this kind: 'with its variegated array of journals, bookstores, publishing companies, film and video distribution networks, lecture series, research centers, academic programs, conferences, conventions, festivals, and local meeting places' (1992: 123).

Fraser notes how the language has been altered by the impacts of this sphere, with terms such as 'sexism', date rape' and 'sexual harassment' becoming part of political and social discourse. This language has in turn made possible shifts in social relations: 'Armed with such language, we have recast our needs and identities, thereby reducing, although not eliminating, the extent of our disadvantage in official public spheres' (1992: 123). Fraser's argument enables a renewed emphasis in the public sphere concept upon symbolic power as relationships of struggle and contest.

In the public sphere concept, as Fraser puts it, 'political participation is enacted through the medium of talk' (Fraser 1992: 110). The problem is that the modern media environment is not characterized by a conversational approach: broadcasting, for example, is a one-way communications system; and even those broadcast formats which have the appearance of conversation — such as talkback radio — are tightly controlled and weighted in favour of the broadcaster (Potts 1990, Adams & Burton 1997, Stanyer 2007). Moreover, if broadcast media are not conversational in character, the emerging twenty-first century media environment is more complex still, with an increasingly networked, global nature. The normative thrust of Habermas's work may offer much that is useful in approaching this global mediascape, but it has little to say in itself about the nature of that environment (Thompson 1993: 185–8).

Despite the many criticisms of the concept and its shortcomings, as an ideal or a positive model of how the media space ought to operate, the public sphere offers a useful standard against which we can measure how the media actually do operate. So how can we weigh contemporary media against this ideal? One way would be to isolate the central features of Habermas's model and use these as a basis against which to gauge the performance of a given media forum or media form.

For example, many commentators have assessed the relevance of the public sphere concept to the Internet (among others Dahlberg 1998, Poster 1997, Rheingold 1993, and Salter 2003). Papacharissi (2002) offers a useful round-up of many of these debates: on the one hand, the Internet offers the potential for more people to access more information which can in turn inform public discussion. But on the other hand, this potential has to be offset against the inequalities of access to the Net and the requirements for new media literacies. Similarly, the Net makes possible discussions on a global level, yet this can also be characterized as further fragmenting public discourse. And the Internet, it must be remembered, exists within broader economic, social and cultural contexts, and will be shaped by these: it is naïve to imagine that use of the Net can change social behaviour without the Net itself being changed as well. We'll return to the Net in Chapter 8.

Taking tabloid media seriously

Critics such as Postman and Franklin see tabloid media as a debasement of the public sphere. But there is another way of reading all this, and that's to consider tabloid media as a key space in which our sense of imagined community gets worked out. Langer argues that the very stories most criticized by what he calls the 'lament' are themselves important objects of study. Indeed, for John Hartley, 'the *mainstream* of contemporary journalism is fashion, gossip, lifestyle, consumerism and celebrity, and "news" is private, visual, narrativized and personalized' (1996: 17, emphasis added). If TV news and current affairs lean heavily on human interest, entertainment, and celebrity stories, if they emphasize the visual and story-telling, if they are often concerned with the domestic and private rather than with the public worlds of politics and the economy, then all of this should be analysed and better understood.

Take celebrity coverage. It's important to bear in mind that the production of celebrity is an *industry*, not just a cultural phenomenon (Turner, Bonner & Marshall 2000). The aims of this industry are both symbolic power and, through it, economic power. Celebrity is an effect of symbolic power, and symbolic power is in turn the goal of celebrity. The exercise of celebrity symbolic power is the marketing of a commodity — there's money in it. But audiences use celebrity too. In his book *Celebrities, Culture and Cyberspace,* McKenzie Wark argues that celebrity works through a complex set of relationships between the *ordinary* and the *extraordinary*. Celebrity stories always involve some kind of tension between these opposing poles:

> The pleasure of celebrity embraces the reciprocal link between the everyday and the fantastic, the banal and the magical [...] Celebrity is not just a trace of the extraordinary in the ordinary. What makes it tangible is that it is also a trace of the ordinary in the extraordinary [...] The celebrity may fascinate, but the trace of the ordinary habits of

> life, from domestic friction to eating disorders, connects even the most worldly celebrity to the mundane (Wark 1999: 49).

This distinction between the ordinary and the extraordinary is, on one level, another way of talking about the private and public spheres. So a celebrity figure like Nicole Kidman on a public level embodies the extraordinary — Oscar winner, works with Stanley Kubrick and Baz Luhrmann and Gus Van Sant. But what we most often read about is her relationships, and how these involve private issues from infidelity to addiction to adoption to pregnancy. Nicole Kidman's private sphere of home and relationships becomes very much part of our public sphere. And the reverse can happen: ordinary people can have celebrity thrust upon them by being caught up in extraordinary situations or simply by appearing in the media — becoming what Couldry (2003) calls 'media people', a category which entrenches the myth, as Couldry sees it, that the media are the centre of society.

Van Zoonen argues that news is gendered in terms of its topics (with the masculine public world of politics, finance and crime set against the feminine private sphere of human interest, culture and consumer items), as well as in its emphasis on facts, its privileging of male sources, and its detached ethical stance of objectivity, all of which van Zoonen codes as masculine (1994, 1998). Commercial news organizations, however, increasingly emphasize human interest stories, sensationalism, emotional investment, and the desires and needs to the audience, all qualities which van Zoonen suggests women journalists are better able to provide (1998). Lumby argues that many criticisms of tabloid media are rooted in a barely disguised 'elitist and authoritarian view of what issues matter and what the public ought to be interested in' (1997b: 117). In this view, critics of tabloid media are trying to maintain a separation of public and private in which the worlds of the domestic, the personal, the feminine, are unfit to be in the news, which is instead the realm of boys' stuff. Tabloid presentation of serious issues can make those issues more accessible and meaningful to many people (Lumby 1999, Marshall 2006). In an important example, Gillespie's ethnographic research into the media use of young Londoners found that people and events on television offer proxies: they provide a vehicle for audiences to explore and form opinions, and to work out how they feel about issues in their own lives (Gillespie 1995).

Kylie's cancer

One example came in May 2005, when singer Kylie Minogue announced that she had breast cancer. The Scottish version of *The Sun* gave its first eight pages over to the story. As well as three full-page colour photos of Kylie and her boyfriend, the paper launched a pink wristband campaign with the Breast Cancer Care charity. It also ran a short piece with the byline of Deputy Health Minister Rhona Brankin, in which she spoke of her own diagnosis with the disease and advised readers on risk factors and check-ups (18 May 2005, p. 7). The *Guardian* also put Kylie on the front page, with a large colour picture above the fold, and other broadsheets, including the *Times* and the *Telegraph* also covered the story. The *Guardian's* daily 'G2' supplement ran a detailed article about risk factors, treatment options and survival rates, as well as a feature piece which explained 'why Kylie's illness matters to us' (18 May 2005, 'G2' pp. 2–3).

As the coverage of Kylie's cancer shows, celebrity stories are not always simple trivia. Celebrities can be the vehicle for public awareness or public health campaigns — 'celebrities can act as prisms through which social complexity is brought back to the human level' (Turner, Bonner & Marshall 2000: 166). To set this claim and those of the previous section in a fuller context, this chapter now turns to a survey of the main ways in which media audiences have been understood. Audiences are central to the processes of news and to its relations of symbolic power.

From vulnerable viewers to creative audiences

One of the defining features of media as they were understood in the twentieth century is what Thompson calls the 'structured break' between media production and media reception (1995: 29). For the most part, the news is produced in one place (such as a TV studio) and received in another (such as your living room). Media producers do not have direct access to media audiences; or rather, they cannot actually witness media consumption. As one commentator puts it, 'media audiences do it in private and do it unobserved' (Turnbull 2006: 78). One consequence of this is the rise of entire industries that attempt to bridge this gap (e.g. ratings, market research, opinion polling). Another consequence is that audience analysis is one of the most contested areas of Media Studies and is particularly open to problems of claim-and-counter-claim. There are, in short, many ways to understand (and misunderstand) media audiences.

There are, of course, different kinds of audience and there is a sense in which academics and media industries alike have to create audiences in order to study them (Ang 1991, Hartley 1992b). In McQuail's (1997) analysis, we might think of an audience as defined by such variables as:

- time — such as the prime-time audience
- medium — such as the TV audience
- geography — such as the local audience or the national audience
- demographics — such as gender, age, income

Each of these can be understood in many different ways. The audience, as Bird writes, 'is everywhere and nowhere' (2003: 4). The history of the development of audience research, from the mid-twentieth century on, can be read as a very gradual recognition that audiences are not only subject to symbolic power but are also able to exercise it. This is of critical importance in the digital media environment, in which audiences have unprecedented opportunities to create, circulate and remix media content of their own. For many people, the media are no longer just what they read, watch or listen to — the media are now also what they *do*.

Those scary media

The first question to be asked seriously of media audiences was *what do the media do to people?* As it turned out, this wasn't a very good question, but it still gets asked today. The 1920s saw the beginnings of radio broadcast networks, the development of a workable television system, the arrival of sound in the movies, and the emergence of a serious public relations industry. Each of these made possible new kinds of audience, new kinds of public. But what kinds? The public were at first seen as a vulnerable mass, swayed by worthless popular culture (Adorno & Horkheimer 1995 [1972], Adorno 2003 [1975]). Early audience research traded on these assumptions as it tried to establish the 'effects' of mass communication. Harold

Lasswell's famous 1948 formulation of communication — 'who says what in which channel to whom with what effect?' — remains an influential approach (1995: 93). But it's a model which assumes a one-way delivery of meaning.

Even early research in this area, such as that by Lazarsfeld, Berelson and Gaudet into election choices, found little evidence of direct media influence on how people voted and more evidence of the importance of social interaction and discussion (2003) [1944]. It turned out, that as Raymond Williams once wrote, there are no masses after all — 'there are only ways of seeing people as masses' (1958: 300). The 'masses', Williams pointed out, were always other people, never ourselves — we all knew ourselves to be more complicated, more discriminating, more distinctive than simply a part of an amorphous mass. Decades of research into audiences have since continued to fail to establish the kinds of direct causal influences that were first assumed (Gauntlett 1998). Hartley suggests that:

> if advertising, propaganda and mass manipulation actually worked, we wouldn't need any of it, because everyone would in fact be buying, doing and believing what they were told. The continual investment in mass persuasion is the strongest evidence that it doesn't work (1996: 7–8).

But the idea of an all-powerful media manipulating vulnerable audiences retains a strong hold on the popular imagination and, unsurprisingly, on the media themselves — school shootings, for example, are always accompanied by a ritual discussion of the shooters' media use, and the particular videogames or movies that might have tipped them over the brink. When one such shooting took place in Montreal, the *Guardian* headline read 'Goth loner loved school massacre video game' (15 September 2006, p. 25). But the article said that the killer had written that he wanted to die 'like Romeo and Juliet'. So, despite the videogame angle, the killer's own stated influence was Shakespeare. But there were no calls to ban his plays or restrict their use by impressionable schoolchildren.

Selling the audience

Another important approach to audiences is the ratings. Commercial TV news organizations have a particular stake in being able to count their audience, which gives the ratings a special currency and importance. But there are problems with this: Gitlin observes that ratings count only the televisions tuned to a particular station — 'not necessarily shows watched, let alone grasped, remembered, loved, learned from, deeply anticipated, or mildly tolerated' (Gitlin 1983: 54). At 9.15pm on 13 April 2005, Sydney's Channel 7 lost power for 15 minutes. The ratings figures later reported that 638,000 viewers watched a blank screen for quarter of an hour (*Sydney Morning Herald,* 15 April 2005, p. 3). This seems very unlikely, and instead points to the interpretation that ratings are a convenient fiction, a simulated currency to be used in the advertising marketplace. The discourse of ratings, as Ang has argued, is not concerned with the actual TV viewing of any actual TV viewers, but rather with the management and marketing of a more abstract 'TV audience' which can be measured and sold (Ang 1991). Indeed, one powerful argument here sees audience members as performing unpaid labour for advertisers (Smythe 1995).

Setting the agenda

Do the news media tell us what to think? They might — but then again we might not pay them any attention. But a different kind of important claim is that, for all matters beyond our immediate daily environment, the news media tell us what to think *about* (Cohen 1963). This perspective is known as agenda-setting (McCombs & Shaw 1999 [1972]). The news media set the agenda for discussion, they identify the issues of the day, they select and focus on some stories and not others, and they define the parameters of debate. In this view, issues given prominent coverage in the news media become prominent in audience members' views of the world (McCombs 1998, 2004). This is doubly true of the largest, most respected and most influential news outlets (such as, in the US context, the *New York Times*), whose selections and emphases are reflected in many smaller outlets, from metropolitan TV stations to individual bloggers, who respond to the agenda set by the *Times*. McCombs and Shaw's 1972 study of voters in a particular election campaign found strong correlations between what people said were the major issues and what the news media had emphasized as the major issues (McCombs and Shaw 1999 [1972]). Agenda-setting does not see the audience as narcotized suckers, swallowing whatever they're told. It allows for diversity in audience response and opinion. But it claims that the audience can only respond to, and hold opinions about, things they hear about. Outside the world represented by the news media, there is nothing but obscurity (Castells 2004).

What use are the media?

What do people do with the media? This question marked an important move beyond the question of effects and informed the tradition known as uses and gratifications research. This asked why people used particular media. For example, challenging the simple assumption that people watch TV to escape their daily lives, McQuail and his collaborators researched viewers' motivations and satisfactions. They found four main types of reason for watching TV — for diversion, for information, to feel part of a group, and to feel like an individual (McQuail, Blumler & Brown 1972).

TV news and pleasure

From a different tradition of psychoanalytic screen theory, Robert Stam considers the role of TV news and its relationships to its spectator, its audience. Drawing on psychoanalytic film theory, Stam takes as his starting point the claim that TV news is 'pleasurable'. TV news extends our perception beyond that which is within our reach — 'It grants us not only ubiquity, but *instantaneous* ubiquity' (2000: 362, original emphasis). More than that, it gives the viewer certain advantages over those bystanders or participants who might actually be present on the scene — the viewer can get instant replays, slow motion, multiple angles, explanatory or expert commentary, while actual witnesses or participants are stuck with the real event. Moreover, TV's emphasis on *liveness* can create genuine suspense. What will happen? With live news we don't know — it hasn't happened yet, and we're there on the scene to see it unfold (Scannell 1996: 84). Such pleasures, Stam suggests, are narcissistic. TV flatters our sense of self: 'television transforms us into armchair imperialists, flattering and reaffirming our sense of power' (2000: 363). (We will discuss the particular qualities of live news further in Chapter 7).

Moreover, Stam suggests that TV news also offers us the pleasures of identification with the people on screen. It offers us newsreaders, Stam says, who may take the roles previously restricted to teachers or priests — 'authentic heroes, whose words have godlike efficacy' (2000: 365). Yet even those presenters with strong journalistic credentials must also be actors, reading a crafted script. They've been cast in the role for their ability to appear credible (and perhaps to appear attractive). They must inhabit a certain role, perform a particular part, embodying authority while simultaneously enacting a simulated one-on-one conversation with the viewer (which is to say with no one in particular). Finally, there are also the pleasures of narrative. Stories, says Stam, are pleasurable because they give shape to the randomness of human life. They offer 'the consolations of form' (2000: 368). From this perspective, every news story is a good story, because it offers the basic pleasures of story-telling itself. However, what Stam overlooks here is that many news stories lack the specific pleasure of narrative closure, the very reason that the news may so often appear to be bad.

What do you mean?

Who decides what something means? An influential model which tried to answer this question was Hall's encoding/decoding model (2006 [1980]), later applied by Morley (1980). This suggested that while producers may have a particular point they wish to get across in a news item (and 'encode' this in their presentation of the story), individual audience members may take — or rather *make* — something quite different (when they 'decode' the news item). Hall proposed three broad kinds of possible meaning that an audience member could make: a *dominant* one, in which the position most clearly foregrounded in the story is broadly accepted; a *negotiated* one, in which the individual's micro-level situation, interests and background are brought to bear on the macro-level perspective of a news story, producing a meaning which is in some way qualified; and an *oppositional* meaning, in which the individual rejects the premises and assumptions of the dominant perspective encoded in the story.

This encoding/decoding model was explored in Morley's 1980 research into the ways in which different groups of people reacted to episodes of the BBC current affairs programme *Nationwide*. Morley showed two episodes of the programme to focus groups of people from different socio-economic and professional backgrounds and then led discussions. His initial assumption was that the different groups would offer different readings of the programme and that these could be expected to vary according to demographic factors, including social class. He found that the different groups did produce very different interpretations of *Nationwide* — bank managers came up with dominant readings but so did working-class apprentices. These results were more complex than the basic hypothesis of class-influence had allowed for, and the research showed that it could be productive to think of the audience as made up of individuals who are in turn part of social and cultural groups, rather than as, on the one hand, a passive mass or, on the other hand, as discrete individuals in search of gratification. The value of the exercise was, as Fiske noted, that it dealt with real people watching real television, rather than an abstract 'audience'. And, he went on, the approach 'acknowledges the differences between people despite their social construction, and pluralizes the meanings and pleasures that they find in television' (Fiske 1987: 63).

This was an important precursor to much subsequent research which saw television news and current affairs as part of everyday life, understood by individuals in particular social and cultural contexts (Morley 1986, 1992). It was no longer sustainable to think of meanings as being firmly set by producers and simply moved from one place to another, as though delivering a pizza; instead meaning could be thought of as a process of translation or negotiation. Media forms could be seen as 'complex ensembles of meaning that can be interpreted and responded to in a variety of ways' (Murdock 2001: 165). Audiences, in other words, have to translate media texts into the language of their own inner lives. A useful word to bring in here is 'assimilation' or 'becoming similar to'. When we watch a movie or a TV programme do we get assimilated to it? Do we become similar to the movie? Do we alter our lives and feelings and experiences to fit the movie? Or do we assimilate it to ourselves? Do we somehow make it our own, measure it against, and match it up with our own experiences, knowledge, situation and desires? (de Certeau 1984).

Active audiences?

Such questions are asked from what is sometimes called the 'active audience' perspective. The word 'active' can be a problem, as it's not always clear or explicit what is to count as audience 'activity' (Barker 1998). What's more, a certain strain of such work tends to fall into simple celebration of consumerism, in which buying a pair of jeans is held up as 'resistance' (Fiske 1989; cf. Morris 1998). This almost certainly underestimates the extent to which dominant meanings are accepted — it overlooks the unequal resources of symbolic power distributed throughout society, and the concentration of symbolic power within media organizations; and in the news context, it overlooks the fact that news stories are coded as true.

One of the best examples of active audience research is Marie Gillespie's book *Television, Ethnicity and Cultural Change*. Gillespie examined the roles played by television in the lives of a group of British teenagers of Punjabi background. These teenagers had multiple cultural influences. They had to negotiate the Punjabi elements of their home and community life within the broader context of growing up in London. A key part of their everyday conversations was what Gillespie calls 'TV talk', the discussion of programmes or other kinds of conversation informed by television. Gillespie argues that such TV talk is 'a crucial forum for experimentation with identities. It is possible to say things in TV talk which would be otherwise embarrassing if not unsayable' (1995: 25). People and events on television offer proxies, and talking about them gives these teenagers a vehicle to explore and form their own opinions about issues in their own lives, as their TV talk shifts from discussing issues in the news to the ways in which they have been framed and presented and to the ways in which they impact on their own lives. Talking about news carries a particular importance as it represents participation in the adult world (Gillespie 1995: 109).

New audiences

The twenty-first century media environment makes possible some different emphases in thinking about audiences. Most audience research has assumed a broadcast model of communication, in which information is sent in only one direction — a model in which media organizations are the only ones who get to produce content and the only ones who make decisions about how and when it's made available (Bordewijk & Kaam 1986). But more and more, audiences are able to make decisions about how and when to access news content — think of the ways in which we might read a news site online (following links, downloading images, saving stories for later, forwarding clips to friends) and how these are different from the experience of watching a TV news bulletin. More and more, audiences have (admittedly limited) scope to register preferences and opinions with news organizations (rating stories, pushing the red button). And more and more, audiences can find avenues to produce and distribute their own media images and texts.

Creative audiences?

In the new media environment, is it more useful to think of audiences as creative? Jenkins describes a figure from an advertising image which takes the concept of the active audience for granted — 'No longer a couch potato, he determines what, when and how he watches media. He is a media consumer, perhaps even a media fan, but he is also a media producer, distributor, publicist and critic' (Jenkins 2002: 157). This captures how the 'structured break' between production and reception is no longer so clear. The people we somehow persist in calling 'audiences' are hard at work creating, remixing and swapping content. Instead of being slumped on the couch in front of the telly, more and more people are busy making media. They're uploading photos to Flickr from their mobiles, customizing their music playlists at Last.fm, writing book reviews at Amazon, tweaking their profiles on Facebook, mashing up video clips at Photobucket, fixing up daft mistakes in Wikipedia, running a blog from their MySpace page, and going to virtual gigs by actual musicians inside *Second Life*. Audiences may have fewer symbolic power resources than, say, Rupert Murdoch, but they have never had so many opportunities to deploy those resources than at present, and the long-term cultural and social consequences of this are not yet clear (Meikle 2008).

Such developments illustrate what Tim Berners-Lee, creator of the web, has termed 'intercreativity' — collaborative creative work made possible through the adoption of digital media technologies (1999: 182–3). For Berners-Lee, the web was never intended to be about delivering content to passive audiences, but to be about shared creativity:

> We ought to be able not only to find any kind of document on the Web, but also to create any kind of document, easily. We should be

> able not only to follow links, but to create them between all sorts of media. We should be able not only to interact with other people, but to create with other people. *Intercreativity* is the process of making things or solving problems together. If *interactivity* is not just sitting there passively in front of a display screen, then *intercreativity* is not just sitting there in front of something 'interactive' (Berners-Lee 1999: 182–3, emphasis in original).

We will pick up this theme in Chapter 8, where we consider some of the most important developments in online news.

Conclusion

Audiences — readers, viewers, and users of news — are central to the symbolic power relations that we call news. They make meanings as well as take them, and, more and more, they make their own media too. But their symbolic power resources are not equal to those of media organizations or, in many instances, powerful sources. To understand news, we have to see the role of audiences as dynamic and active, yet operating within constraints imposed by other actors in the processes of news.

The next two chapters focus on some of the technological possibilities that enable and extend the exercise of symbolic power. Chapter 7, 'Totally Wired' shows how the adoption and adaptation of new technical possibilities can enable new kinds of news institution, able to exercise symbolic power in new ways, in relation to new kinds of audience.

Chapter 7

Totally Wired

> *'We are in great haste to construct a magnetic telegraph from Maine to Texas; but Maine and Texas, it may be, have nothing important to communicate. [...] We are eager to tunnel under the Atlantic and bring the old world some weeks nearer to the new; but perchance the first news that will leak through into the broad, flapping American ear will be that the Princess Adelaide has the whooping cough'* (Thoreau 1854: unpaginated).

Photographs from the Abu Ghraib prison began to appear in May 2004 — the image of American reservist Private Lynndie England grinning as a naked and hooded Iraqi prisoner was made to masturbate for the camera. The photograph of Private England posing behind a human pyramid of naked prisoners. And the picture of Private England dragging a naked prisoner across the floor on a leash — a photograph that the UK tabloid *The Sun* ran on its front page under the one-word headline 'Witch' (7 May 2004). When the pictures surfaced, then-US Defence Secretary Donald Rumsfeld told a Senate committee: 'People are running around with digital cameras and taking these unbelievable photographs and then passing them off, against the law, to the media, to our surprise' (*New York Times,* 9 May 2004, section 4, p. 13).

Rumsfeld should not have been so surprised — when people get access to new communications technologies, such as digital cameras and email networks, they tend to use them in unexpected ways. As cyberpunk science fiction novelist William Gibson observed, 'the street finds its own uses for things' (1986: 215). The second Iraq conflict was one in which the coalition troops were able to communicate with their families by email and by sending digital photographs home; some even kept blogs. In effect, these troops had a double role, augmenting their combat duties with working as witnesses and archivists, as sources, chroniclers and amateur reporters of the conflict in real time. It would have been more remarkable if some of this material had *not* found its way into the news.

News changes when its means of production, distribution and reception change. All of us are familiar with developments in technology from the point of view of media reception — better remote controls, faster downloads, sharper TV pictures. But as the circulation of images from Abu Ghraib illustrates, new communications technology can also make possible changes in the production and distribution of media texts and images (a lesson the US military had perhaps learned by May 2007, when it placed a ban on troops in Iraq using its network to access certain websites, including MySpace, Photobucket and YouTube).

Of particular interest here, and examined throughout this and the following chapter, are the ways in which developments in media technologies can broaden the range of those who are able to contribute to the news, thus enabling a redistribution of symbolic power resources. Think, for example, of the footage of the beating of Rodney King, which eventually led to the Los Angeles riots of 1992; of the planes crashing into the World Trade Center on September 11 2001; or of the 2004 Indian Ocean tsunami surging through the streets of Banda Aceh in Indonesia. In each case, iconic images of the event were captured by amateur onlookers with video cameras rather than professional news teams.

When London was bombed on 7 July 2005, some of the most widely-seen images were taken with mobile phones (Goggin 2006: 147). The BBC received fifty images from onlookers within an hour of the first explosion, the number later growing to the thousands; Sky News aired a camera-phone video within 20 minutes of receiving it (Marriott 2007: 113). A public equipped with camera-phones leads to the potential for what Margaret Morse has termed 'continuous surveillance of a society from below without pause, always' (1998: 59) — a point which was proved by the circulation of mobile phone images and video of the execution of Saddam Hussein.

Most people perhaps most commonly think of the media as institutions or organizations — the TV network, the radio station, the newspaper; CNN, the BBC, the *New York Times*. Yet everything that we think of as media are also technologies, or else depend on assemblages of technologies for their production, distribution and reception. This is as true of the local community newspaper, put together by phone, email and desktop publishing software, as it is true of CNN, with its use of satellite news gathering equipment.

This chapter explores how certain key media technologies — the telegraph, broadcasting, satellites — have been exploited to create new kinds of media institutions. These change the distribution of symbolic power as well as creating new means for its exercise. First, the transnational news agency, built on harnessing the potential of telegraphy. Second, the national public service broadcaster, creating and serving a new kind of public through the capacity to address enormous simultaneous audiences under a specific kind of licence to inform, educate and entertain. And third, the 24-hour television news providers, using satellite and telecommunications networks to offer the striking phenomenon of live news in real time.

The message

Many scholars have produced critical considerations of media that take their technological form as the object of analysis. Joshua Meyrowitz terms such studies *medium theory*: 'the historical and cross-cultural study of the different cultural environments created by different media of communication' (1985: 16). This is not really a method, so much as it is a perspective: a way in to asking questions about the social and cultural roles of media by asking questions about the technological forms of the media, about their fixed properties and their mutable uses:

> Broadly speaking, medium theorists ask: What are the relatively fixed features of each means of communicating and how do these features make the medium physically, psychologically, and socially different from other media and from face-to-face interaction? (Meyrowitz 1994: 50).

In turning our attention to the media as technologies in this way, it is important to be conscious of the reductive trap of technological determinism (Smith & Marx 1994). This can be thought of as an emphasis on the effects of technologies while downplaying or ignoring their causes. This doctrine holds that the development of apparently neutral technology drives social change. It assumes, as one commentator puts it, that 'technology impinges on society from the outside' (Wajcman 1994: 3). Technological determinism is a common and influential discourse (and certainly the most common way in which technological developments are reported and discussed in the news media). But it is a deeply problematic one.

In media scholarship, this perspective is most closely associated with the work of Marshall McLuhan. 'Societies', wrote McLuhan, 'have always been shaped more by the nature of the media by which men communicate than by the content of the communication' (McLuhan & Fiore 1967: 8). This argument and the technological determinist perspective are both encapsulated in his aphorism 'the medium is the message' (1964: 7). In saying this, McLuhan was trying to draw scholars away from the then-prevailing emphasis on analysing media content. The real message of any communications technology, argued McLuhan, was 'the change of scale or pace or pattern that it introduces into human affairs' (1964: 8). He uses electric light as an example, suggesting that it is pure information — we only recognize it as having a message at all when it's shaped into a word (such as 'TAXI'). But for McLuhan, the real message of electric light is rather the changes made possible in societies and human relationships by the introduction and applications of that technology — the uncoupling of the working day from the rising and setting of the sun; the expansion of industry made possible when factories could operate around the clock in shifts; and the expansion of reading made possible by electric light.

McLuhan is often criticized (most famously in Williams 1974) for abstracting technologies from the contexts in which they are developed. Missing from McLuhan's analysis is any sense of the reality that media are developed in specific economic, regulatory and political environments and may be further adapted as they reach different cultural contexts (Gibson's 'street uses', for example). Media technologies are not independent causal agents and they do not develop in isolation (MacKenzie & Wajcman 1999). Rather, as technology critic Langdon Winner observes, 'deliberate choices about the relationship between people and new technology are made by someone, somehow, every day of the year' (1999: 216–17). This 'social shaping of technologies' perspective is endorsed widely, but as Sonia Livingstone points out, 'it seems in continual need of restatement' (2002: 18). Livingstone notes that the determinist world-view is deeply entrenched in media and other discourses about technology — one factor here, perhaps, is the ways in which a determinist perspective, in which technologies are actors, agents or characters, is well suited to prevailing narrative forms of the kinds discussed in Chapter 3.

This chapter starts from the position that the introduction of new technologies creates certain possibilities, but does not necessarily determine outcomes. From this perspective, for example, we could say that the introduction of the telegraph contributed to major shifts in the production, distribution and reception of news. We could also say that it made possible new types of media institution, from Western Union to Reuters. To say these things is not to argue that the telegraph *determined* the nature of such media organizations, but rather that certain developments were made possible by both the adoption and the adaptation of the technology. Institutional and cultural factors, of course, affect the nature of the news, as we have seen in earlier chapters, but technology also both enables and constrains. The medium might not be the message — but it does matter.

Touching from a distance (further all the time)

Telegraphy, writes James Carey, 'permitted for the first time the effective separation of communication from transportation' (1989: 203). For the first time, it was possible for a message to travel faster than a person (or a horse or a pigeon) could carry it. There had, of course, been important precursors to this development (Standage 1998). There was a history of optical telegraphy, there were line-of-sight systems of signalling and semaphore, there were smoke signals (Headrick 2003). But electrical telegraphy was a qualitative transformation, a decisive break with the past. All of these earlier systems had been in some way tied to the body: the receiver had to be in sight of the message. But electrical telegraphy sent messages across vast distances at unprecedented speeds.

Along with related developments in railways and shipping, the telegraph contributed to changes in the experience of both space and time — what David Harvey (1989) has labelled time-space compression. For example, in the 1820s, to send a message by mail from Calcutta in India to Falmouth in England could take four months; by 1906, the same feat could be accomplished in just 35 minutes (Chapman 2005: 67). The speed of news would continue to accelerate (Hartley 2003, Stephens 2007) and this would enable a rethinking of distance — in May 2007, a news organization in California recruited two journalists based in India to cover the Pasadena local council beat without leaving India. The reporters, one in Mumbai, one in Bangalore, were to follow Pasadena council meetings live online and write daily reports (*Guardian Weekly*, 25 May 2007, p. 39).

As we will discuss below, in relation to CNN and Al Jazeera, time-space compression is a process with which we are still coming to terms in the twenty-first century. For now, however, we can note that electrical telegraphy marked the beginning of a decisively new phase in the exercise of symbolic power, one that can be characterized by McKenzie Wark's term *telesthesia*, or perception at a distance: 'From the telescope to the telegraph and telephone,' writes Wark, 'from television to telecommunications, the development of telesthesia means the creation of, literally, *dislocated* perception and action' (1994: 43, original emphasis). If printing had made possible the development of the nation-state as an imagined community, telegraphy made possible an imagined community on the scale of a global village.

If the telegraph solved problems of communicating across space, it opened up time as a new arena for commercial competition and expansion (Carey 1989). In this sense, the gradual emergence of 24-hour broadcasting schedules is traceable to the telegraph. A key legacy of this is the rise to primacy of CNN and its imitators, from Fox News to Al Jazeera, offering round-the-clock news coverage; we will return to this aspect later in this chapter. Telegraphy introduced a new imperative to be *first* with a story. Nineteenth-century reporters would tie up the telegraph office all day when they were expecting an important story to send on: in some cases, if a story was not yet ready, then rather than lose a chance to beat the opposition, they would head down to the telegraph office and prevent others from using it by transmitting the Bible word-by-word (Blondheim 1994: 61). By 1855, newspapers in northern England could receive by telegraph a daily digest of what the London papers were reporting and circulate it through the region in their own daily edition hours before copies of those London newspapers could arrive by train (Reeve 1855: 497).

Before the telegraph, news was predominantly local and was not subject to the same imperatives of frequency or timeliness as it would become. In countries as large as the US, the speed of the postal service acted as the regulator of the speed of news, as most newspapers got their news from other newspapers, exchanged by mail (Blondheim 1994: 15). The telegraph made possible a new way of thinking about news: as a commodity (Postman 1985: 67). The Associated Press (AP) was formed in 1848 to exploit the telegraph's speed in distribution (Schudson 1978: 4). This meant that the same reports were, for the first time, being distributed by the new wire service wholesale across broad territories. Because AP reports were compilations, not representing any particular jurisdiction, the perception was that they were free from vested interests. This was augmented by the practice of requiring reporters to keep their texts as spare and unadorned as possible, excluding all personal perspectives and local colour (Blondheim 1994: 195). 'If the same story were to be understood in the same way from Maine to California,' Carey writes, 'language had to be flattened out and standardized' (1989: 210). Local colour was leached out of news reports to make them saleable in a market unconstrained by geography. 'The origins of objectivity', Carey argues, 'may be sought, therefore, in the necessity of stretching language in space over the long lines of Western Union' (1989: 210).

The telegraph also made possible the rise of the global news agencies such as the British-based Reuters. In the nineteenth century the news agencies — including not just Reuters but also the American AP, the German Wolff and the French Havas — emerged as a significantly new kind of media organization in many ways. For our present discussion we will confine ourselves to two of these: the transnational operation of the agencies (whose cartel agreement meant a network that became genuinely global in scope), and their telegraph-enabled emphasis on speed.

Reuters

In Rupert Murdoch's estimation, 'Reuters is a key story in the information revolution. A real key' (quoted in Shawcross 1992: 238). Reuters is the largest and best-known international news agency in the world. As a wholesaler of news to other media organizations, Reuters claims to publish some eight million words a day. According to the company's website, it employs 2,300 journalists, editorial staff, photographers and camera operators, and has almost 200 bureaux in 130 countries <http://about.reuters.com/aboutus/overview/facts

/index.asp>. However, as leading scholars of news agencies point out, some of these key words are open to more than one interpretation and, as with any other publicity material, we should be cautious about taking it entirely at face value (Boyd-Barrett 1998: 29). One analyst, for example, suggests that what a news agency calls a 'bureau' might constitute 'a lone stringer with an obsolete camera' (Paterson 1998: 86). Like all the major news agencies, Reuters operates across the full spectrum of news provision: print, radio, television, photography and Internet (for an account of Reuters' difficulties in adapting to the Internet see Mooney & Simpson 2003). Reuters television service sends packaged news reports (video and sound, without narration) by satellite to its subscribers. These clients can then add their own commentary before transmission, with the option of using a script provided by Reuters, or in some cases can broadcast a complete finished package — 'for the broadcaster unwilling to invest in actual journalism' as agency scholar Chris Paterson puts it (1998: 79).

A useful distinction with which to clarify the activities of the news agencies is that between 'retail' and 'wholesale' news provision (Boyd-Barrett & Rantanen 1998). Retail news services supply news directly to audiences; wholesale services provide news material to retailers (although, while still useful, this distinction has been blurred since the advent of cable and satellite television news services such as BBC World and CNN, who offer retail services direct to watching viewers as well as providing wholesale services to other news organizations). From a wholesale perspective, it is easy to take for granted how much of our daily news has been supplied by news agencies such as Reuters, but the figures can be striking. For example, consider a random edition of the *Sydney Morning Herald*, from Saturday 28 August 2004. In this issue there were six pages of world news, with a total of 36 stories. Of those, no fewer than eight were attributed to Reuters. A further four were sourced from the Associated Press, and a further three from the French news agency AFP. So Reuters were the source of almost a quarter of the world news in that paper, and the three big news agencies taken together accounted for a little over 40%. By way of a comparison, *Sydney Morning Herald* writers contributed just five of the 36 articles, mostly analysis and comment pieces (for very thorough discussions of the extent to which UK news media rely on agency copy from the Press Association, see Lewis, Williams & Franklin 2008a, 2008b; Davies 2008).

The commercial success of Reuters and the other agencies has always been predicated on the fastest communications technology (Boyd-Barrett 1998). Indeed, before founding the company in London in 1851, Paul Julius Reuter had successfully closed a gap in the still-developing European telegraph network by using *pigeons.* His fleet of 45 pigeons could transfer information between Belgium and Germany in two hours, which was six hours faster than the train (Levinson 1997: 53). Reuters made its name when it reported US President Lincoln's assassination in 1865 earlier than anyone else, with a two-hour exclusive on the news. Lincoln was shot on 14 April, and the news reached Ireland by boat on 26 April at 9.45 am; by 11.30 a message with the dateline 'New York, 15 April, 9 a.m.' had been dispatched to London newspapers, where the news was so shocking that it was first thought to be a hoax (Read 1999: 43). But when other sources confirmed it, hours later, Reuters' reputation was made (Levinson 1997: 53–5). News of Lincoln's death took 12 days to cross the Atlantic in 1865, but when US President Garfield was shot in 1881, it made the British papers within 24 hours, thanks to the development of transatlantic cable. Garfield's death was marked in Britain more extensively than had been Lincoln's; as Reuters historian Donald Read notes, the rapid transmission of information meant there could now be 'a sense of shared experience' (1999: 97). This is an early example of Wark's telesthesia.

From the beginning, Reuters had globalizing ambitions. The company established offices throughout Europe in the 1850s. In 1865, they opened an Alexandria office, the first outside Europe. Their first office in Asia opened in Bombay in 1866, their first in South Africa in Cape Town in 1876; Hong Kong was reached by cable in 1871, Australia in 1872, Tokyo and Shanghai in 1873 (Read 1999). In October 2006, Reuters opened a bureau inside the virtual world *Second Life* <http://secondlife.reuters.com>, suggesting those globalizing ambitions are still strong.

John Thompson has argued that the emergence of Reuters and the other major international news agencies was one of the most important developments in the globalization of communications, for three reasons. First, for the agencies, news was something to be gathered and distributed systematically, rather than haphazardly — and to be gathered and distributed, moreover, by telegraph, which is to say *quickly*. Second, the agencies divided up the world between them, each specializing in different regions: the effect of this was, in Thompson's words, to create 'a multilateral ordering of communication networks which was effectively global in scope' (1995: 154). And third, this systematic and global gathering of news was allied to emerging print networks, and subsequently radio, TV and Internet networks, that would reach ever larger audiences. Boyd-Barrett and Rantanen (1998: 2) have further pointed out that global news agencies are not just major agents of globalization themselves, but that their activities are also central to the activities of other agents of globalization (other corporations, other media firms, the banking and finance sectors). So from this perspective, the news agencies are central to the development of not just news but also of modernity, capitalism and globalization.

Cultural imperialism?

Any force of such influence and scope as the news agencies is inevitably going to be controversial. Reuters and the other major agencies contribute such a huge proportion of the world's news that there has been widespread concern about their influence. This was a major factor in the cultural imperialism debates, most notably in the UNESCO push in the 70s and 80s for what became known as a New World Information and Communication Order (NWICO), seeking ways to establish balance in global information flows (Picard 1991, MacBride & Roach 2000). As John Tomlinson (1991, 1997) has shown, the cultural imperialism discourse actually encompasses not one but a range of inter-related debates. Among these is the idea that the media are the vehicle for spreading ideas and values from a supposedly dominant, central culture to supposedly weaker, peripheral ones: this is encapsulated in Herbert Schiller's phrase 'the developing world under electronic siege' (1971: 109) and in the full title of Edward Herman and Robert McChesney's 1997 book *The Global Media: The New Missionaries of Corporate Capitalism*. In this view, globally exported media products (including news) are the vehicle for spreading certain ideas about, for example, trade, consumerism and government. Globalization is seen to be bound up with the exercise of symbolic power.

While the cultural imperialism issue eventually grew to encompass concerns about perceived western dominance in the international trade in entertainment programming, advertising, and technological development, its starting point was the news (MacBride & Roach 2000). Specifically, it grew out of concern about the extent to which the major news agencies dominated the flow of news in and out of developing countries. This dominance was seen by some to manifest itself in restricted — even distorted — representations of developing countries (UNESCO 1980). The Nigerian journalists observed in Golding and Elliott's study of broadcast news production made precisely these complaints about the western news agency reports they received (1979: 103–10). Among the counter-arguments offered was Reuters' contention that this was to blame the news agencies for the news selections of their subscribers: that the agencies did indeed provide material on developing countries but that their clients did not use it unless there was a coup or an earthquake (Read 1999: 393–4). While the UNESCO-sponsored debates lost some momentum in the 1980s (in part because the US and UK both withdrew from the organization), their influence on perceptions of — and responses to — globalization continues to be felt: despite its many flaws, the cultural imperialist perspective remains one of the key frames within which globalization is discussed, including in the news media. We will return to these questions in the final section of this chapter.

Radio Active

In the 1920s, two key types of media institution developed in the US and the UK — commercial networks in the US, and public service broadcasting (PSB) in the UK. What's the difference? For commercial broadcasters, the audience is a means to the end of selling advertising; for public service broadcasters, the audience is an end in itself. Both models offered centralized transmission to individual households: in the US model by advertising-funded commercial stations and networks; in the British model, by state-funded networks with a public service brief to, as the BBC's charter put it, 'inform, educate and entertain'. These became the templates for the development of radio broadcasting in other contexts. Moreover, they provided a basis for the development of television. Broadcasting brought together a number of preceding communications technologies: telegraphy, telephony, wireless telephony. Crisell suggests we can usefully think of as radio technology as 'broadcast wireless telephony' (1997: 10).

One important antecedent to broadcasting was the telephone, whose significance was that it made possible new kinds of *simultaneous* communication. The fact that anyone could listen in on telephone calls at first seemed like a problem, but was quickly seen to offer possibilities as well: using telephone lines, it was possible to send messages that were *intended* to be heard by anyone at all. Invented in 1876, the telephone was being used for what we can consider broadcasts by as early as 1879 (Kern 1983: 69). The most famous example is the case of Hungary, where a system called the Telefon Hirmondó network delivered news, drama and music programming over the phone system from 1893 until 1925, when it merged with the state radio broadcaster (Marvin 1988: 222–31). Writing of the Hirmondó system, Stephen Kern emphasizes that the key elements of broadcasting were already in place and that these rested on *simultaneity*:

> It focused the attention of the inhabitants of an entire city on a single experience, regulated their lives according to the program schedules, and invaded their privacy with an emergency signal that enabled the station to ring every subscriber when special news broke. (Kern 1983: 69).

Wireless telegraphy was another antecedent. Marconi developed a system for sending Morse code messages without wires in 1894 (Kern 1983: 68, Crowley & Heyer 2003). By 1901 it was possible to transmit such messages across the Atlantic. Among the commercial applications of this introduced by Marconi was the first wireless news service, sending transmissions between Britain and the US each night from 1904 (Kern 1983: 68). The uses of the wireless in the *Titanic* disaster in 1912 drew widespread attention to the possibilities of the new medium; by then wireless was not only widely used at sea, but was also well-established on land with hobbyists and amateurs, creating an appetite and a potential market for further developments in broadcast communication (Douglas 1987).

In 1920 David Sarnoff of RCA proposed a business plan in which people would buy a radio and subscribe to the *Wireless Age* magazine. The necessary investment would be underwritten by the sales of radio receivers as well as subscriptions and advertising (Flichy 1995: 108). The demands of larger urban environments, more mobile and diverse populations, and a social emphasis on the private sphere and the family home, created the demand for a form of mass broadcasting (Williams 1974). Wireless sets were produced on an industrial scale and marketed successfully by companies who broadcast programming as a means of generating sales of radios. The enormous size of the simultaneous audiences created huge interest: in 1923 a speech by the then-US President Harding was heard by over a million people; as Patrice Flichy writes, 'In a society in which urban change was rapid and cultures with rural origins had disappeared, radio provided a link with society.' (1995: 111).

The BBC

The British Broadcasting Company (later Corporation) was created in response to such US developments. Georgina Born sums up the creation of the BBC as 'a pragmatic arrangement between the Post Office and a cartel of radio-set manufacturers intended to provide radio content so as to promote the sale of wirelesses' (2004: 26). The BBC made its first transmissions on 14 November 1922. The following year, a government committee introduced the idea that broadcasting should be a public utility, utilizing as it did the public resource of the airwaves, in deliberate contrast to the emerging American commercial model. The implications of this were to be fleshed out by the BBC's first general manager John Reith: in his view, broadcasting should inform, the better to foster an engaged citizenry; it should educate; and it should entertain, though not purely for the sake of it.

> *'Broadcasting brings relaxation and interest to many homes where such things are at a premium. It does far more; it carries direct information on a hundred subjects to innumerable men and women, who thereby will be enabled not only to take more interest in events which were formerly outside their ken, but who will after a short time be in a position to make up their own minds on many matters of vital moment, matters which formerly they had either to receive according to the dictated and partial versions and opinions of others, or to ignore altogether. A new and mighty weight of public opinion is being formed, and an intelligent concern on many subjects will be manifested in quarters now overlooked.'* (Reith 1924: 18–19).

Jacka notes how Reith's original vision emphasized educational and instructional programming: 'It would stretch and extend the audience. It would make them better than they were' (2006: 346).

In Scannell and Cardiff's synopsis, the Reithian view of PSB is of 'a cultural, moral and educative force for the improvement of knowledge, taste and manners' (1991: 7). This organization was transformed into the British Broadcasting Corporation on 1 January 1927, with a now-formal government mandate to inform, educate and entertain, as well as with a guarantee of funding through the sale of licences to users and strict prohibitions on advertising and editorializing (Crisell 1997: 22)

On one level, PSB is publicly-funded media; however, on another level, the term describes an entire philosophy of broadcasting. Curran and Seaton suggest the approach has three central components: 'serving the needs of democracy, generating content that has cultural value, and promoting social inclusion' (2003: 401). Richard Collins distinguishes between approaches to PSB as 'ises' and 'oughts'. The former are descriptive, inductive analyses of what PSB is; the latter are normative, deductive arguments about what PSB should be. Studies that examine the 'ises' of public service broadcasting tend to emphasize diversity, universality and impartiality as its central attributes (Collins 2004: 41). Studies that focus on the 'oughts' of public service broadcasting emphasize the cultural leadership role of such broadcasters and may draw on the concept of the public sphere (see Chapter 6) in arguing against market forces in broadcasting (Collins 2004). A good example of an 'oughts' approach to PSB is Tracey (1998), who identifies eight basic principles which underlie the concept. In his words, these are:

- Universality of availability
- Universality of appeal
- Provision for minorities, especially those disadvantaged by physical or social circumstances
- Serving the public sphere
- A commitment to the education of the public
- Public broadcasting should be distanced from all vested interests
- Broadcasting should be so structured as to encourage competition in good programming rather than competition for numbers
- The rules of broadcasting should liberate rather than restrict the programme-maker (Tracey 1998: 26–32).

Why does the public service approach to broadcasting matter? The BBC invested vast sums to ensure that their broadcasts were available even in very remote parts of the country, to a degree that commercial networks would probably not have matched otherwise (Hesmondhalgh 2002: 121). This commitment to national availability, and the BBC's policy of programming a wide range of different types of material were of crucial importance. Broadcasting brought the public into the private and took the private into the public (Meyrowitz 1985). More than this, it made possible the creation of a new kind of *general* public — 'one commensurate with the whole of society' (Scannell 1989, Scannell & Cardiff 1991: 14).

The process of developing a distinctive broadcast style of news delivery took years. Until as late as 1938, BBC news was hobbled by restrictions designed to protect the newspaper industry. For example, the BBC was at first required to take its news from agencies, including Reuters, and these reports were written in a style quite unsuitable for broadcast (Crisell 1997: 15). Moreover, until 1927, the BBC was restricted to broadcasting news after 7pm (Schlesinger 1987: 16). Such constraints led to some daft results: for example, forbidden to broadcast any news that had not already been in the papers, the BBC's coverage of the Derby race in 1926 involved their being able to transmit the sounds of the race but not the results (Scannell & Cardiff 1991: 25).

Schlesinger highlights the importance of the early use of news agency copy: it meant that the BBC began by adopting the agencies' wholesale emphasis and their sense of news value. This has led, he suggests, to an ongoing correspondence between the agencies' credo of objectivity and the BBC's ethos of impartiality. Both, suggests Schlesinger, 'appeal to the same Western liberal doctrine of truth' (1987: 15). The difference is that the agencies developed this approach for economic reasons, whereas the BBC did so for political ones. Scannell and Cardiff comment on the 'austere conception of news values' that characterized early BBC radio: if there was deemed to be not enough news of the BBC's standards, bulletins would simply be cut short. On one famous occasion (Good Friday 1930), the news editors decided there was nothing worth broadcasting, and the BBC announced 'there is no news tonight' (Scannell & Cardiff 1991: 118).

In 1930 the BBC negotiated the right to rewrite its agency copy into a more listenable style. Coverage of crises such as the General Strike of 1926, the death of King George V, the Munich Crisis of

1938, all demonstrated the advantages that broadcast news could offer over print (Crisell 1997: 26–7). The General Strike in particular was important not least because the BBC was politicized as an instrument of the government, but also because it provided the impetus for the BBC to actually gather and create its own news for the first time (Schlesinger 1987: 18–19).

The BBC was involved in the development of television from the late 1920s, and launched an experimental TV service in 1936 — with viewers then referred to as 'lookers' (Küng-Shankleman 2000: 69) — although the service was suspended for the duration of World War II. Early BBC TV news resisted the possibilities of the new medium, preferring to replicate existing approaches. Until 1954, BBC TV offered nothing more than a version of the radio news, accompanied by still photographs (Crisell 1997: 92, Curran & Seaton 2003: 168, Born 2004: 39), and a nightly ten-minute newsreel with voiceover commentary (a form, as Crisell notes, derived from cinema). Newsreaders did not appear on screen until 1955, in a development prompted, like many subsequent ones, by the arrival of competition from ITV in September 1955. ITN's newsreaders (or newscasters as ITN called them) rewrote their own scripts to suit their individual delivery. ITN used more visuals, longer bulletins, more actuality and vox pops (Crisell 1997: 93). Until then, the BBC had seen itself as delivering an audio version of *The Times,* with visuals held by some in the News Division as an unacceptable pandering to the lowest common denominator (Schlesinger 1987: 40). ITN provided the impetus to move beyond this. A so-called 'news explosion' followed throughout the 1950s, as new techniques, approaches and technologies were developed, particularly in the field of current affairs programming, such as *Panorama.* Current affairs, with its focus on interpretation provided a politically useful counterpart to news, with its focus on reporting (Schlesinger 1987: 46).

Creeber (2004) argues that the commercial ITN news was responsible for some of the most significant developments in UK TV news. Beginning in 1967, *News At Ten* was a 30-minute broadcast, longer than the standard, allowing for more detail. It aimed for greater accessibility and involvement than the BBC. And the presence of commercials led to a rethink of sequencing: as audiences were believed to switch channels during the ads, ITN introduced trailers and previews of upcoming stories to sustain interest, with some important stories held over till after the break.

Competition has increased ever since. There have been new channels (Channel 4 was launched in 1982), new systems (Murdoch's satellite service began in 1989) and new formats (from breakfast TV to 24-hour news channels; BBC News 24 was launched in 1997 and renamed the BBC News Channel in 2008). This, together with the emphasis on deregulation of the Thatcher government, and the subsequent rise of new technological delivery and reception systems, put significant pressure on the BBC.

The successes of the public service approach to broadcasting are clear. And yet the sector appears to operate in an environment of almost continuous crisis. In 2007, for example, the BBC was battered by a string of fakery scandals, ranging from deceptive editing of footage of the Queen, to a rigged vote to name the new pet kitten on kids' magazine TV show *Blue Peter*. It also flagged controversial cuts to some services, including news, with around 1,800 redundancies scheduled.

What are the challenges faced by this broadcasting model in the early twenty-first century? Küng-Shankleman (2000) notes that almost all of the structuring assumptions that underpinned the development of PSB are now in question — from the ideological environment to the nature of the audience, from the geographical reach of the broadcaster to their financial resources. Küng-Shankleman also draws attention to the changing demands of a broad range of 'stakeholders' with an interest in PSBs, from employees and executives, to competitors and international regulatory bodies (2000: 96).

One very real challenge to PSB is a prevailing neo-liberal ideological climate, which is antithetical to the idea of 'public' services: this has led, in Australia, for example, to a steady decline in funding for PSBs (in real terms), and to the persistent use of organized 'flak' (Herman and Chomsky 1988) against the perceived biases of the national PSB, the Australian Broadcasting Corporation (ABC). In Australia, both Labor and Liberal federal governments have accused the ABC of bias against them, which suggests, if anything, that something is going right. The accusation of bias often serves to direct attention away from the facts of the matter; it challenges the motives of the broadcaster, while sidestepping what they have actually said or asked. This climate also manifests itself in what some commentators have seen as an excessively managerial approach at the BBC: for example, radio and TV newsgathering operations were combined in 1991, which led to a perception among staff that individual programmes became more homogenous, functioning more as outlets for centrally-prepared content, than as distinctive, independent facets of the BBC (Born 2004: 389). In November 2007, the BBC combined its radio, TV and online news departments into a single multimedia newsroom.

Another challenge is posed by the proliferation of new media. In a post-broadcast environment, characterized by convergent delivery platforms (digital TV, cable TV, the Internet), it becomes harder to make the case that the established public service broadcasters are entitled to special government funding and support (Tracey 1998, Steemers 1999). The additional content made available by these new platforms also poses a problem for the argument that PSBs cater for audiences that would otherwise go unaddressed, redressing what economists term 'market failure' (Jacka 2006: 350). BBC news and current affairs faced problems in adapting to the challenges and possibilities posed by developments such as the innovations of CNN from 1980 onwards, and the availability of video, satellite, and digital production facilities. With newsgathering centralized, and news outlets within the BBC proliferating (such as the 1991 launch of the international rolling news service BBC World), journalists found themselves under greater time pressure, and would re-purpose the same material across different outlets. The result, as Born puts it, was contradictory: 'new means of delivery and new formats were countered by greater uniformity of content; an appearance of diversity disguised the considerable pressures for editorial conformity' (Born 2004: 404).

While acknowledging the problems facing the sector, it is also important to emphasize its ongoing successes. These successes are reflected in the new charter which the BBC received in 2007. This restated its mission to 'inform, educate and entertain' and also redefined its public purposes as:

(a) sustaining citizenship and civil society;
(b) promoting education and learning;
(c) stimulating creativity and cultural excellence;
(d) representing the UK, its nations, regions and communities;
(e) bringing the UK to the world and the world to the UK;
(f) in promoting its other purposes, helping to deliver to the public the benefit of emerging communications technologies

> and services and, in addition, taking a leading role in the switchover to digital television.
> <http://www.bbc.co.uk/bbctrust/framework/charter.html>.

For example, in a world increasingly conscious of globalization, the BBC World Service remains a highly significant news operation, broadcasting to more than 150 million people in dozens of languages. Moreover, the BBC is a major innovator in the field of new media — some 45% of UK Net users regularly visit BBC websites (Born 2004: 9) and its creation of the Freeview digital TV system was an important contribution to the new media environment, as was the launch of the online iPlayer service in 2007. The PSB ethos works well with the Net, and the BBC has been an important player in the development of experimental forms such as digital storytelling, which encourages users to use their own symbolic power resources (Meadows 2003).

Satellite of love?

CNN was launched on 1 June 1980, the creation of Ted Turner, who had been an early adopter of satellite broadcast technology. Turner reportedly launched the channel with the following address to staff: 'See, we're gonna take the news and put it on the satellite, and then we're gonna beam it down into Russia, and we're gonna bring world peace, and we're gonna get rich in the process!' (quoted in Whittemore 1990: 124). Turner's approach to broadcasting had become possible in 1975 with the launch of RCA's first commercial satellite, and HBO's subsequent successful introduction of a cable movie service using the satellite for networking (Friedland 1992). Turner began networking his small Atlanta TV station across the US as early as 1976 and quickly saw the potential for more. CNN was the first television station devised around the concept of continuous live news. Turner's initial concept was based on popular magazines — *Time, Sports Illustrated, People, Fortune*: the station's format would offer 30 minutes of features modeled on the content of each, in a repeating two-hour block (Whittemore 1990: 30–1, Volkmer 1999: 132).

Communications satellites were first launched early in the 1960s, but it was not until the following decade that TV networks and telecommunications providers began to use these for signal distribution (Volkmer 1999). The success of first HBO and later CNN, coupled with widespread international trends towards re-regulation of broadcasting systems, generated a global boom in satellite distribution of media forms, and a large industry demand for transponder access. Although beginning in the US, these developments were by no means confined there, and satellite broadcasting arrived in Europe in the 1980s (Curran & Seaton 2003: 277). Satellite-driven cable channels emerged in India, Mexico and Taiwan, and reached China in the form of covert access to Murdoch's Hong Kong based STAR TV (Hilmes 2002). One consequence of these developments was that much cheap American programming was made available internationally, fuelling concerns about cultural imperialism discussed elsewhere in this chapter.

TV's particular quality of 'liveness' has always been central to attempts to understand and theorize television (Scannell 1996, Bourdon 2000, Crisell 2006, Marriott 2007). News has always placed particular emphasis on being broadcast live, even though much of a given bulletin may have been pre-recorded and edited. But the key innovation of CNN was *continuous* live news, which they conceived of as re-making the role of the audience, drawing them into the process of the news and keeping them there as they waited (like the journalists themselves!) to find out what happened. CNN's anchors at times had to ad lib for hours over raw video footage of an event in progress, a method which has been widely adopted by CNN's imitators. In the UK on 9 September 2007, this approach reached some kind of nadir with both the BBC and Sky News transmitting hours of raw live coverage of the parents of missing toddler Madeleine McCann driving to a Portuguese airport and then arriving in the UK, a journey entirely untouched by incident. This approach instead works best at times of crisis, when large numbers of people are drawn to follow a breaking story. CNN's early reputation was partly built on such dramas — the attempted assassination of US President Reagan in 1981, the *Challenger* space shuttle disaster in 1986, the student protests in Beijing's Tiananmen Square in 1989. *Challenger* in particular brought CNN to international attention, and the network began to function as a kind of wire service or wholesaler to other news organizations in Europe and elsewhere (Whittemore 1990: 272). However, unlike the established news agencies, who could fact-check and edit before releasing a story, CNN aired everything live. This gave the network an important agenda-setting role (Friedland 1992).

In covering such stories, CNN were forced to put details to air as they received them: the audience knew as much as the reporters did, and there was new scope for mistakes (Meyrowitz 1985: 111–12). Barbie Zelizer has argued that CNN's approach to news is not an entirely new form, but rather: 'just faster, more continuous, less polished, and less edited journalism' (1992: 78). In this analysis, CNN is news-as-usual, except that the audience is exposed to different aspects of the news-making process. Others, however, have argued that CNN's approach has had more important implications and have seen more serious changes in the live, rolling news format: for Elihu Katz, CNN's Gulf War coverage of 1990–91 was 'the beginning of the end of journalism as we have known it' (1992: 9). It is news, in this analysis, that is predicated upon immediate updating and correction, upon interruption and contradiction. News moves from reporting what has happened to speculating about what *might* happen (Ellis 2000: 75). The whole idea of being live all the time is that things will change, amending the situation presented a moment ago. In minimizing the potential for editing, for shaping and interpretation, CNN offers news, suggests Katz, which 'almost wants to be wrong' (1992: 9). On 13 October 2005, UK rolling news service Sky News offered a vivid example to support this view, with host Ginny Buckley offering the following indelible live report: 'Joining you now with some breaking news here at the Sky News Centre, we have Howard... *Harold* Pinter, who's joining us ... the playwriter [*sic*] Harold Pinter, I believe, has just died... news just... has won the Nobel Prize for Literature. Apologies for that.'

How the news changes the news

As McKenzie Wark has pointed out, a 24-hour continuous news service is not ideally compatible with the established narrative strategies of news. Rather than cutting and shaping events to fit familiar narrative forms, CNN instead introduced an emphasis on what Wark calls 'the queer concept of "live" news coverage — an instant audiovisual presence on the site of an event' (1994: 38). This focus on speed and immediacy, on being the first on the scene, leads to news that is all event and no process. More than this, it leads at times to revealing moments when CNN-style coverage becomes obvious as a component part of the event it purports to cover (Gurevitch 1991, MacGregor 1997). An early example was a 1987 incident in which an unguarded remark on CNN by US President Reagan about the value of the US dollar caused the currency to fall before his meeting with reporters was over (the run on the currency was quickly halted by — of course — a second statement on CNN). As Lewis Friedland puts it: 'No longer did the network merely report events, but through its immediate reportage, CNN actually shaped the events and became part of them' (1992: 2).

MacGregor offers a clear example of this:

> On 18 April 1995 a catamaran ferry went aground off the coast of Jersey. No one was killed and it was hardly the story of the century. Nevertheless CNN had a live feed from the scene as the Harbour Office, the local lifeboat, a Customs helicopter, the police, fire and ambulance services together conducted the rescue of the 300 passengers. The local emergency services used the live CNN pictures from the scene to coordinate the rescue work. (1997: 4).

The September 11 attacks also illustrated how live news of an event can change that event, perhaps most vividly in the case of the fourth plane, United 93, which never reached the hijackers' intended destination after a struggle with passengers who had been alerted by mobile phones from people on the ground watching the news.

The defining example of this came with the Tiananmen Square crisis of 1989. Not only did cameras make possible a global audience for this event (and for subsequent examples such as the toppling of Saddam's statue in Baghdad in 2003), and not only did cameras influence the construction of public opinion on a global scale — the presence of cameras also influenced the actors involved; the act of observing changed the course of what was being observed. CNN broadcast live a confrontation with Chinese officials over the shutdown of the network's satellite transmission, which in a sense served in a small way as an illustration of the repressive regime in operation (it may have drawn attention to, and dramatized, the nature of the regime, although of course it did not prevent what was to follow) (Whittemore 1990: 289–98, Friedland 1992: 6). In his analysis of the Tiananmen media event Wark argues that the media event appeared as 'a positive feedback loop' (1994: 22). The Beijing students' perceptions of Western accounts of their demands and motives became caught up in the students' own accounts of their own motives, their own demands: Western interpretations of what was happening in Beijing, Wark writes, 'fed back into the event itself via a global loop encompassing radio, telephone, and fax vectors. They impacted back on the further unfolding of the event itself' (1994: 22). Friedland's account of the attempted Soviet coup of 1991 draws a similar conclusion: 'an act of repression was monitored by the outside world, and the act of monitoring altered, however subtly, the course of events' (1992: 42).

An often-remarked-upon phenomenon is the extent to which world leaders have been prepared to admit their dependence on CNN for information. In his account of the 2001 US-led conflict in Afghanistan, Bob Woodward recounts a Northern Alliance victory over the Taliban in Afghanistan in November 2001. He writes how then-National Security Adviser Condoleeza Rice received a report that the city of Mazar had been taken, but was unsure of the situation. Woodward writes: 'What does the national security adviser do in such a situation? She turned on CNN, which confirmed the reports, and called Rumsfeld to tell him the news' (2002: 302). More than this, leaders have at times used CNN as a kind of diplomatic channel, making statements to and for each other in the knowledge that these will be seen on TV — a phenomenon sometimes known as 'airwave diplomacy' (Volkmer 1999: 139).

Al Jazeera

Al Jazeera became a major global news force on 7 October 2001. As the only channel with a 24-hour live satellite link to Kabul, Al Jazeera found its footage being fed to key news services around the world when US bombs started to land in the Afghan campaign. On the same night, the station received a video message from Osama bin Laden, in which he admitted responsibility for the September 11 attacks, and put it straight to air (el-Nawawy & Iskandar 2002: 21). This was the first time Al Jazeera drew much international notice, and it's worth noting here that this attention was drawn by the station as a news wholesaler — the significance of this, and of its other roles as a retailer, is the focus of this section. As el-Nawawy and Iskandar observe: 'Al Jazeera is an unofficial two-way communications channel between the Arab and Western worlds. The Arab world tunes in for information, and foreign networks tune in for material and footage' (2002: 156).

Al Jazeera's origins can be traced to 1994 with a joint BBC-Saudi venture, which collapsed because of heavy-handed Saudi editorial constraints (Flew 2007). This Arabic project within the BBC had been developed from the idea that BBC World Service Arabic Radio with 14 million listeners in 1994 could be adapted for TV and become a major media player in the region (el-Nawawy & Iskandar 2002: 31–3). In a sense, then, Al Jazeera is a legacy of the public service broadcasting tradition of the BBC, whose early involvement created a pool of trained staff that the new channel could use (McNair 2006: 111). The emir of Qatar bankrolled the nascent Al Jazeera in November 1996. By 2001, the station would be able to claim a staff of around 350 reporters in 31 countries, with viewer numbers estimated at 35 million, and its website drawing far larger audiences than that (el-Nawawy & Iskandar 2002: 34, 65). The target audience has been described as 'the emerging politically critical middle class in politically divided Arab countries' (Volkmer 2002: 241), although the importance of its international reach to diasporic communities should be emphasized (Sinclair, Jacka & Cunningham 1996, Cunningham & Sinclair 2001). Its reach continues to broaden, with the launch of its English-language channel in November 2006 — with presenters David Frost and Rageh Omaar on board — and its own YouTube channel in April 2007.

The 2003 Iraq conflict brought Al Jazeera into the media mainstream, just as the previous one had done for CNN (el-Nawawy and Iskandar 2004). In the first week of the 2003 fighting, the station claimed to double their subscriber numbers in Europe, from four million to eight million in a few days. To counter the electronic siege on their website from hackers, Al Jazeera started up an SMS news update service, which soon became available to over 130 countries in both English and Arabic, using the same infrastructure provider as does CNN for its text service. And they won the annual Freedom of Expression award from the respected watchdog group Index on Censorship, which praised its independence.

Providing material to other networks, as a wholesaler, is a key part of Al Jazeera's success. For example, following September 11, Al Jazeera and CNN signed a deal, which would give CNN exclusive rights to rebroadcast Al Jazeera material for six hours after broadcast, while Al Jazeera in turn would get access to CNN equipment and footage. This arrangement is unremarkable in itself, as CNN has many affiliates; of more interest is the fact that the other major US networks ignored this exclusivity deal, rebroadcasting Al Jazeera footage and citing fair use and national interest for doing so (el-Nawawy & Iskandar 2002: 163–5).

Yet as a news wholesaler, Al Jazeera became caught up in the conflict in ways that represented them to western viewers as some kind of enemy. Western politicians, such as Donald Rumsfeld, criticized Al Jazeera for screening images of dead US troops as well as for showing bin Laden's communiqués. The images from Al Jazeera were incorporated into western news texts in ways that led to misunderstandings and conflict, with the channel seen by the Bush administration as a participant in events instead of an observer (McNair 2006: 114). Some American TV viewers actually rang the station's US bureau to ask why Al Jazeera was beheading prisoners (Azran 2004: 84). They broadcast film of American prisoners being interrogated, of dead US troops, of civilian casualties. Their Baghdad base was bombed by a US plane, killing a cameraman (Knightley 2003: 539). As was discussed in a previous chapter, John Hartley has argued that the news works through inclusion and exclusion, through the construction of realms of Wedom and Theydom (1992a). For Al Jazeera, as a news wholesaler, providing images and texts to be used by western networks, their material is going to rub up against the operation of — in Daniel Hallin's terms — the sphere of consensus, the media realm where journalists speak for 'us' and take for granted a national, cultural consensus on the meaning and significance of an event. Al Jazeera's ideas and approach, their structures of feeling, can't really be fitted into a journalistic moment that is very much about constructing a sense of Wedom. They can only be understood, as Hartley would put it, within our Theydom.

What of Al Jazeera as a news retailer? Here it is worth picking up the discussion of globalization begun earlier in this chapter. Rather than the linear flows assumed by proponents of cultural imperialism, it is necessary to see globalization as a complex set of processes without a single centre (Tomlinson 1997). As Appadurai (1990) has argued in an influential essay, there are flows of people, of technology, of media and images, of finance, and of ideas and ideologies. These flows are not complementary but are processes characterized by 'disjuncture'. Transnational satellite news services combined with diasporic communities make possible new kinds of public spheres — 'diasporic public spheres' for Appadurai (1996); 'microspheres' for Volkmer (2005). As el-Nawawy and Iskandar point out, Al Jazeera is a 'major stakeholder' in the 'Arab peoples' experience of globalization, migration, and emigration' (2002: 19). The rise to prominence of Al Jazeera reveals these complex, disjunctive flows in operation, as satellite transmission of Arab structures of feeling meets exile communities around the world. Al Jazeera points to the complex possibilities of particular imagined communities on the scale of a global village.

Conclusion

On 22 September 2005 JetBlue Flight 292 had a problem with its landing gear and was forced to circle the airport in Long Beach, California for three hours before a successful emergency landing. On board, the 140 passengers spent the time watching live news coverage of their own predicament on seat-back satellite TVs. Some recorded farewell messages to loved ones on their camcorders; others rang them on their mobiles. One passenger used their phone's camera to record images from the live TV coverage of the incident — images that were in turn later broadcast by TV news networks. In one sense, this was a very twenty-first century media event — a weird kind of reality TV. But in another sense, it was a nineteenth century media event — one descended from the initial breakthrough of the telegraph in separating the communication and the transportation of information. The JetBlue incident captured the ways in which the almost instantaneous transmission of information between any two points on a network can become part of the events it presents: in this case, bringing live news of an unfolding drama even to those caught up in it.

This chapter has traced some of the innovations in news made possible by the uses of a range of media technologies, showing how these uses have made possible new kinds of news organization, and in turn reshaping resources and strategies of symbolic power. The next chapter extends this analysis to the Internet, considering the implications for the news of a media environment built around networked communication between peers.

Chapter 8

News 2.0?

'In our time reality is scarce because of access: so few command the machinery for its determination. Some get to speak and some to listen, some to write and some to read, some to film and some to view' (Carey 1989: 87).

'"Read-only." Passive recipients of culture produced elsewhere. Couch potatoes. Consumers. This is the world of media from the twentieth century. The twenty-first century could be different. This is the crucial point: It could be both read and write' (Lessig 2004: 37).

In the year 2015 the Museum of Media History prepares an exhibition outlining the main developments in media ownership and use throughout the previous decade. Looking back to 2005, a visitor would be struck by the dramatic ways in which long-standing assumptions about the nature of news have been overturned. The BBC, CNN, the *New York Times* — none of these is to become the dominant force in the media environment of 2015. Instead, the emerging digital mediascape is to be shaped by newer players — Google, Amazon, Microsoft — and by newer approaches: by new opportunities to automate, to personalize and to participate. If news is the organized daily production, distribution and uses of nonfiction drama, every key term in that definition is to be open to challenge and change.

The exhibition might recall how in 2008 Google merged with Amazon to form Googlezon. The new entity combined Google's search capacities and its automated Google News service with Amazon's personalized recommendations software to offer news assembled and edited by computer and tailored to the specifications of each individual user. Meanwhile, Microsoft developed a social networking news service, enabling any user to comment publicly on any content within extended networks of readers and writers. The resulting competition was brutal, driving the previously dominant news organizations out of business — by 2014 even the *New York Times* had retreated offline, reduced to a 'print-only newsletter for the elite and the elderly'.

This story is told in *EPIC 2015*, an eight-minute Flash animation by Robin Sloan and Matt Thompson, which was widely circulated online in early 2005. It's a text which both captures and dramatizes key trends and themes in the study of new media and their implications for news and current affairs. From one perspective, *EPIC 2015* is about aspects of *convergence*, from multi-platform publishing to concentrated ownership — the comings-together of content, communications and computing; of industries and audiences; of models and modes (Pool 1983, Rice 1999, Castells 2000, Jenkins 2001, 2004, 2006, Boczkowski 2004). But from another perspective, it's concerned with the opposites of convergence, with ways in which Net use can enable new configurations of news production, distribution and reception; new modes of authorship and audiencehood; new kinds of producer and consumer: pluralization, multiplication, fragmentation — *divergence* (Lovink 2002, Meikle 2002, Deuze 2003, Atton 2004, Bruns 2005). The two epigraphs for this chapter point to these rapid changes. Carey, writing in 1989, surveyed a media landscape built around a one-way broadcast paradigm; Lessig, 15 years later, saw the development of a participatory media environment. It is this shift which is the main focus of this chapter.

Brian McNair points to two key trends which were influential in the development of online journalism in the first decade of the Net as a mass medium — continuity and transformation, or in McNair's words, 'established professionalism and iconoclastic amateurism' (2006: 119). On the one hand, attempts to apply long-established principles to the new medium; on the other hand, experiments with new modes. McNair suggests that this interplay between old and new led to four identifiable kinds of online news producer. In his words these are:

1. *Professional-institutional actors,* including the BBC, CNN, Al Jazeera and other transnational satellite broadcasters; the

websites of newspapers and national broadcasters; and the websites of internet-only journalistic organizations, such as *Slate;*

2. *Professional-individual actors,* such as Andrew Sullivan, Glenn Reynolds, the Baghdad Blogger, and a few others, numbering in the hundreds at most (I refer here only to English-language outlets);
3. *Non-professional-institutional actors,* including government agencies, NGOs, political parties, campaigning and lobby groups, and terrorist organizations such as Al Qaida and the proliferation of web-savvy Islamic groups that support them;
4. *Non-professional-individual actors,* or private bloggers, numbering in their millions (McNair 2006: 119).

This chapter, taken together with the earlier discussion of blogging in Chapter 4, includes examples of each of these four categories. The final section of this chapter is an extended discussion of one of McNair's third category, non-professional institutional actors, the Indymedia network.

Convergence and divergence

If convergence is the coming together of things that were previously separate, what kinds of things are converging? There are different ways of answering this question. First, we might point to industry or corporate convergence, the ongoing processes of mergers, acquisitions and alliances, most famously still in the ill-fated 2000 union between Time-Warner and AOL (Bagdikian 2004). Second, we could focus on content convergence, as the same stories, ideas or characters are refashioned and re-purposed across different media forms: the comic that becomes a film that becomes a game that becomes a ringtone (Marshall 2002). A further layer of complexity is that, in news terms, convergence often refers specifically to multi-platform publishing (Hall 2004: 5); in the US, notes Quinn, convergence often refers to partnership agreements between local TV stations and newspapers, seeking to combine the reach and brand of the former with the larger reporting staff of the latter (2004: 112).

However, for the purposes of this chapter, the key aspect of convergence is technological, as media content, telecommunications and computing become ever more integrated, and as people find new ways to exploit this potential. This perspective focuses on the so-called three C's of convergent media: content, computing and communications (Bolter & Grusin 1999, Rice 1999, Barr 2000, Pavlik 2001, Flew 2005). The most straightforward illustration of this is an email (Barr 2000: 22), which comprises a written message — *content* — composed on a *computer* and sent through the phone system (*communications*). In the 1990s, convergence was something of a buzzword, focused on future possibilities. Today, however, it's an almost banal description of daily media reality — computers increasingly offer television functions, televisions are increasingly computer-like, and telephones are increasingly like both. New media do not render existing media obsolete but can come to complement (or supplement) them. And this process can make itself felt in both directions — so not only does the CNN website borrow from the immediacy of CNN's television coverage (and from newspaper layout design), but also the presentation of that television news coverage is increasingly influenced by the windowed environment of computer media. What we see on screen in a TV news report is now likely to resemble what we see on our computer desktops, with, for example, an anchor asking questions of a foreign correspondent, each framed in a separate on-screen window, against a background marked by logos and graphics, with a scrolling text across the bottom of the screen (Bolter & Grusin 1999). Indeed, for some commentators, the fact that telephony, moving image forms, and computers have been studied separately until now is beginning to seem something of a historical oversight (Friedberg 2002).

Does convergence imply homogenization? Yes and no. Castells notes the increasing diversity of media messages and the ongoing fragmentation of the 'mass' audience into ever-more specialized niches; but he also notes the increasingly entrenched control of major corporations, and the ongoing search for synergies through patterns of acquisitions, alliances and mergers. Certain genres and narrative types, programming formulas, circulate globally, but there are local inflections and variations. The synthesis of this, for Castells, is that '*we are not living in a global village, but in customized cottages globally produced and locally distributed*' (Castells 2000: 370, original emphasis). For Mark Poster, the coming together (and integration) of things that were previously separate is the harbinger of 'a second media age', one which moves beyond the broadcast, few-to-many paradigm that characterized the twentieth century. Poster pointed out that technological convergence could make possible a new era of media *divergence*, characterized by many-to-many, decentralized communication — 'a system of multiple producers/distributors/consumers, an entirely new configuration of communication relations in which the boundaries between those terms collapse' (Poster 1995: 3).

A common criticism of the rhetoric of convergence, as expressed in concepts such as a 'second media age', is that it can display a certain teleology. In this view, to talk about convergence implies that there is an end-point or destination to the process. This end-point is usually either a utopian version ('isn't new technology great?') or else an undesirable dystopian one ('isn't new technology scary?'). This kind of criticism ties in with a critique of the concept of convergence which sees it as technologically determinist (Silverstone 1995). For example, two recent major histories of media forms (Briggs & Burke 2005, Winston 2005) conclude with chapters called 'convergence', adding to the sense of teleology. And yet, as one of these authors puts it, in seeming exasperation: 'That people can listen to their radio over their digital television — so what? That they can make telephone calls on their computers — so what?' (Winston 2005: 377). This chapter sets out to take this 'so what?' question as a real one, not a rhetorical one. To ask 'so what?' in a serious way is to ask what is at stake in a given debate or situation — and more is at stake in the new media environment than Winston's brief dismissal allows. This chapter argues that technological convergence matters more than Winston suggests, as it makes possible new approaches to news.

Three dimensions of online news

12 December 1998. You log on to the BBC News website. US President Bill Clinton faces impeachment for perjury. There's a 500-word report for you to read, and links to a brief video clip and three audio clips from BBC correspondents and from the House of Representatives vote to impeach the president. (This page, as well as many others, can still be viewed through the remarkable Wayback Machine at <http://www.archive.org/index.php>). In 1998, BBC News Online was a simple, straightforward, text-based site, built around the visual metaphor of a newspaper front page. It offered the user great content but few options. In the late nineties, online news was essentially a novel means of distribution.

6 November 2006. You log on to the BBC News website. Former Iraqi President Saddam Hussein has been sentenced to death. In 2006, BBC News Online boasted an enormous amount of content, with considerably more graphics, video and audio resources. But what else has changed in eight years? The site has developed in ways that exploit three central possibilities offered by convergent media. First, it offers more *automated* services — email digests and headlines; news feeds to your mobile phone; news alerts sent straight to your desktop; RSS feeds; and audio and video podcasts, including edited versions of the key TV current affairs shows *Newsnight* and *Question Time.* Second, it offers more scope for the user to *personalize* the site — for example, to choose between international and UK versions, more or fewer graphics, and from text offered in a range of languages, including Spanish and Chinese. And third, it offers some modest possibilities for the user to *participate* in the news process — there's a 'Have Your Say' section, a vox pop with automated forms. More significantly, readers are invited to submit story ideas, pictures or video, with the iconic mobile phone images of the London bombing included on the page as a reminder of how user-generated content can become central to even the biggest news stories. By the middle of the first decade of the twenty-first century, online news was not just about new methods of distribution, but about new possibilities for production and reception, and a blurring of the lines between the two.

Automation, personalization, participation. Here are three central dimensions of online news, each made possible by media convergence, and each being explored in different ways by different organizations (and individuals) — often in far more radical ways than those offered by the BBC. These three characteristics often overlap and reinforce each other in practice — we may use an automated publishing function to personalize our blog, for instance. But in order to give enough attention to each, we will take them separately in the following sections. This chapter expands on each of these three trends before a more extended discussion of one Net phenomenon which illustrates all three — the global online news network, Indymedia.

Automatic for the people

At noon Sydney time on 6 November 2006, Google News had as its lead story 'Saddam Hussein Sentenced to Death'. This event was always going to be number one that day. But Google News's choice of source was perhaps less obvious — its lead story was sourced, not from CNN or the *Washington Post,* but from MTV.com. Why would MTV.com, in this instance, rank as a more prominent news source than the *Times*? The essential thing to note about Google News is the line at the foot of its page — 'The selection and placement of stories on this page were determined automatically by a computer program'. Google News is, to date, the highest-profile fully-automated news portal. It aggregates stories from more than 4,000 sources. When I logged on to check on the Saddam Hussein verdict, the reason that MTV.com was placed first was that it had been the most recently updated. Google News points to developments which could challenge the relationships that news organizations aim to develop with their audiences — it enables the user to first decide what they want to read about and then which news site they will get it from, rather than the more usual other way round, and so places a question mark against notions of habitual use. However, we should also note that early research suggests that, for the most part, large commercial news providers are highly ranked in Google News searches, and that much of such news is re-purposed newspaper content, which points to an extension of the reach and influence of the established news media in the online environment (Elmer, Devereaux & Skinner 2006). That said, newspapers can lose valuable advertising revenue by relying on Google or Yahoo!, as these aggregator sites lead readers to stories buried deep in their website, whereas if readers come in through the main page of a newspaper's site, that paper can charge more for display advertising on that page (*Economist,* 24 August 2006, p. 54).

The automated approach of Google News, like everything else in the media, has its histories and antecedents. For example, Pavlik records the existence of automated story-writing software, dating from the early 1990s, which could replace journalists in the production of routine reports. One such programme, called 'SportsWriter', used form data supplied by team coaches by phone after a game, to generate simple stories — one Nebraska newspaper fired its sports reporter after buying a copy of the software, which cost them $100 as opposed to the journalist's $1,500 a month (Pavlik 1998: 200–2).

Automated functions are becoming central to many news websites. RSS feeds (the abbreviation variously standing for Rich Site Summary or Really Simple Syndication) make it possible to subscribe to news sites, with updates being automatically pushed to your browser, rather than having to check back frequently at the site to pull out the latest stories for yourself. But while convenient, there are drawbacks to RSS — Gillmor points out that, for one thing, it strips away the individuality of many blogs, presenting the subscriber with only brief summaries or headlines (2004: 40). And it's possible for RSS to complicate our information diet rather than simplifying it — instead of streamlining the news, RSS feeds can create a sense of pressure or information overload, with each update presenting yet more stuff to read, yet more potentially crucial stories (Jordan 1999: 117–27). One experimental project that makes use of RSS is *News at Seven* <http://www.newsatseven.com>. This website uses a videogame engine, RSS feeds and speech-generation technology to enable users to generate a customized news bulletin, presented by animated avatars.

Podcasting is another automated function that offers new possibilities for news and current affairs. An awkward hybrid of iPod and broadcasting, the term denotes a simple system for syndicating audio and/or video. It makes it possible for a broadcaster (whether the BBC or your next-door neighbour) to make available online regular updates of their programming and for subscribers to receive this automatically. Podcasting makes possible not just time-shifting (listening to or watching a broadcast on your own schedule rather than the network's) but also space-shifting (taking broadcast content away from the dominant domestic context and into new kinds of public space), creating new potentials for news distribution and consumption.

One example of the potential of automation is offered by the website *10x10*, which offers a visual representation of the key news stories of the hour <http://www.tenbyten.org/10×10.html>. Every hour, using updates from automated RSS feeds from Reuters, the BBC and the *New York Times*, the *10×10* database establishes the 100 key words of the last hour's news, and represents each with a photograph sourced from the same news providers. The visitor to the site sees the result as a matrix of 100 photographs, with a matching list of key words down the right-hand side of the screen. Selecting a photograph will bring up the relevant headline, and the user can click through to the original story. So, for example, at 2pm

Sydney time on Monday 6 November 2006, the top three key words were *climate, Saddam* and *talks*; Saddam Hussein, who had been sentenced to death a day earlier, was represented by a picture of then-UK Foreign Secretary Margaret Beckett, who had just issued a statement on the death sentence. Clicking on Beckett's photo would open up a small window containing links to the relevant stories on the BBC, Reuters and *New York Times* websites. *10x10* is a powerful illustration of the potential of automation to re-work our news diet in original ways.

Up close and personal

In his best-selling 1995 book *Being Digital*, Nicholas Negroponte looked ahead to ways in which digital media would enable an extreme personalization of news:

> Imagine a future in which your interface agent can read every newswire and newspaper and catch every TV and radio broadcast on the planet, and then construct a personalized summary. This kind of newspaper is printed in an edition of one (Negroponte 1995: 153).

Negroponte called this imaginary newspaper *The Daily Me*. Personalization on this scale would change the economics of the news industry, broaden the scope of usable items, and bring users' preferences and interests to the fore. The vision of *The Daily Me* made some commentators uneasy, suggesting visions of greater social fragmentation and incoherence as each of us retreated into a new solipsism, secure in our individual news cocoons, choosing to ignore whole swathes of public debate. Others noted that really important stories would remain hard to miss, and that customized news would be more about ruling things into our daily news diet than about screening things out. As Pavlik puts it: 'audience fragmentation is inevitable but [...] social disintegration is not' (2001: 191).

A decade on from Negroponte's description of *The Daily Me*, it is no longer speculative — now many of us read it every day. The websites of major news providers invite us to customize our page, to subscribe to automated updates of favourite sections, to save stories to a personal archive (Project for Excellence in Journalism 2007). Google News, for example, features a large box at the top right-hand-side of the screen: 'Personalize this page'. Users can drag sections and headings around, so that sports news or tech stories always appear at the top of the page, or to omit that business section altogether. Moreover, they can create 'custom sections' to be filled with stories only on topics of particular interest to them, in languages of their choice — want your Google News to only offer stories about Nintendo or carbon-trading or Spanish actresses? *The Daily Me* is now a daily reality. However, what Negroponte didn't canvass was that we'd not just read *The Daily Me* — now we can all *write* it as well, as we'll discuss below.

Mobile news

The ubiquitous availability of camera phones (Levinson 2004) also adds a dimension of personalization, which has as yet uncertain relationships to more public forms of news — what Gerard Goggin calls 'the intimate turn of news' (2006: 148).

> The locus and matrix of news appears to move from the professionalised routines and forms of circulation and production of newsrooms to the micro-arenas of personal life with their rules of relevance and tiny audiences defined by the individual, and their immediate friends, colleagues, family, and networks (Goggin 2006: 148).

As people record and share more and more of their everyday lives through phone cameras, blogs, and social networking websites, the limits of news as 'public' are being tested. Micro-blogging services such as Twitter allow users to send an ongoing stream of tiny updates on their lives, in messages no longer than 140 characters: while many users concentrate on private trivia for friends and family, it is possible for any other user to subscribe to their stream; at the same time, the service has also been adopted by the BBC <http://twitter.com/bbc>, the *New York Times* <http://twitter.com/nytimes> and the *Guardian* <http://twitter.com/guardiantech>. The resulting blend of private trivia with public headlines illustrates Goggin's 'intimate turn of news'. And as established news outlets that publish invitations to submit photos are joined by dedicated photo blogs and mobile blogs, and by services such as Scoopt, each providing opportunities for users to send in their everyday images, there emerges the potential for people to personalize the news in a new way — not just by customizing their reception of news, but also by intervening in its production, by sharing or publicizing their own everyday record.

This kind of reshaping of the public and the private is characteristic of all major developments in media forms. In the case of mobile phones, McKenzie Wark argues that mobiles are the cancer cells of the social body, and that they are breaking down the cell walls that separate the public from the private: 'Cellphones break down space in much the same way that a digital sampler breaks down beats. In cellspace, there's no place that can't be connected to another space' (Wark 2000).

Sadie Plant observes that the fixed line phone, and later the Internet, took communications links into the homes and workplaces of the developed world. The mobile is different because it puts such communications links not into fixed places, such as homes and offices, but into the hands of individuals — and this time not just in the developed world:

> On a wooden ship moored in Dubai's busy creek, a Somali trader dozes in the shade of a tarpaulin sheet. He wakes to the opening bars of Jingle Bells. 'Hallo? Aiwa... la... aiwa... OK.' The deal is done. This trader, Mohammed, exports small electrical goods, including mobile phones, to East Africa. 'It's my livelihood,' he says of the mobile phone. 'No mobile, no business.' It multiplies his opportunities to make contacts and do deals as he moves between cities and ports, and the short, instantaneous messages and calls to which the mobile lends itself are perfectly suited to the small and immediate transactions in which he is engaged. He now has access to intelligence about the movements of goods, ships, competitors and markets. Information that was once way beyond his reach is now at his fingertips (Plant 2002: 74).

Plant argues that if the landline telephone arrived at a historical moment marked by the emergence of unified nation-states and urban expansion, the mobile has arrived in 'a new era of mobility' — similar to what Manuel Castells (2000) has described as a shift from a space of places to a space of flows. This new era, argues Plant, is characterized by 'increasing connectivity, unprecedented mobility, and the emergence of new cultures, communities and collectivities' (2002: 76). As Manuel Castells and his collaborators have argued, perhaps the real significance of the mobile phone is not mobility as such, but *connection*. When mobile phones were first introduced, people used them as a substitute for a fixed landline, when they happened to be out and about. Now, write Castells *et al*:

> 'mobile communication now represents the individualized, distributed capacity to access the local/global communication network from any place at any time. This is how it is perceived by users, and this is how it is used. With the diffusion of wireless access to the Internet, and to computer networks and information systems everywhere, mobile communication is better defined by its capacity for ubiquitous and permanent connectivitity rather than by its potential mobility' (Castells *et al* 2007: 248).

News is already being affected by all of this. The capacity to personalize our news intake can be seen as part of broader shifts in our relationships with information.

News, argue Burnett and Marshall, has become 'a subset of a wider search for information by Web users' (2003: 206) and this in turn has seen 'a shift in how we recontextualize news around a much larger search for information' (2003: 152). The idea of searching offers a new perspective on the news. News has traditionally emphasized narrative, as was explored in Chapter 3. However, the convergent media era, according to Lev Manovich, places a new emphasis on the database form. Stories have beginnings, middles and endings; they are organized in cause-and-effect sequences; they display development. Databases, in contrast, are collections of discrete items, none more significant than another, each open to random access, combination and search (Manovich 2001: 218). Websites are examples of this database form, with each being a collection of discrete elements.

Database and narrative, Manovich suggests, can be thought of as: 'two competing imaginations, two basic creative impulses, two essential responses to the world' (2001: 233). He notes, for example, that the ancient Greeks composed not only the Homeric epics (a narrative form), but also early encyclopaedias (a database form). News websites are built around the capacity to 'view, navigate, search' (Manovich 2001: 219), and this gives a qualitative difference to the experience of using a database form to using a narrative form. I might consult, for example, the *New York Times* website, searching for a key term or for columns by a particular commentator; downloading various stories for later, bookmarking others, forwarding still others to friends; I might copy to disk a photo from the site, rework it in Photoshop, or embed the image within a new context, a new collection, a new database.

In the move from a narrative environment to a database one, audience members are transformed into researchers (Burnett & Marshall 2003). On the one hand, we become comfortable with getting our news from a broader range of sources; but at the same time we search for new ways to hierarchize those sources, to establish some as more legitimate than others. The result, according to Burnett and Marshall, is 'a shifted boundary of what constitutes news' (2003: 167) — what they term 'informational news', a search-driven response to a database-driven media environment. But this concept of informational news is largely cast in terms of reception and consumption: the practices of these new informational news researchers are discussed in terms of information retrieval, not production — even blogs are considered as additional sources for information retrieval, rather than as new avenues for new kinds of journalists to develop and publish new kinds of news.

Over to you

The third key characteristic of the emerging online news environment is participation. One very visible manifestation of media participation made possible by convergence is offered by social network (or networking) sites such as Facebook, which allow users to construct a profile of themselves, to develop a list of other users with whom they have some form of relationship or connection (called 'friends' on Facebook, although this may be best seen as a metaphor) and to maintain these relationships through the site (boyd and Ellison 2007). Each user of Facebook has a profile page which they can customize by adding small software applications: at the time of writing in May 2008, these include headline feeds from the BBC and CNN; links to YouTube channels, including those of established news organizations; branded content streams from *The Australian* and *The Washington Post*; clips of Jon Stewart's *The Daily Show*; and a small game that challenges you to whack Rupert Murdoch on the head with a mallet.

Thinking about participation makes it possible to distinguish between two dimensions of new media — the *New Old Media* and the *New New Media* (Young 2007). *New Old Media* offer more of the same; *New New Media* offer something that we haven't seen before. The term *New Old Media* describes uses of the convergent media environment which update or extend the textual forms and business models of the twentieth century. It's the same old media but with a digital spin. *New Old Media* use the digital environment, and the convergence of communications and computing, to distribute their content. It's the move from the *New York Times* on paper to the *New York Times* online at <nytimes.com>; the move from the BBC news on your radio to a stream of the BBC news on your computer. The old media made new.

A central challenge for established media organizations is to develop ways of using the new media environment which fully exploit its potential. This is where, so far, many have failed. Boczkowski (2004) has shown how new technological possibilities are initially viewed by news organizations from the standpoint of their established practices. From his analysis of the online 'Technology' section of the *New York Times,* the 'Virtual Voyager' project of the *Houston Chronicle*, and the 'Community Connection' initiative of a group of New Jersey media outlets, Boczkowski concludes that print newspapers have been constrained in their extensions online by a reactive stance, a desire to protect their existing turf, and an aversion to the risks of long-term development strategies. The Net was not seen as an entirely blank slate of communicative possibilities, but rather as a new means of extending existing business models and journalistic forms. *New Old Media.*

Terry Flew identifies three main factors which established media businesses have seen as inducements to enter the digital media arena: reduced costs of archiving and distributing information; the ability to re-purpose and re-use existing content and to cross-promote; and the potential to customize delivery systems (2005: 85–6). Over time, new approaches will develop out of this exchange, and the web presence of many newspapers has indeed changed considerably since the mid-nineties, but these new approaches will be inscribed with the initial assumptions that were carried over to the new medium from the old. *New Old Media.*

In contrast, the *New New Media* build original models and forms that take full advantage of the Net's potential for participation and collaboration. They blur the lines between producer and receiver, creating the potential for every reader to become a writer. As Hartley points out, this poses fundamental challenges to the nature of news and journalism: 'This is where journalists have had the upper hand for so long: they can "write" in public. But now, worryingly for them, anyone can join them; readers are transforming into writers in the interactive media.' (Hartley 2000: 42–3).

To illustrate this, we can first recap on the key features of the old media environment — with the twentieth-century, broadcast model of communication. Thompson's (1995) analysis of this type of communication identifies five key characteristics.

- First, such communication involves the development of certain types of industry which exploit the potential offered by new communications technologies.
- Second, such communication involves, in Thompson's phrase, the 'commodification of symbolic forms' — ideas and images, stories and songs, information and entertainment are assigned an economic value.
- Third, such communication extends the availability of information in space and time.
- Fourth, its products are, in principle, available to anyone with the necessary equipment — (such as a TV set — and the necessary skills and competencies — such as the ability to read a newspaper.
- And fifth, there is what Thompson calls the 'structured break' between media production and media reception.

This fifth characteristic is the one which is most challenged by the emerging convergent media environment. The 'structured break' can now be bridged by anyone with a Net connection. The result is an emerging media culture built around participation. *New New Media*.

The Net is a vivid example of the possibilities of participatory culture (Jenkins 2003, Pew Internet & American Life Project 2006a & 2006b, Deuze, Bruns & Neuberger 2007, Bruns 2008a, Leadbeater 2008, Shirky 2008). At the time of writing in May 2008 (no doubt some will have changed by the time of reading), the websites provoking the most excitement are those which allow users to create and distribute, to archive and comment, to remix, rework and recontextualize — YouTube for online video, Flickr and Photobucket for online photos, Last.fm and Pandora for online music, and MySpace or Facebook for all of the above. Collaborative creativity is the fuel for popular projects such as Wikipedia, Livejournal, Second Life, and Indymedia.

To capture these practices of remixing and reworking, Hartley proposes the terms 'redaction' and 'redactors' (essentially, this refers to editing, though he deliberately avoids this term as it has established uses as well as connotations of agenda-setting, gate-keeping and so on). Redaction refers to processes of preparation, arrangement, editing, revision, shaping:

> Is it possible to tell a society by how it edits? Is redaction a symptom of the social? [...] Are we in a period where it is not information, knowledge or culture as such that determine the age but how they are handled? If so, then a redactional society is one where such processes are primary, where matter is reduced, revised, prepared, published, edited, adapted, shortened, abridged to produce, in turn, the new(s) (Hartley 2000: 44).

What are the possible consequences of this? At one extreme, journalists may increasingly be no longer needed; alternatively, the profusion of information in the new media environment may make journalists more valuable than ever, as filters, explicators and guides — 'Journalism evolves from the provision of facts to the provision of meaning' (Bardoel 1996: 297).

Henry Jenkins (2003: 286) has shown how the contemporary participatory media environment, centring on the Net, draws together several decades of developments in media forms, each of which reinforced the idea of media as something we not only consume but also produce:

- the photocopier, whose adoption by small presses, alternative media groups and fanzine publishers enabled a broadening of sub-cultural expression.
- the VCR, which made it possible for audiences to exploit broadcast material, to assemble personal archives, and to edit their own amateur productions.
- the camcorder, which enabled anyone to make their own home movies or to create footage for documentary production.
- videogames, which fostered a sense of immersion, participation and engagement with media stories.

- digital cameras and photo manipulation software, and music sampling and editing programmes — each of these too made possible new forms of production.

This participatory culture is becoming more mainstream than some may think, and it's not just confined to the young. The Pew Internet & American Life Project (2007) released research on how Americans used the Net in the 2006 mid-term election campaigns. It found that 11% of US Internet users (some 14 million people) used the Net not just to get news and information about the campaigns, but also to write, to blog, to comment, to forward, and to distribute their own audio and video material. That's a lot of people who see politics as something they're part of; a lot of people who see media as something they do, rather than just watch, listen to or read.

It would, of course, be possible to point to older historical examples of participatory media. According to Boczkowski (2004: 141), the sole issue of *Publick Occurrences,* the first American newspaper, in September 1690, had four pages — three were printed, but the fourth was left blank for the reader to add their own notes, comments, contributions or stories before passing the paper on to others. Lessig (2004) points to the introduction of the cheap, push-button Kodak camera, and the cultural transformations made possible by making photography something that anyone can do. But for the most part, twentieth-century broadcast and print media were not open to participation by just anyone. Jenkins's timeline of developments enables us to set the Internet in a fuller media context. The case study of Indymedia which comprises the remainder of this chapter is just one of the more substantial recent developments in this direction — it does not represent any kind of end-point.

Indymedia

This section will briefly introduce the nature and scope of the Indymedia movement, which offers a vivid illustration of participatory culture online. Indymedia is a global network of independent news websites, each using a local version of the common domain name <indymedia.org>, as in, for example, <sydney.indymedia.org>, <madrid.indymedia.org> or <scotland.indymedia.org>. Each site publishes news stories and other items submitted by anyone who wishes to contribute; while this policy is evolving and subject to local variation, the defining principle of Indymedia is this ethos of 'open publishing'. Each Indymedia Centre (IMC) is administered by a local editorial collective; some also operate physical spaces, but many do not. Something of the flavour of the movement is captured in the self-definition offered at the 'global' site <www.indymedia.org>:

> The Independent Media Center is a network of collectively run media outlets for the creation of radical, accurate, and passionate tellings of the truth. We work out of a love and inspiration for people who continue to work for a better world, despite corporate media's distortions and unwillingness to cover the efforts to free humanity <http://www.indymedia.org/en/static/about.shtml>.

Why does this project matter? Indymedia points to potentially significant shifts in:

- news *production*, as a forum for non-professional journalists
- news *distribution*, through the network's spectacular growth and its promotion of 'open publishing' models, as well as through its convergent nature and dependence on computing and telecommunications for the production, distribution and reception of its media content
- and in news *reception*, through its blurring of the lines between writers and readers.

For these reasons, Indymedia has attracted a great deal of research attention. Some of this work addresses Indymedia's connections to the so-called 'anti-globalization' movement (Downing 2002, 2003a, Kidd 2003, Lovink 2003, Kahn & Kellner 2004, Coyer 2005). Other studies have focused on the tensions or successes of developing and sustaining such a large network of quasi-autonomous collectives, and on the tensions between its voluntarist ethos and the ongoing need for funding (Halleck 2003, Pickard 2006). There are also significant studies which focus on Indymedia's challenge to established practices of news and journalism (Platon & Deuze 2003, Downing 2003b, Atton 2004, Allan 2006, Garcelon 2006). And there are studies which engage with the network's central ethos of open publishing (Arnison 2001, Meikle 2002, Bruns 2005).

The first Indymedia website <http://www.indymedia.org> was established as an online focal point for the demonstrations against the World Trade Organization (WTO) meeting in Seattle in November 1999 (Meikle 2002, Platon & Deuze 2003). It provided news coverage uploaded by anyone who wanted to contribute. As riots broke out in Seattle and the WTO meeting was temporarily suspended, the nascent Indymedia drew a claimed 1.5 million hits (Kidd 2003). In the following months, the site was refocused around several subsequent protests, before local collectives began to appear and form their own Indymedia centres. Within a year of the first IMC, a network of more than 30 Indymedia sites had been set up. By March 2002 there were more than 70 nodes in the network, from India to the Czech Republic, from Italy to the Congo (Meikle 2002). By January 2004 there were more than 120 IMCS — in Melbourne, Jakarta and Buenos Aires; in Poland, Japan and South Africa (Meikle 2004). By September 2006 there were 136 active Indymedia centres, while a further 22 sites were no longer operating (Coopman 2006). By any measure, the development of this network is a striking phenomenon. One thing that is particularly impressive is that the Indymedia network has been established largely by volunteers and donations (Halleck 2003, Pickard 2006). Indymedia has not always maintained the standards set in its first few years. Bruns suggests that, by 2008, the main Indymedia newswire had been reduced to 'a mere clearinghouse for activist press releases' (2008b: 250). Nevertheless, the network still demands serious attention — as one of the longest-established participatory online projects, it offers great scope for analysis and for gaining perspective on newer developments that follow in its wake.

There are important precursors and antecedents here. Jesse Drew offers an account of alternative TV and video networks, tracing connections from Paper Tiger TV and the Deep Dish network to the Indymedia network. Drew stresses the importance of recognizing the social and cultural dimensions to the success of these earlier networks. On the one hand, Deep Dish depended on the proliferation of camcorders to enable community groups to contribute reports on ongoing projects or campaigns or issues. In this, there is a technological analogue to the role of the Net in making Indymedia possible. On the other hand, Drew emphasizes the need to interrogate structures and organizations in networks, to go beyond the usual easy assumption that networks are necessarily positive. 'Networks', writes

Drew, 'must be scrutinized for their social impact, and not just their technical achievement' (2005, p. 222).

Like any other complex phenomenon, the story of the development of Indymedia can be told in many different ways, each emphasizing a different dimension: three are introduced here.

Open source

The first version would emphasize the technology of Indymedia and the relationships between open source software (Raymond 1997) and the Indymedia philosophy of 'open publishing' (Arnison 2001, Meikle 2002). Such an Indymedia narrative would centre around the Active software developed by Sydney's Catalyst tech collective. This software was developed to run the Active Sydney site <http://www.sydney.active.org.au>, launched in January 1999, an online hub for Sydney activists to promote events from direct actions to screenings and seminars. Active Sydney was a key prototype for Indymedia — part events calendar, part meeting place, part street paper. Using the Active open source software, anyone anywhere could add a report, a video clip, a photo or an audio file, and see it instantly added to the database, as though posting to a blog. Catalyst members collaborated online with organizers in Seattle to establish the first Indymedia site, taking the Active software system as the initial basis, and while the Active software is no longer the only platform used for Indymedia, it made a huge contribution to the movement's explosive growth (see Arnison 2001, Hintz 2003, Meikle 2002).

DIY news

A second version of the story would approach Indymedia as part of what cultural studies academic George McKay terms 'DiY Culture'. McKay defines this as 'a youth-centred and -directed cluster of interests and practices around green radicalism, direct action politics, new musical sounds and experiences' (1998: 2). For this version of the story, a useful analogy would be with punk — not with the music so much as with its DIY access principle ('here's three chords, now form a band'). DIY was the key to Richard Hell's much-misunderstood lyric 'I belong to the blank generation' — the idea of the blank was that you were supposed to fill it in for yourself, to define your own identity, rather than sign up to someone else's agenda.

To consider Indymedia as part of this DIY spirit would be to see it as the expression of a blank generation in this original sense — not a vacant generation, but one prepared to offer their own self-definitions and to create their own media networks to do it. More than this, it would also be to place Indymedia within the frameworks of independent production and distribution which were the real impact of punk — independent record labels changed music more than any of their records, while photocopied zines opened up new possibilities for self-expression. Just as the real importance of punk wasn't in the individual songs, the importance of Indymedia isn't in this or that news story posted to this or that site. Instead, it's in its DIY ethos and its commitment to establishing new, participatory networks.

Indymedia and alternative media

A third version of the story would place Indymedia within the long traditions of alternative media (Downing 2001, Atton 2002, Couldry & Curran 2003, Coyer, Dowmunt & Fountain 2007). The concept of 'alternative' media demands care, as it needs to be defined and used more strictly than simply in opposition to 'mainstream'. Atton refers to 'media projects, interventions and networks that work against, or seek to develop different forms of, the dominant, expected (and broadly accepted) ways of "doing" media' (2004: ix). While this opens up a large range of issues, this section will confine itself to four points which are salient in the analysis of Indymedia.

First, there is the acknowledgment of history — the precursors, traditions and models upon which contemporary alternative media build (Downing *et al* 2001, Atton 2002, Drew 2005). Much Internet commentary focuses on transformation, on the shock of the new, and on the possibilities for developing new modes of media production, distribution, reception — and analysis. However, the continuities are at least as important as the transformations. This also applies to the relative reach of alternative and mainstream news organizations online. A Pew study of US Net users in 2006 found that established media organizations such as MSNBC or CNN drew the most online visitors (Pew Internet & American Life Project 2006c). Similarly, in the UK, the BBC, the *Mail*, the *Telegraph* and the *Guardian* have substantial leads over other sources of online news (Jenkins 2003, Pew

Internet & American Life Project 2006, Deuze, Bruns & Neuberger 2007, Bruns 2008a, Leadbeater 2008, Shirky 2008).

Second, there is the emphasis within the alternative media literature on modes of organization, in particular upon independence and self-management or self-organization (Downing 1995). The question of alternative media has often been addressed in terms of control and ownership, of political economy, and such issues have their own specificity in relation to the Internet. It is of course true that the Internet remains far from universally available — Sparks points out that even electricity is beyond the reach of vast sections of the global population (2005). Nevertheless, for those who do have ready access to the Net, the obstacles to establishing an online presence are significantly different from those involved in creating a broadcast network.

Third, such projects can be approached in terms of their content: textual forms, narrative strategies, modes of address, visuality, or ideological orientation. Of particular significance are the ways in which Internet projects construct forums for viewpoints which are not usually expressed within the established media consensus about what counts as news and who counts as an authoritative source. Indymedia illustrates Atton's analysis of the style of activist journalism that is emerging online: 'Its practices emphasise first-person, eyewitness accounts by participants; a reworking of the populist approaches of tabloid newspapers to recover a "radical popular" style of reporting' (Atton 2004: 26).

A fourth important dimension of online alternative media strategies is the extent to which these emphasize and foster horizontal connections and open participation, in contrast to the vertical flows of the established news media — a common emphasis is on the potential of communication between participants, rather than to audiences (Downing, 1995, 2001, 2003a). As Atton and Couldry note (2003), those who create alternative media are those who are dissatisfied with the established relations of symbolic power. The open access provisions of projects such as Indymedia, and their collaborative, intercreative ethos, enact particular visions of journalistic potential: '... collective and anti-hierarchical forms of organisation which eschew demarcation and specialisation — and which importantly suggest an inclusive, radical form of civic journalism' (Atton 2004: 26).

Atton and Couldry (2003) note that arguments for the salience of alternative media often turn on questions of citizenship. In this regard Rodriguez's concept of 'citizens' media' is useful in considering Indymedia (2001, 2002). Rodriguez argues for a participation-centred approach to alternative media, suggesting we examine such projects 'in terms of the transformative processes they bring about within participants and their communities' (2002: 79). From this perspective, the significance of Indymedia may lie in the resources it offers users to create their own media, to participate in debates, and to act as citizens as well as audiences — with citizenship thought of here as a concept defined 'on account of one's ability to gather forces that shape one's symbolic and material world' (Rodriguez 2002: 79).

To tell the Indymedia story from an alternative media perspective would be to highlight its independence and self-management, and the autonomy of each local editorial collective in running each Indymedia centre. It would be to acknowledge and explore the precursors and models upon which Indymedia built (Drew 2005). It would be to emphasize Indymedia as a forum for viewpoints which are not usually expressed within the established media's consensus about what is and isn't news. And, perhaps most importantly, to tell the Indymedia story as one in the alternative media tradition would be to focus on the extent to which this movement fosters horizontal connections and open participation, in contrast to the vertical flows of the established broadcast and print media (Downing 1995, 2001).

Open publishing

The three approaches to Indymedia introduced above — open source, DIY, alternative — share an important characteristic. Each stresses new avenues and methods for new people to create news; each shifts the boundary of who gets to speak; each highlights an emphasis on access and participation. These three different versions intersect in the concept of open publishing. Matthew Arnison of Catalyst, who played a key role in developing the Active software, offers a working definition of open publishing which is worth quoting in full:

> Open publishing means that the process of creating news is transparent to the readers. They can contribute a story and see it instantly appear in the pool of stories publicly available. Those stories are filtered as little as possible to help the readers find the stories they want. Readers can see editorial decisions being made by others. They can see how to get

> involved and help make editorial decisions. If they can think of a better way for the software to help shape editorial decisions, they can copy the software because it is free and change it and start their own site. If they want to redistribute the news, they can, preferably on an open publishing site (Arnison 2001).

Of course, news that absolutely anyone can write demands active, questioning readers — but then so does professional news. Google News temporarily suspended San Francisco Indymedia stories from its service in May 2003, due to concerns about the absence of editorial supervision. But they didn't remove the *New York Times* when it emerged in the same month that its rising star Jayson Blair had fabricated a shocking number of stories; and one of the key questions raised by the Blair story is that of how widespread such practices are — after all, if the *New York Times* can't be trusted, then what of less illustrious news outlets? This is not an argument in favour of knee-jerk cynicism: instead, it's a reminder that we should always be active, questioning participants in the news process, whether we are reading an online open publishing site or reading the *New York Times*.

Indymedia is by no means the only project exploring these possibilities. One of the most elaborate — and successful — experiments in participatory news is the Korean website OhmyNews <http://www.ohmynews.com>. OhmyNews employs a staff of 60, which includes 35 staff reporters, but also recruits citizen reporters who register with the site, creating individual profiles and agreeing to observe a set of ethical guidelines: the site launched in February 2000 with 727 registered citizen reporters; as of January 2005, 36,657 people had signed up (Kim & Hamilton 2006: 546). What's remarkable about OhmyNews is that these citizen reporters generate by far the majority of the site's output, typically contributing between 150 and 200 articles each day (Kim & Hamilton 2006: 545).

The established media are beginning to experiment with the potential of participatory news and current affairs. One example would be the *Los Angeles Times*'s 'wikitorial' experiment — on 17 June 2005 the paper made available an editorial on the Iraq war on their website, inviting readers to make any changes they wished; the experiment lasted two days before the plug was pulled after various acts of vandalism <http://www.latimes.com/news/opinion/editorials/la-wiki-splash,0,1349109.story>. Another would be the *Guardian*'s re-branding of its online op-ed page as a blog titled 'Comment Is

Free' ('... but facts are sacred' as their former editor C. P. Scott had it), with some columns now attracting hundreds of follow-up posts from readers. Still another would be the *International Herald Tribune* signing a deal with OhmyNews, whereby stories written by its non-professional 'citizen reporters' could be carried on the *Herald Tribune*'s website, and perhaps in the newspaper itself.

These examples could be seen as realizations of the Internet's democratic potential for wider participation in relation to news. Or they could be seen as part of processes of absorption and normalization of the Net, with the established news media extending their influence and reach into the online environment, thus consolidating their positions. Participatory media raise a number of questions. In particular, intellectual property questions are of urgent importance in a communications environment whose most influential framework is a creative industries policy discourse that attempts to articulate the role of media and related industries in an increasingly global and digital context (Leadbeater 1999, Department for Culture, Media and Sport [UK] 2001, Howkins 2001, Florida 2002, Leadbeater & Miller 2004, Hartley 2005). The creative industries discourse relies upon audiences who increasingly participate in new ways; moreover, it sees intellectual property as a central engine of wealth creation (Lessig 2004, Wark 2004). A major question yet to be faced by many people who may not expect it, could be the extent to which they find their online creations subject to claims to be 'owned', 'managed', or accommodated within regimes of intellectual property.

Conclusion

The adoption and the adaptation of digital media are making possible new opportunities for audiences to exercise symbolic power in new ways. However, many observers, especially those with a substantial stake in the established media, are not keen on these developments. Documentary film-maker Adam Curtis, for example, creator of the series *The Power of Nightmares,* contributed a three-minute history of modern journalism to an episode of Charlie Brooker's satirical TV review show *Screenwipe* on 9 October 2007. Curtis ended his piece with an assessment of participatory news:

> Now our presenters plead with us to send in our photos and videos. They proudly present it as a new kind of open democracy. But in

> reality it's something very different. Because the journalists don't understand what is going on in today's complex, chaotic world, they have had to revert to their old habit of finding someone in authority who will tell them. But this time, it's not the politicians — it's us, the audience, that they've turned to. The only problem is that *we* don't have a clue what's going on. Particularly because the journalists have given up on their job of explaining the world to us.

Curtis, as ever, makes his point with some force. But he leaves unexplored the question of whether other kinds of voice, other kinds of story-telling, and other kinds of news, can have valid claims on our attention. Is there a new role for those whom Jay Rosen (2006) has termed 'the people formerly known as the audience?' It is this final question to which we turn to conclude the book.

Afterword

On 15 October 2004, Jon Stewart, the host of Comedy Central's *The Daily Show*, appeared as a guest on CNN's debate programme *Crossfire*. Not many people saw the show go out — at least not compared to the millions who downloaded the clip afterwards, as it became one of the most-watched online clips and most-blogged topics of the year. Stewart delivered a damning indictment of television current affairs, calmly taking apart *Crossfire*'s hosts Tucker Carlson and Paul Begala for their formulaic and aggressive staged debates. Stewart compared the show to Pro Wrestling and argued that *Crossfire* cheated its audience out of genuine discussion, that it was all heat and no light — 'You're doing theatre', he told the hosts, 'when you should be doing debate.'

In other words, Jon Stewart wanted CNN's current affairs show to be driven more by authentic discussion of matters of public importance, and less by entertainment. But on the other side, Carlson criticized Stewart for not asking hard-hitting journalistic questions of presidential candidate John Kerry when he had appeared on *The Daily Show*. In other words, Carlson wanted the satirical comedy show to be driven more by authentic discussion of matters of public importance, and less by entertainment.

Stewart responded that if CNN was looking to Comedy Central to uphold journalistic standards, then everyone's in trouble — 'You're on CNN', he told Carlson. 'The show that leads into me is puppets making crank phone calls. What is wrong with you?' Maybe Stewart was onto something — maybe presenting serious issues in an entertainment format, as *Crossfire* tried to, contributes to a culture where everyone is well-entertained but ill-informed. But perhaps Carlson was onto something too — perhaps as a satirist Stewart has a more important and honest role in public debate than CNN.

Satirists, like Jon Stewart, are more valuable than ever in our twenty-first century media environment. One 2007 Pew Report on public knowledge of news and current affairs found that those who were best-informed were most likely to be regular viewers of satire programmes *The Daily Show* and *The Colbert Report.* Like journalists, satirists are licenced agents of symbolic power, but they work to undermine it — Stephen Colbert's word 'truthiness' nailed the Bush administration and its communication strategies more effectively than the *New York Times* admitting it had been taken in on the invasion of Iraq.

The *Crossfire* event captures a number of the key trends that characterize the emerging news environment of the early twenty-first century: the tensions between information and entertainment, between news as 'nonfiction' and news as 'drama'; the rise of online distribution; the ascendancy of participatory culture. Jon Stewart forced a public discussion about the exercise of symbolic power — about the place of the news media, the roles of journalists, the legitimacy of speech.

This book has argued that news can be analysed and understood as a field of symbolic power relations. It has argued that news is both a particular kind of product (one created by news organizations and shaped by cultural expectations which it in turn shapes) and particular kinds of processes of production, distribution and reception. In the networks of symbolic power relations between organizations, journalists, sources and audiences, news is the organized daily production, distribution and uses of nonfiction drama.

This book has argued more than once that an analysis of key aspects of news shows how those aspects could be different. News values are not handed down from the sky but rather suit the imperatives and conventions of news organizations — they could be changed. News stories are often built around predictable narrative forms, but here again we are dealing with questions of organizational convention and convenience — they could be changed. These coordinates of news — *organized, daily, production, distribution, uses, nonfiction, drama* — can all be reworked for the twenty-first century. The news environment will be shaped by both contested continuities and emergent transformations. The news is changing — that's always true; as this book has shown, the news is always in transition as new organizations, new technologies, new approaches emerge. At the time of writing, Indymedia, OhmyNews, Wikinews, Twitter, Slashdot, Digg and several million blogs offer a radical set of challenges to established ideas about what news is and who makes it. They suggest a potential reshuffling of the coordinates of news, and a corresponding potential realignment of symbolic power resources. New kinds of organization. New conceptions of news-time. New ways of producing and distributing news. New kinds of uses from new kinds of users. New possibilities for story-telling. New kinds of emphasis, in new kinds of community, sharing new approaches to the rituals of news. Symbolic power resources are likely to remain concentrated in media organizations, but those organizations will have to change.

One direction for such change is suggested by the Indymedia slogan 'everyone is a journalist'. What does this mean? If it's a provocation, then whom and what is it meant to provoke? Obviously, 'everyone' is not a journalist — at least not if journalists are seen as employees of news institutions and news businesses, employees with some kind of training in research methods and narrative construction. But to say that 'everyone is a journalist' is not to claim that everyone has such institutional affiliation, or that everyone has such training or expertise. Instead, the tactic here seems to be to inflate something out of all proportion in order to draw attention to the core smaller truth that may otherwise go unnoticed. Specifically in this case, what authorizes some to be story-tellers and not others? From this perspective, the slogan reads like a claim for difference, a claim that other kinds of expertise and other kinds of know-how also have valid claims on our attention, and that these too can make valid contributions to the more plural media environment made possible — but not guaranteed — by the Net. It's a claim that the licence to tell stories should be shared around.

References

Achbar, Mark (ed.) (1994) *Manufacturing Consent: Noam Chomsky and the Media*, Montreal: Black Rose Books.
—— and Wintonick, Peter (directors) (1992) *Manufacturing Consent: Noam Chomsky and the Media* (1992), documentary film, Montreal.
Adams, Phillip and Burton, Lee (1997) *Talkback: Emperors of Air*, Sydney: Allen & Unwin.
Adorno, Theodor W. (2003) [1975] 'Culture Industry Reconsidered', in Will Brooker and Deborah Jermyn (eds) *The Audience Studies Reader*, London: Routledge, pp. 55–60.
—— and Horkheimer, Max (1995) [1972] 'The Culture Industry: Enlightenment as Mass Deception', in Oliver Boyd-Barrett and Chris Newbold (eds) *Approaches to Media*, London: Arnold, pp. 77–80.
Alexander, Jeffrey C. and Jacobs, Ronald N. (1998) 'Mass Communications, Ritual and Civil Society', in Tamar Liebes and James Curran (eds) *Media, Ritual and Identity*, London: Routledge, pp. 23–41.
Allan, Stuart (2004) *News Culture* (second edition), Maidenhead: Open University Press.
—— (2005) 'Hidden in Plain Sight – Journalism's Critical Issues', in Stuart Allan (ed.) *Journalism: Critical Issues*, Maidenhead: Open University Press, pp. 1–15.
—— (2006) *Online News: Journalism and the Internet*, Maidenhead: Open University Press.
Allen, Robert C. and Hill, Annette (2004) 'Spaces of Television', in Robert C. Allen and Annette Hill (eds) *The Television Studies Reader*, London: Routledge, pp. 105–9.
Althusser, Louis (1984) *Essays on Ideology*, London: Verso.
Anderson, Benedict (1991) *Imagined Communities* (revised edition) London: Verso.
Ang, Ien (1991) *Desperately Seeking the Audience*, London: Routledge.
Appadurai, Arjun (1990) 'Disjuncture and Difference in the Global Cultural Economy', *Theory, Culture & Society*, vol. 7, nos. 2–3, pp. 295–310.
—— (1996) *Modernity At Large: Cultural Dimensions of Globalization*, Minneapolis: University of Minnesota Press.
Arnison, Matthew (2001) 'Open Publishing is the Same as Free Software', <http://www.cat.org.au/maffew/cat/openpub.html>, accessed 23 February 2004.
Atton, Chris (2002) *Alternative Media*, London: Sage.
—— (2004) *An Alternative Internet*, Edinburgh: Edinburgh University Press.
—— and Couldry, Nick (2003) 'Introduction to Special Issue of *Media, Culture & Society* on Alternative Media', *Media, Culture & Society*, vol. 25, no. 5, pp. 579–86.
Azran, Tal (2004) 'Resisting Peripheral Exports: Al Jazeera's War Images on US Television', *Media International Australia*, no. 113, pp. 75–86.

Bagdikian, Ben H. (1983) *The Media Monopoly*, Boston: Beacon Press.
—— (2004) *The New Media Monopoly*, Boston: Beacon Press.
Bangs, Lester (1987) *Psychotic Reactions and Carburettor Dung*, New York: Vintage.
Bantz, Charles R. (1997) [1985] 'News Organizations: Conflict as a Crafted Cultural Norm', in Dan Berkowitz (ed.) *Social Meanings of News*, Thousand Oaks: Sage, pp. 123–37.
Bardoel, Jo (1996) 'Beyond Journalism: A Profession between Information Society and Civil Society', *European Journal of Communication*, vol. 11, no. 3, pp. 283–302.
Barker, Martin (1998) 'Critique: Audiences 'R' Us', in Roger Dickinson, Ramaswami Harindranath and Olga Linné (eds) *Approaches To Audiences: A Reader*, London: Arnold, pp. 184–91.
Barthes, Roland (1974) *S/Z*, New York: Hill and Wang.
—— (1977) *Image, Music, Text*, New York: Hill and Wang.
—— (1981) *Camera Lucida*, London: Vintage.
Baudrillard, Jean (1995) *The Gulf War Did Not Take Place*, Sydney: Power Publications.
Becker, Karin E. (2003) 'Photojournalism and the Tabloid Press', in Liz Wells (ed.) *The Photography Reader*, London: Routledge, pp. 291–308.
Bell, Allan (1991) *The Language of News Media*, Oxford: Blackwell.
Bennett, W. Lance and Edelman, Murray (1985) 'Toward a New Political Narrative', *Journal of Communication*, vol. 35, no. 4, pp. 156–71.
Berkowitz, Dan (1999) [1990] 'Refining the Gatekeeping Metaphor for Local Television News', in Dan Berkowitz (ed.) *Social Meanings of News*, Thousand Oaks: Sage, pp. 81–93.
Berners-Lee, Tim (1999) *Weaving the Web*. London: Orion Business Books.
Bird, S. Elizabeth (1992) *For Enquiring Minds: A Cultural Study of Supermarket Tabloids*, Knoxville: University of Tennessee Press.
—— (2002) 'Taking It Personally: Supermarket Tabloids After September 11', in Barbie Zelizer and Stuart Allan (eds) *Journalism After September 11*, London: Routledge, pp. 141–59.
—— (2003) *The Audience in Everyday Life: Living in a Media World*, New York: Routledge.
—— and Dardenne, Robert W. (1997) [1988] 'Myth, Chronicle and Story: Exploring the Narrative Qualities of News', in Dan Berkowitz (ed.) *Social Meanings of News*, Thousand Oaks: Sage, pp. 333–50.
Bleske, Glen L. (1997) [1991] 'Ms. Gates Takes Over: An Updated Version of a 1949 Case Study', in Dan Berkowitz (ed.) *Social Meanings of News*, Thousand Oaks: Sage, pp. 72–80.
Blondheim, Menahem (1994) *News Over The Wires: The Telegraph and the Flow of Public Information in America, 1844–1897*, Cambridge, Massachusetts: Harvard University Press.
Blood, Rebecca (2002) 'Introduction', in Rebecca Blood (ed.) *We've Got Blog: How Weblogs Are Changing Our Culture*, Cambridge, Massachusetts: Perseus, pp. ix–xiii.
Boczkowski, Pablo J. (2004) *Digitizing the News: Innovation in Online Newspapers*, Cambridge, Massachusetts: MIT Press.

Bolter, Jay David and Grusin, Richard (1999) *Remediation: Understanding New Media,* Cambridge, Massachusetts: MIT Press.

Boorstin, Daniel (1992) [1961] *The Image*, New York: Vintage.

Bordewijk, Jan L. and van Kaam, Ben (1986) 'Towards a New Classification of Tele-Information Services', *Intermedia,* vol. 14, no. 1, pp. 16–21.

Bordwell, David and Thompson, Kristin (1999) *Film Art: An Introduction* (fifth edition), New York: McGraw-Hill.

Born, Georgina (2004) *Uncertain Vision: Birt, Dyke and the Reinvention of the BBC,* London: Secker & Warburg.

Bourdieu, Pierre (1991) *Language and Symbolic Power,* Cambridge: Polity.

—— (1998) *On Television,* New York: The New Press.

Bourdon, Jérôme (2000) 'Live Television Is Still Alive: On Television As An Unfulfilled Promise', *Media, Culture and Society,* vol. 22, no. 5, pp. 531–56.

Boyce, George (1978) 'The Fourth Estate: the Reappraisal of a Concept', in George Boyce, James Curran and Pauline Wingate (eds) *Newspaper History: From the Seventeenth Century to the Present Day,* London: Constable, pp. 19–40.

boyd, danah (2006) 'A Blogger's Blog: Exploring the Definition of a Medium', *Reconstruction,* vol. 6, no. 4, <http://reconstruction.eserver.org/064/boyd.shtml>, accessed 27 July 2007.

—— and Ellison, Nicole B. (2007) 'Social Network Sites: Definition, History and Scholarship', *Journal of Computer-Mediated Communication,* vol. 13, no. 11, <http://jcmc.indiana.edu/vol13/issue1/boyd.ellison.html>, accessed 17 December 2007.

Boyd-Barrett, Oliver (1995) 'Conceptualizing the "public sphere"', in Oliver Boyd-Barrett and Chris Newbold (eds) *Approaches to Media: A Reader,* London: Arnold, pp. 230–4.

—— (1998) '"Global" News Agencies', in Oliver Boyd-Barrett and Terhi Rantanen (eds) *The Globalization of News,* London: Sage, pp. 19–34.

—— and Rantanen, Terhi (1998) 'The Globalization of News', in Oliver Boyd-Barrett and Terhi Rantanen (eds) *The Globalization of News,* London: Sage, pp. 1–14.

Breed, Warren (1999) [1955] 'Social Control in the Newsroom: A Functional Analysis', in Howard Tumber (ed.) *News: A Reader,* Oxford: Oxford University Press, pp. 79–84.

Briggs, Asa and Burke, Peter (2005) *A Social History of the Media: from Gutenberg to the Internet* (second edition) Cambridge: Polity.

Brighton, Paul and Foy, Dennis (2007) *News Values,* London: Sage.

Bruns, Axel (2005). *Gatewatching: Collaborative Online News Production.* New York: Peter Lang.

—— (2008a) *Blogs, Wikipedia, Second Life and Beyond: From Production to Produsage*, New York: Peter Lang.

—— (2008b) 'Gatewatching, Gatecrashing: Futures for Tactical News Media', in Megan Boler (ed.) *Digital Media and Democracy: Tactics in Hard Times*, Cambridge, MA: MIT Press, pp. 247–70.

—— and Jacobs, Joanne (eds) (2006) *Uses of Blogs*, New York: Peter Lang.

Burnett, Robert and Marshall, P. David (2003) *Web Theory: An Introduction*, London: Routledge.

Calhoun, Craig (1992) 'Introduction: Habermas and the Public Sphere', in Craig Calhoun (ed.) *Habermas and the Public Sphere,* Cambridge, Massachusetts: MIT Press, pp. 1–48.
Campbell, Alastair (2007) *The Blair Years,* London: Hutchinson.
Carey, James (1989) *Communication as Culture,* New York: Routledge.
—— (1998) 'Political Ritual on Television: Episodes in the History of Shame, Degradation and Excommunication', in Tamar Liebes and James Curran (eds) *Media, Ritual and Identity,* London: Routledge, pp. 42–70.
—— (2000) 'Some personal notes on US journalism education', *Journalism: Theory, Practice and Criticism,* vol. 1, no. 1, pp. 12–23.
—— (2002) 'American Journalism On, Before, and After September 11', in Barbie Zelizer and Stuart Allan (eds) *Journalism After September 11.* New York: Routledge, pp. 71–90.
Castells, Manuel (2000) *The Rise of the Network Society* (second edition), Oxford: Blackwell.
—— (2004) *The Power of Identity* (second edition), Oxford: Blackwell.
—— (2007) 'Communication, Power and Counter-Power in the Network Society', *International Journal of Communication,* vol. 1, no. 1, pp. 238–66.
——, Fernandez-Ardevol, Mireia, Linchuan Qiu, Jack, and Sey, Araba (2007) *Mobile Communication and Society: A Global Perspective,* Cambridge, MA: MIT Press.
Chambers, Deborah, Steiner, Linda and Fleming, Carole (2004) *Women and Journalism,* London: Routledge.
Chapman, Jane (2005) *Comparative Media History,* Cambridge: Polity.
Chenoweth, Neil (2001) *Virtual Murdoch,* London: Secker & Warburg.
Chomsky, Noam (2001a) *9–11,* New York: Seven Stories Press.
—— (2001b) 'What Makes Mainstream Media Mainstream', in Russ Kick (ed.) *You Are Being Lied To,* New York: Disinformation, pp. 20–4.
Cohen, Bernard (1963) *The Press and Foreign Policy,* Princeton: Princeton University Press.
Cohen, Stanley (2002) [1972] *Folk Devils and Moral Panics* (third edition), London: Routledge.
Collins, Richard (2004) '"Ises" And "Oughts": Public Service Broadcasting in Europe', in Robert C. Allen and Annette Hill (eds) *The Television Studies Reader,* London: Routledge, pp. 33–51.
Conboy, Martin (2004) *Journalism: A Critical History,* London: Sage.
—— (2006) *Tabloid Britain: Constructing A Community Through Language,* London: Routledge.
—— (2007) *The Language of the News,* London: Routledge.
Conley, David (1997) *The Daily Miracle,* Melbourne: Oxford University Press.
Coopman, Ted (2006) 'Indymedia as a Global Free Media Infrastructure', paper presented to the Association of Internet Researchers Conference in Brisbane, 29 September.
Cottle, Simon (2003a) 'Media Organisation and Production: Mapping the Field', in Simon Cottle (ed.) *Media Organization and Production,* London: Sage, pp. 3–24.
—— (ed.) (2003b) *Media Organization and Production,* London: Sage.
—— (ed.) (2003c) *News, Public Relations and Power,* London: Sage.
Couldry, Nick (2000) *The Place of Media Power,* London: Routledge.

—— (2003) *Media Rituals,* London: Routledge.
—— and Curran, James (eds) (2003) *Contesting Media Power: Alternative Media in a Networked World,* Lanham, Maryland: Rowman & Littlefield.
Coyer, Kate (2005) 'If It Leads It Bleeds: The Participatory Newsmaking of the Independent Media Centre', in Wilma de Jong, Martin Shaw and Neil Stammers (eds) *Global Activism, Global Media,* London: Pluto, pp. 165–78.
——, Dowmunt, Tony, and Fountain, Alan (eds) (2007) *The Alternative Media Handbook,* London: Routledge.
Creeber, Glen (2004) 'News At Ten', in Glen Creeber (ed.) *Fifty Key Television Programmes,* London: Arnold, pp. 144–8.
Crisell, Andrew (1997) *An Introductory History of British Broadcasting,* London: Routledge.
—— (2006) *A Study of Modern Television: Thinking Inside the Box,* Basingstoke: Palgrave Macmillan.
Critcher, Chas (2003) *Moral Panics and the Media,* Buckingham: Open University Press.
—— (2006) 'Introduction: More Questions Than Answers', in Chas Critcher (ed.) *Critical Readings: Moral Panics and the Media,* Buckingham: Open University Press, pp. 1–24.
Croteau, David and Hoynes, William (2005) *The Business of Media: Corporate Media and the Public Interest,* Thousand Oaks, California: Pine Forge Press.
Crowley, David and Heyer, Paul (eds) (2003) *Communication in History: Technology, Culture, Society* (fourth edition), Boston: Allyn and Bacon.
Cunningham, Stuart and Sinclair, John (eds) (2001) *Floating Lives: The Media and Asian Diasporas,* Lanham: Rowman & Littlefield.
Curran, James (1978) 'The Press as an Agency of Social Control: an Historical Perspective', in George Boyce, James Curran and Pauline Wingate (eds) *Newspaper History: From the Seventeenth Century to the Present Day,* London: Constable, pp. 51–75.
—— (2002) *Media and Power,* London: Routledge.
—— and Seaton, Jean (2003) *Power Without Responsibility: The Press, Broadcasting, and New Media in Britain* (sixth edition), London: Routledge.
Dahlberg, Lincoln (1998) 'Cyberspace and the Public Sphere: Exploring the Democratic Potential of the Net', *Convergence,* vol. 4, no. 1, pp. 70–84.
Davis, Aeron (2003) 'Public Relations and News Sources', in Simon Cottle (ed.) *News, Public Relations and Power,* London: Sage, pp. 27–42.
Davies, Nick (2008) *Flat Earth News*, London: Chatto & Windus.
Dayan, Daniel and Katz, Elihu (1992) *Media Events: The Live Broadcasting of History,* Cambridge, Massachusetts: Harvard University Press.
de Certeau, Michel (1984) *The Practice of Everyday Life*, Berkeley: University of California Press.
Department for Culture, Media and Sport [UK] (2001) *Creative Industries: Mapping Document 2001.* London: Department for Culture, Media and Sport.
Deuze, Mark (2003) 'The Web and Its Journalisms: Considering the Consequences of Different Types of Newsmedia Online', *New Media & Society*, vol. 5, no. 2, pp. 203–30.
——, Bruns, Axel and Neuberger, Christoph (2007) 'Preparing For An Age Of Participatory News', *Journalism Practice,* vol. 1, no. 3, pp. 322–38.

Douglas, Susan J. (1987) *Inventing American Broadcasting, 1899–1922*, Baltimore: Johns Hopkins University Press.

Downing, John D. H. (1995) 'Alternative Media and the Boston Tea Party', in John Downing, Ali Mohammadi and Annabelle Sreberny-Mohammadi (eds) *Questioning The Media* (second edition) Thousand Oaks, California: Sage, pp. 238–52.

—— (2002) 'Independent Media Centres: A Multi-local, Multi-media Challenge to Global Neo-liberalism', in Marc Raboy (ed.) *Global Media Policy in the New Millennium*, Luton: University of Luton Press, pp. 215–32.

—— (2003a) 'Audiences and readers of alternative media: the absent lure of the virtually unknown', *Media, Culture & Society*, vol. 25, no. 5, pp. 625–45.

—— (2003b) 'The Independent Media Center Movement and the Anarchist Socialist Tradition', in Nick Couldry and James Curran (eds) *Contesting Media Power: Alternative Media in a Networked World*, Lanham, Maryland: Rowman & Littlefield, pp. 243–57.

—— with Tamara Villarreal Ford, Geneve Gil and Laura Stein (2001) *Radical Media: Rebellious Communication and Social Movements*, Thousand Oaks, California: Sage.

Doyle, Gillian (2002a) *Media Ownership*, London: Sage.

—— (2002b) *Understanding Media Economics*, London: Sage.

Drew, Jesse (2005) 'From the Gulf War to the Battle of Seattle: Building an International Alternative Media Network', in Annmarie Chandler and Norie Neumark (eds) *At a Distance: Precursors to Art and Activism on the Internet*, Cambridge, Massachusetts: MIT Press, pp. 210–24.

Dunn, Anne (2005) 'Television News as Narrative', in Helen Fulton, Rosemary Huisman, Julian Murphet and Anne Dunn *Narrative and Media*, Melbourne: Cambridge University Press, pp. 140–52.

Eagleton, Terry (2007) *Ideology: An Introduction* (second edition), London: Verso.

Eisenstein, Elizabeth (1993) *The Printing Revolution in Early Modern Europe*, Cambridge: Cambridge University Press.

Eliasoph, Nina (1997) 'Routines and the Making of Oppositional News', in Dan Berkowitz (ed.) *Social Meanings of News*, Thousand Oaks: Sage, pp. 230–53.

Ellis, John (1982) *Visible Fictions*, London: Routledge.

—— (2000) *Seeing Things*, London: I. B. Tauris.

Elmer, Greg, Devereaux, Zach and Skinner, David (2006) 'Disaggregating Online News: The Canadian Federal Election, 2005–2006', *Scan*, vol. 3, no. 1 <http://www.scan.net.au/scan/journal/display.php?journal_id=72>, accessed 19 October 2006.

el-Nawawy, Mohammed and Iskandar, Adel (2002) *Al Jazeera: How the Free Arab News Network Scooped the World and Changed the Middle East*, Cambridge, Massachusetts: Westview.

—— (2004) 'Al Jazeera and War Coverage in Iraq: The Media's Quest for Contextual Objectivity', in Stuart Allan and Barbie Zelizer (eds) *Reporting War*, London: Routledge, pp. 315–32.

Ericson, Richard V., Baranek, Patricia M. and Chan, Janet B. L. (1987) *Visualizing Deviance: A Study of News Organization*, Milton Keynes: Open University Press.

—— (1989) *Negotiating Control: A Study of News Sources,* Milton Keynes: Open University Press.
Evans, Harold (1978) *Pictures on a Page,* London: Pimlico.
Evans, Jessica and Hall, Stuart (1999) 'What is Visual Culture?', in Jessica Evans and Stuart Hall (eds) *Visual Culture: The Reader*, London: Sage, pp. 1–7.
Ewen, Stuart (1996) *PR! A Social History of Spin,* New York: Basic Books.
Febvre, Lucien and Martin, Henri-Jean (1976) *The Coming of the Book: the Impact of Printing 1450–1800,* London: NLB.
Fetveit, Arild (1999) 'Reality TV in the Digital Era: A Paradox in Visual Culture?', *Media, Culture and Society,* vol. 21, no. 6, pp. 787–804.
Fishman, Mark (1980) *Manufacturing The News,* Austin: University of Texas Press.
Fiske, John (1987) *Television Culture*, London: Methuen.
—— (1989) *Understanding Popular Culture,* London: Routledge.
Flew, Terry (2005) *New Media: An Introduction* (second edition), Melbourne: Oxford University Press.
—— (2007) *Understanding Global Media*, Basingstoke: Palgrave.
Flichy, Patrice (1995) *Dynamics of Modern Communication: The Shaping and Impact of New Communication Technologies*, London: Sage.
Florida, Richard (2002) *The Rise of the Creative Class.* New York: Basic Books.
Forde, Eamonn (2001) 'From Polyglottism to Branding: On The Decline of Personality Journalism in the British Music Press', *Journalism: Theory, Practice, Criticism,* vol. 2, no. 1, pp. 23–43.
—— (2003) 'Journalists With A Difference: Producing Music Journalism', in Simon Cottle (ed.) *Media Organisation and Production,* London: Sage, pp. 113–30.
Foucault, Michel (1978) *The Will to Knowledge: The History of Sexuality*, vol. 1, London: Penguin.
—— (1980) *Power/Knowledge: Selected Interviews and Other Writings 1972–1977,* Brighton: Harvester Press.
—— (2000) *Power: Essential Works of Foucault 1954–1984, Volume Three,* London: Penguin.
Franklin, Bob (1997) *Newszak and News Media,* London: Arnold.
—— (2003) '"A Good Day to Bury Bad News?": Journalists, Sources and the Packaging of Politics', in Simon Cottle (ed.) *News, Public Relations and Power,* London: Sage, pp. 45–61.
—— (2004) *Packaging Politics: Political Communications in Britain's Media Democracy* (second edition), London: Arnold.
Fraser, Nancy (1992) 'Rethinking the Public Sphere: A Contribution to the Critique of Actually Existing Democracy', in Craig Calhoun (ed.) *Habermas and the Public Sphere,* Cambridge, Massachusetts: MIT Press, pp. 109–42.
Friedberg, Anne (2002) 'CD and DVD', in Dan Harries (ed.) *The New Media Book*, London: British Film Institute, pp. 30–9.
Friedland, Lewis A. (1992) *Covering the World: International Television News Services,* New York: Twentieth Century Fund.
Fulton, Helen (2005) 'Print News as Narrative', in Helen Fulton, Rosemary Huisman, Julian Murphet and Anne Dunn *Narrative and Media,* Melbourne: Cambridge University Press, pp. 218–44.

Gaber, Ivor (2000) 'Government By Spin: An Analysis of the Process', *Media, Culture & Society*, vol. 22, no. 4, pp. 507–18.
Galtung, Johan and Ruge, Mari Holmboe (1965) 'The Structure of Foreign News', *Journal of Peace Research*, vol. 2, no. 1, pp. 64–91.
—— (1981) 'Structuring and Selecting News', in Stanley Cohen and Jock Young (eds) *The Manufacture of News* (revised edition), London: Constable, pp. 52–63.
Gans, Herbert J. (1979) *Deciding What's News*, New York: Pantheon.
García Márquez, Gabriel (1978) [1970] *One Hundred Years of Solitude*, London: Picador.
Garcelon, Marc (2006) 'The "Indymedia" Experiment', *Convergence*, vol. 12, no. 1, pp. 55–82.
Garnham, Nicholas (1992) 'The Media and the Public Sphere', in Craig Calhoun (ed.) *Habermas and the Public Sphere*, Cambridge, Massachusetts: MIT Press, pp. 359–76.
Gauntlett, David (1998) 'Ten Things Wrong With the "Effects" Model', in Roger Dickinson, Ramaswami Harindranath and Olga Linné (eds) *Approaches To Audiences: A Reader*, London: Arnold, pp. 120–30.
Gibson, William (1986) 'Burning Chrome', collected in (1995) *Burning Chrome and Other Stories*, London: HarperCollins.
Gieber, Walter (1999) [1964] 'News is What Newspapermen Make It', in Howard Tumber (ed.) *News: A Reader*, Oxford: Oxford University Press, pp. 218–23.
Gillespie, Marie (1995) *Television, Ethnicity and Cultural Change*, London: Routledge.
Gillmor, Dan (2004) *We The Media: Grassroots Journalism by the People, for the People*, Sebastopol, California: O'Reilly.
Gitlin, Todd (1980) *The Whole World Is Watching: Mass Media in the Making and Unmaking of the New Left*, Berkeley: University of California Press.
—— (1983) *Inside Prime Time*, New York: Pantheon.
Glasgow University Media Group (1976) *Bad News*, London: Routledge & Kegan Paul.
—— (1995a) *Glasgow Media Group Reader, Volume 1*, London: Routledge.
—— (1995b) *Glasgow Media Group Reader, Volume 2*, London: Routledge.
Goggin, Gerard (2006) *Cell Phone Culture*, London: Routledge.
Golding, Peter and Elliott, Philip (1979) *Making The News*, London: Longman.
Goode, Erich and Ben-Yehuda, Nachman (1994) *Moral Panics: the Social Construction of Deviance*, Oxford: Blackwell.
Gorman, Lyn and McLean, David (2002) *Media and Society in the Twentieth Century: A Historical Introduction*, Oxford: Blackwell.
Gramsci, Antonio (1971) *Selections from the Prison Notebooks*, London: Lawrence and Wishart.
Greenslade, Roy (2003) *Press Gang: How Newspapers Make Profits From Propaganda*, London: Pan Macmillan.
Greenwald, Robert (dir.) (2004) *Outfoxed: Rupert Murdoch's War on Journalism*, documentary film.
Gripsrud, Jostein (2000) 'Tabloidization, Popular Journalism, And Democracy', in Colin Sparks and John Tulloch (eds) *Tabloid Tales: Global Debates Over Media Standards*, Lanham, Maryland: Rowman and Littlefield, pp. 285–300.

—— (2006) 'Semiotics: Signs, Codes and Cultures', in Marie Gillespie and Jason Toynbee (eds) *Analysing Media Texts,* Maidenhead: Open University Press, pp. 9–41.
Gurevitch, Michael (1991) 'The Globalization of Electronic Journalism', in James Curran and Michael Gurevitch (eds) *Mass Media and Society,* London: Edward Arnold, pp. 178–93.
Habermas, Jürgen (1974) 'The Public Sphere: an Encyclopedia Article', *New German Critique,* vol. 1, no. 3, pp. 49–55.
—— (1989) *The Structural Transformation of the Public Sphere,* Cambridge, Massachusetts: MIT Press.
—— (1992) 'Concluding Remarks', in Craig Calhoun (ed.) *Habermas and the Public Sphere,* Cambridge, Massachusetts: MIT Press, pp. 462–79.
Halavais, Alexander (2006) 'Scholarly Blogging: Moving Toward the Visible College', in Axel Bruns and Joanne Jacobs (eds) *Uses Of Blogs,* New York: Peter Lang, pp. 117–26.
Hall, Jim (2004) 'Editorial', *Convergence,* vol. 10, no. 4, pp. 5–7.
Hall, Stuart (1981) 'The Determinations of News Photographs', in Stanley Cohen and Jock Young (eds) *The Manufacture of News* (revised edition), London: Constable, pp. 226–43.
—— (1984) 'The Narrative Construction of Reality: An Interview', *Southern Review,* vol. 17, no. 1, pp. 3–17.
—— (2006) [1980] 'Encoding/Decoding', in Douglas Kellner and Meenakshi Gigi Durham (eds) *Media and Cultural Studies: KeyWorks* (revised edition), Malden, Massachusetts: Blackwell, pp. 163–73.
—— and Critcher, Chas, Jefferson, Tony, Clarke, John and Roberts, Bryan (1978) *Policing The Crisis,* London: Macmillan.
Halleck, DeeDee (2003) 'Indymedia: Building an International Activist Internet Network', *Media Development,* vol. 50, no. 4, pp. 11–15.
Hallin, Daniel C. (1986) *The 'Uncensored War': The Media and Vietnam,* Berkeley: University of California Press.
Harcup, Tony and O'Neill, Deirdre (2001) 'What Is News? Galtung and Ruge Revisited', *Journalism Studies,* vol. 2, no. 2, pp. 261–80.
Harris, Michael (1978) 'The Structure, Ownership and Control of the Press, 1620–1780', in George Boyce, James Curran and Pauline Wingate (eds) *Newspaper History: From the Seventeenth Century to the Present Day,* London: Constable, pp. 82–97.
Hartley, John (1982) *Understanding News,* London: Methuen.
—— (1992a) *The Politics of Pictures,* London: Routledge.
—— (1992b) *Tele-ology: Studies in Television,* London: Routledge.
—— (1996) *Popular Reality,* London: Arnold.
—— (1998) 'Juvenation: News, Girls and Power', in Cynthia Carter, Gill Branston and Stuart Allan (eds) *News, Gender and Power,* London: Routledge, pp. 47–70.
—— (1999) *Uses Of Television,* London: Routledge.
—— (2000) 'Communicative democracy in a redactional society: the future of journalism studies', *Journalism: Theory, Practice and Criticism,* vol. 1, no. 1, pp. 39–48.
—— (2001) 'The Infotainment Debate', in Glen Creeber (ed.) *The Television Genre Book,* London: British Film Institute, pp. 118–20.

—— (2003) 'The Frequencies of Public Writing: Tomb, Tome, and Time as Technologies of the Public', in Henry Jenkins and David Thorburn (eds) *Democracy and New Media*, Cambridge, Massachusetts: MIT Press, pp. 247–69.
—— (ed.) (2005) *Creative Industries*, Malden, MA: Blackwell.
Harvey, David (1989) *The Condition of Postmodernity*, Oxford: Blackwell.
Headrick, Daniel (2003) 'The Optical Telegraph', in David Crowley and Paul Heyer (eds) *Communication in History: Technology, Culture, Society* (fourth edition), Boston: Allyn and Bacon, pp. 123–31.
Herman, Edward S. (1995) 'Media in the U.S. Political Economy', in John Downing,, Ali Mohammadi and Annabelle Sreberny-Mohammadi (eds) *Questioning The Media*, Thousand Oaks, California: Sage (second edition), pp. 77–93.
—— (2000) 'The Propaganda Model: a Retrospective', *Journalism Studies*, vol. 1, no. 1, pp. 101–12.
—— and Chomsky, Noam (1988) *Manufacturing Consent*, New York: Pantheon.
—— and McChesney, Robert (1997) *The Global Media: The New Missionaries of Corporate Capitalism*, London: Cassell.
—— and Peterson, David (1999) 'Bomb the *New York Times*?', *Z Magazine*, 31 May, <http://www.zmag.org/Sustainers/Content/1999–05/may_31herman.htm>, accessed 31 March 2006.
Hesmondhalgh, David (2002) *The Cultural Industries*, London: Sage.
Hilmes, Michele (2002) 'Cable, Satellite and Digital Technologies', in Dan Harries (ed.) *The New Media Book*, London: British Film Institute, pp. 3–16.
Hintz, Arne (2003) 'Indymedia Germany: A Local Node of the Global Network', *Media Development*, vol. 50, no. 4, pp. 21–5.
Hoggart, Richard (1976) 'Foreword', in Glasgow University Media Group *Bad News*, London: Routledge & Kegan Paul, pp. ix–xiii.
Holland, Patricia (1998) 'The Politics of the Smile: "Soft News" and the Sexualisation of the Popular Press', in Cynthia Carter, Gill Branston and Stuart Allan (eds) *News, Gender and Power*, London: Routledge, pp. 17–32.
Howkins, John (2001) *The Creative Economy*, London: Penguin.
Jacka, Elizabeth (2006) 'The Future of Public Service Broadcasting', in Stuart Cunningham and Graeme Turner (eds) *The Media and Communications in Australia* (second edition), Sydney: Allen & Unwin, pp. 344–56.
Jenkins, Henry (2001) 'Convergence? I Diverge', *Technology Review*, June, p. 93.
—— (2002) 'Interactive Audiences?', in Dan Harries (ed.) *The New Media Book*, London: British Film Institute, pp. 157–70.
—— (2003) 'Quentin Tarantino's Star Wars? Digital Cinema, Media Convergence, and Participatory Culture', in David Thorburn and Henry Jenkins (eds) *Rethinking Media Change*, Cambridge, Massachusetts: MIT Press, pp. 281–312.
—— (2004) 'The Cultural Logic of Media Convergence', *International Journal of Cultural Studies*, vol. 7, no. 1, pp. 33–43.
—— (2006) *Convergence Culture*, New York: New York University Press.
Jones, Nicholas (1995) *Soundbites and Spin Doctors: How Politicians Manipulate the Media – and Vice Versa*, London: Cassell.
—— (1999) *Sultans of Spin: The Media and the New Labour Government*, London: Orion.
—— (2001) *The Control Freaks: How New Labour Gets Its Own Way*, London: Politico's.

—— (2006) *Trading Information: Leaks, Lies and Tip-Offs*, London: Politico's.

Jordan, Tim (1999) *Cyberpower: the Culture and Politics of Cyberspace and the Internet*, London: Routledge.

Kahn, Richard and Kellner, Douglas (2004) 'New Media and Internet Activism: From the "Battle of Seattle" to Blogging', *New Media & Society*, vol. 6, no. 1, 87–95.

Katz, Elihu (1992) 'The End of Journalism? Notes on Watching the War', *Journal of Communication*, vol. 42, no, 3, pp. 5–13.

Keane, John (1991) *The Media and Democracy*, Cambridge: Polity Press.

Kent, Nick (1994) *The Dark Stuff*, London: Penguin.

Kern, Stephen (1983) *The Culture of Time and Space 1880–1918*, Cambridge, Massachusetts: Harvard University Press.

Kidd, Dorothy (2003) 'Indymedia.org: A New Communications Commons', in Martha McCaughey and Michael D. Ayers (eds) *Cyberactivism: Online Activism in Theory and Practice*, New York: Routledge, pp. 47–69.

Kim, Eun-Gyoo and Hamilton, James W. (2006) 'Capitulation to Capital? OhmyNews as Alternative Media', *Media, Culture & Society*, vol. 28, no. 4, pp. 541–60.

Klaehn, Jeffery (2002) 'A Critical Review and Assessment of Herman and Chomsky's "Propaganda Model"', *European Journal of Communication*, vol. 17, no. 2, pp. 147–82.

Knightley, Phillip (2003) [1975] *The First Casualty: The War Correspondent as Hero, Propagandist and Myth-Maker from the Crimea to Iraq* (updated edition), London: André Deutsch.

Küng-Shankleman, Lucy (2000) *Inside the BBC and CNN: Managing Media Organisations*, London: Routledge.

Langer, John (1980) 'The Structure and Ideology of the "Other News" on Television', in Patricia Edgar (ed.) *The News in Focus: The Journalism of Exception*, Melbourne: Macmillan, pp. 13–43.

—— (1998) *Tabloid Television: Popular Journalism and the 'Other News'*, London: Routledge.

Lasswell, Harold D. (1995) [1948] 'The Structure and Function of Communication in Society', in Oliver Boyd-Barrett and Chris Newbold (eds) *Approaches to Media*, London: Arnold, pp. 93–4.

Lazarsfeld, Paul F., Berelson, Bernard and Gaudet, Hazel (2003) [1944] 'The People's Choice: How The Voter Makes Up His Mind In A Presidential Campaign', in Will Brooker and Deborah Jermyn (eds) *The Audience Studies Reader*, London: Routledge, pp. 13–18.

Leadbeater, Charles (1999) *Living on Thin Air*, London: Vintage.

—— (2008) *We-Think*, Profile, London.

—— and Miller, Paul (2004) *The Pro-Am Revolution: How Enthusiasts are Changing Our Economy and Society*, London: Demos.

Lessig, Lawrence (2004) *Free Culture*, New York: Penguin.

Levinson, Paul (1997) *The Soft Edge: A Natural History and Future of the Information Revolution*, London: Routledge.

—— (2004) *Cellphone*, New York: Palgrave Macmillan.

Lewis, Justin, Williams, Andrew and Franklin, Bob (2008a) 'A Compromised Fourth Estate?', *Journalism Studies*, vol. 9, no. 1, pp. 1–20.

—— (2008b) 'Four Rumours and an Explanation', *Journalism Practice,* vol. 2, no. 1, pp. 27–45.
Lippmann, Walter (1922) *Public Opinion*, New York: Free Press.
Livingstone, Sonia (2002) 'Introduction to Part One: The Changing Social Landscape', in Leah A. Lievrouw and Sonia Livingstone (eds) *Handbook of New Media: Social Shaping and Consequences of ICTs*, London: Sage, pp. 17–21.
Lichtenberg, Judith (2000) 'In Defence of Objectivity Revisited', in James Curran and Michael Gurevitch (eds) *Mass Media and Society* (third edition), London: Arnold, pp. 238–54.
Lovink, Geert (2002) *Dark Fiber: Tracking Critical Internet Culture*, Cambridge, Massachusetts: MIT Press.
—— (2003) *My First Recession: Critical Internet Culture in Transition,* Rotterdam: V2_Publishing/Nai Publishers.
Lumby, Catharine (1997a) 'Panic Attacks: Old Fears in a New Media Era', *Media International Australia,* no. 85, November, pp. 40–6.
—— (1997b) *Bad Girls: The Media, Sex and Feminism in the '90s*, Sydney: Allen & Unwin.
—— (1999) *Gotcha: Life in a Tabloid World*, Sydney: Allen & Unwin.
—— (2002) 'The Future of Journalism', in Stuart Cunningham and Graeme Turner (eds) *The Media and Communications in Australia,* Sydney: Allen & Unwin, pp. 320–9.
Lury, Karen (2005) *Interpreting Television,* London: Hodder Arnold.
Lyotard, Jean-Francois (1984) *The Postmodern Condition: A Report on Knowledge*, Manchester: Manchester University Press.
MacBride, Sean and Roach, Colleen (2000) [1989] 'The New International Information Order', in Frank J. Lechner and John Boli (eds) *The Globalization Reader*, Oxford: Blackwell, pp. 286–92.
MacGregor, Brent (1997) *Live, Direct and Biased? Making Television News in the Satellite Age,* London: Arnold.
MacKenzie, Donald and Wajcman, Judy (eds) (1999) *The Social Shaping of Technology* (second edition), Buckingham: Open University Press.
Manning, Paul (2001) *News and News Sources,* London: Sage.
Manovich, Lev (2001) *The Language of New Media*, Cambridge, Massachusetts: MIT Press.
—— (2003) 'The Paradoxes of Digital Photography', in Liz Wells (ed.) *The Photography Reader,* London: Routledge, pp. 240–9.
Marcus, Greil (1975) *Mystery Train,* London: Faber.
Marr, David and Wilkinson, Marian (2003) *Dark Victory,* Sydney: Allen & Unwin.
Marriott, Stephanie (2007) *Live Television: Time, Space and the Broadcast Event,* London: Sage.
Marshall, P. David (2002) 'The New Intertextual Commodity', in Dan Harries (ed.) *The New Media Book*, London: British Film Institute, pp. 69–81.
—— (2006) 'Intimately Intertwined in the Most Public Way: Celebrity and Journalism', in P. David Marshall (ed.) *The Celebrity Culture Reader,* New York: Routledge, pp. 315–23.
Marvin, Carolyn (1988) *When Old Technologies Were New: Thinking About Communications in the Late Nineteenth Century*, New York: Oxford University Press.

Marx, Karl and Engels, Friedrich (2006) [1845] 'The Ruling Class and the Ruling Ideas', in Douglas Kellner and Meenakshi Gigi Durham (eds) *Media and Cultural Studies: KeyWorks* (revised edition), Malden, Massachusetts: Blackwell, pp. 9–12.
Matheson, Donald (2004) 'Negotiating Claims to Journalism: Webloggers' Orientation to News Genres', *Convergence*, vol. 10, no. 4, pp. 33–54.
McChesney, Robert W. (1999) *Rich Media, Poor Democracy: Communication Politics in Dubious Times*, Urbana: University of Illinois Press.
—— (2002) 'September 11 and the Structural Limitations of US Journalism', in Barbie Zelizer and Stuart Allan (eds) *Journalism After September 11*, London: Routledge, pp. 91–100.
McCombs, Maxwell (1998) 'News Influence on our Pictures of the World', in Roger Dickinson, Ramaswami Harindranath and Olga Linné (eds) *Approaches To Audiences: A Reader*, London: Arnold, pp. 25–35.
—— (2004) *Setting The Agenda: The Mass Media and Public Opinion*, Cambridge: Polity.
—— and Shaw, Donald L. (1976) 'Structuring the "Unseen Environment"', *Journal of Communication*, vol. 26, pp. 18–22.
—— and Shaw, Donald L. (1999) [1972] 'The Agenda-Setting Function of Mass Media', in Howard Tumber (ed.) *News: A Reader*, Oxford: Oxford University Press, pp. 320–8.
McKay, George (1998) 'DiY Culture: Notes Towards an Intro', in George McKay (ed.) *DiY Culture: Party & Protest in Nineties Britain*, London: Verso, pp. 1–53.
McLuhan, Marshall (1964) *Understanding Media*, London: Routledge.
—— and Fiore, Quentin (1967) *The Medium is the Massage*, San Francisco: Hardwired.
McNair, Brian (1998) *The Sociology of Journalism*, London: Arnold.
—— (2003) *An Introduction to Political Communication* (third edition), London: Routledge.
—— (2006) *Cultural Chaos: Journalism, News and Power in a Globalised World*, London: Routledge.
McPherson, Tara (2006) 'Reload: Liveness, Mobility, and the Web', in Wendy Hui Kyong Chun and Thomas Keenan (eds) *New Media Old Media: A History and Theory Reader*, New York: Routledge, pp. 199–208.
McQuail, Denis (1997) *Audience Analysis*, Thousand Oaks, California: Sage.
—— (2000) *McQuail's Mass Communication Theory* (fourth edition), London: Sage.
——, Blumler, Jay G. and Brown, J. R. (1972) 'The Television Audience: A Revised Perspective', in Denis McQuail (ed.) *Sociology of Mass Communications*, Harmondsworth: Penguin, pp. 135–65.
McQuillan, Martin (ed.) (2000) *The Narrative Reader*, London: Routledge.
McRobbie, Angela and Thornton, Sarah (2006) 'Re-Thinking "Moral Panic" For Multi-Mediated Social Worlds', in Chas Critcher (ed.) *Critical Readings: Moral Panics and the Media*, Buckingham: Open University Press, pp. 266–76.
Meadows, Daniel (2003) 'Digital Storytelling: Research-Based Practice in New Media', *Visual Communication*, vol. 2, no. 2, pp. 189–93.
Meikle, Graham (2002) *Future Active: Media Activism and the Internet*, New York: Routledge.

—— (2004) 'Networks of Influence: Internet Activism in Australia and Beyond', in Gerard Goggin (ed.) *Virtual Nation: the Internet in Australia*, Sydney: UNSW Press, pp. 73–87.
—— (2008) 'Whacking Bush: Tactical Media as Play', in Megan Boler (ed.) *Digital Media and Democracy: Tactics in Hard Times*, Cambridge, MA: MIT Press, pp. 367–82.
Melucci, Alberto (1996) *Challenging Codes: Collective Action in the Information Age*, Cambridge: Cambridge University Press.
Merrill, John Calhoun (1974) *The Imperative of Freedom: A Philosophy of Journalistic Autonomy*, New York: Hastings House.
Meyrowitz, Joshua (1985) *No Sense of Place*, New York: Oxford University Press.
—— (1994) 'Medium Theory', in David Crowley and David Mitchell (eds) *Communication Theory Today*, Cambridge: Polity Press, pp. 50–77.
—— (1995) 'Mediating Communication: What Happens?', in John Downing, Ali Mohammadi and Annabelle Sreberny-Mohammadi (eds) *Questioning the Media*, Thousand Oaks, California: Sage, pp. 39–53.
Mill, James (1992) [1823] 'Liberty of the Press', in his *Political Writings*, ed. Terence Ball (1992), Cambridge: Cambridge University Press, pp. 95–135.
Mill, John Stuart (1991) [1859] *On Liberty and Other Essays*, ed. John Gray, Oxford: Oxford University Press.
Milton, John (1990) [1644] 'Areopagitica', in Gordon Campbell (ed.) *John Milton: Complete English Poems, Of Education, Areopagitica* (fourth edition), London: Everyman's Library, pp. 575–618.
Mirzoeff, Nicholas (1999) *An Introduction To Visual Culture*, London: Routledge.
Mitchell, Peter R. and Schoeffel, John (eds) (2002) *Understanding Power: The Indispensable Chomsky*, New York: The New Press.
Molotch, Harvey and Lester, Marilyn (1981) [1974] 'News as Purposive Behaviour: on the Strategic Use of Routine Events, Accidents, and Scandals', in Stanley Cohen and Jock Young (eds) *The Manufacture of News* (revised edition), London: Constable, pp. 118–37.
Mooney, Brian and Simpson, Barry (2003) *Breaking News: How the Wheels Came Off at Reuters*, Chichester: Capstone.
Moore, Martin (2006) *The Origins of Modern Spin: Democratic Government and the Media in Britain, 1945–51*, Basingstoke: Palgrave Macmillan.
Morgan, Piers (2005) *The Insider*, London: Ebury Press.
Morley, David (1980) *The Nationwide Audience*, London: British Film Institute.
—— (1986) *Family Television: Cultural Power and Domestic Leisure*, London: Routledge.
—— (1992) *Television, Audiences and Cultural Studies*, London: Routledge.
—— (2004) 'Broadcasting and the Construction of the National Family', in Robert C. Allen and Annette Hill (eds) *The Television Studies Reader*, London: Routledge, pp. 418–41.
Morris, Meaghan (1998) 'Banality in Cultural Studies', *Discourse*, vol. 10, no. 2, pp. 3–29.
Morse, Margaret (1998) *Virtualities: Television, Media Art, and Cyberculture*, Bloomington: Indiana University Press.
Munster, George (1985) *A Paper Prince*, Harmondsworth: Penguin.

Murdoch, Rupert (2005) 'Speech to the American Society of Newspaper Editors', 13 April, available at <http://www.newscorp.com/news/news_247.html>, accessed 31 July 2006.

Murdock, Graham (1982) 'Large Corporations and the Control of the Communications Industries', in Michael Gurevitch, Tony Bennett, James Curran and Janet Woollacott (eds) *Culture, Society and the Media,* London: Routledge, pp. 118–50.

—— (1990) 'Redrawing the Map of the Communications Industries: Concentration and Ownership in the Era of Privatization', in Marjorie Ferguson (ed.) *Public Communication: The New Imperatives*, London: Sage, pp. 1–15.

—— (2001) 'Reservoirs of Dogma: An Archaeology of Popular Anxieties', in Martin Barker and Julian Petley (eds) *Ill Effects: the Media/Violence Debate* (second edition), London: Routledge, pp. 150–69.

—— and Golding, Peter (1978) 'The Structure, Ownership and Control of the Press, 1914–76', in George Boyce, James Curran and Pauline Wingate (eds) *Newspaper History: From the Seventeenth Century to the Present Day,* London: Constable, pp. 130–48.

Murphet, Julian (2005) 'Stories and Plots', in Helen Fulton, Rosemary Huisman, Julian Murphet and Anne Dunn *Narrative and Media,* Melbourne: Cambridge University Press, pp. 47–59.

Negroponte, Nicholas (1995) *Being Digital*, London: Hodder and Stoughton.

Neil, Andrew (1996) *Full Disclosure,* London: Macmillan.

News Corporation (2006) *Annual Report,* <http://www.newscorp.com/investor/Annual_Reports.html>, accessed 16 July 2007.

—— (2007) *Annual Report*, <http://www.newscorp.com/Report2007/Annual-Report2007/HTML2/default.htm>, accessed 13 May 2008.

OFCOM (Office of Communications) (2006) *Media Literacy Audit: Report on Adult Media Literacy,* <http://www.ofcom.org.uk/advice/media_literacy/medlit-pub/medlitpubrss/medialit_audit>, accessed 17 December 2007.

Orwell, George (1961) [1946] 'Politics and the English Language', in his *Collected Essays*, London: Secker & Warburg, pp. 353–67.

Page, Bruce with Potter, Elaine (2003) *The Murdoch Archipelago,* London: Simon & Schuster.

Papacharissi, Zizi (2002) 'The virtual sphere: the internet as a public sphere', *New Media & Society,* vol. 4, no. 1, pp. 9–27.

Park, Robert E. (1967) [1940] 'News as a Form of Knowledge', in his *On Social Control and Collective Behavior* (ed. Ralph H. Turner), Chicago: University of Chicago Press, pp. 33–52.

Parliament of Australia (2002) *Senate Select Committee for an Inquiry into a Certain Maritime Incident – Report,* <http://www.aph.gov.au/Senate/committee/maritime_incident_ctte/ report/index.htm>, accessed 12 April 2007.

Paterson, Chris (1998) 'Global Battlefields', in Oliver Boyd-Barrett and Terhi Rantanen (eds) *The Globalization of News,* London: Sage, pp. 79–103.

Pavlik, John V. (1998) *New Media Technology: Cultural and Commercial Perspectives* (second edition), Boston: Allyn and Bacon.

—— (2001) *Journalism and New Media*, New York: Columbia University Press.

Pew Internet & American Life Project (2006a) 'Bloggers: A Portrait of the Internet's New Storytellers', <http://www.pewinternet.org/PPF/r/186/report_display.asp>, accessed 1 August 2006.

—— (2006b) 'Riding the Waves of "Web 2.0"', <http://www.pewinternet.org/PPF/r/189/report_display.asp>, accessed 3 August 2007.

—— (2006c) 'Online News: For many home broadband users, the internet is a primary news source' <http://www.pewinternet.org/PPF/r/178/report_display.asp>, accessed 3 August 2007.

—— (2007) 'Election 2006 Online', <http://www.pewinternet.org/PPF/r/199/report_display.asp>, accessed 3 August 2007.

Pew Research Center for the People & the Press (2006) 'Online Papers Modestly Boost Newspaper Readership' <http://people-press.org/reports/display.php3?ReportID=282>, accessed 3 August 2007.

—— (2007) 'Public Knowledge of Current Affairs Little Changed by News and Information Revolutions', <http://people-press.org/reports/display.php3?ReportID=319>, accessed 3 August 2007.

Picard, Robert G. (1991) 'Global Communications Controversies', in John C. Merrill (ed.) *Global Journalism* (second edition), New York: Longman, pp. 73–87.

Pickard, Victor W. (2006) 'United Yet Autonomous: Indymedia and the Struggle to Sustain a Radical Democratic Network', *Media, Culture & Society*, vol. 28, no. 3, pp. 315–36.

Pilger, John (2004) (ed.) *Tell Me No Lies: Investigative Journalism and its Triumphs*, London: Jonathan Cape.

Plant, Sadie (2002) *On The Mobile: The Effects of Mobile Telephones on Social and Individual Life,* <http://www.motorola.com/mot/doc/0/234_MotDoc.pdf>, accessed 27 July 2007.

Platon, Sara and Deuze, Mark (2003) 'Indymedia journalism: a radical way of making, selecting and sharing news?', in *Journalism: Theory, Practice and Criticism,* vol. 4, no. 3, pp. 336–55.

Pool, Ithiel de Sola (1983) *Technologies of Freedom*, Cambridge, Massachusetts: Belknap Press of Harvard University Press.

Poster, Mark (1995) *The Second Media Age*, Cambridge: Polity Press.

—— (1997) 'Cyberdemocracy: Internet and the Public Sphere', in David Porter (ed.) *Internet Culture*, New York: Routledge, pp. 201–17.

Postman, Neil (1985) *Amusing Ourselves to Death,* London: Methuen.

—— and Powers, Steve (1992) *How To Watch TV News,* New York: Penguin.

Pöttker, Horst (2003) 'News and its Communicative Quality: The Inverted Pyramid – When and Why did it Appear?', *Journalism Studies*, vol. 4, no. 4, pp. 501–11.

Potts, John (1990) *Radio in Australia*, Sydney: University of New South Wales Press.

Project for Excellence in Journalism (2007) *The State of the News Media 2007,* <http://stateofthemedia.org/2007>, accessed 16 January 2008.

Quinn, Stephen (2004) 'An Intersection of Ideals: Journalism, Profits, Technology and Convergence', *Convergence*, vol. 10, no. 4, pp. 109–23.

Raymond, Eric S. (1997) 'The Cathedral and the Bazaar', <http://www.catb.org/~esr/writings/cathedral-bazaar>, accessed 23 February 2004.

Read, Donald (1999) *The Power of News: The History of Reuters* (second edition), Oxford: Oxford University Press.

Redden, Guy (2003) 'Read the Whole Thing: Journalism, Weblogs and the Re-Mediation of the War in Iraq', *Media International Australia incorporating Culture and Policy*, no. 109, pp. 153–65.

Reeve, Henry (1855) 'The Newspaper Press', *Edinburgh Review*, vol. 102, no. 208, October, pp. 470–98.
Reith, J. C. W. (1924) *Broadcast Over Britain*, London: Hodder and Stoughton.
Remnick, David (2005) 'Exile on Main Street: Don DeLillo's Undisclosed Underworld', in Thomas DePietro (ed.) *Conversations With Don DeLillo*, Jackson: University Press of Mississippi, pp. 131–44.
Reynolds, Simon (2005) *Rip It Up And Start Again*, London: Faber.
Rheingold, Howard (1993) *The Virtual Community: Homesteading on the Electronic Frontier*, Reading, Massachusetts: Addison-Wesley.
Rice, Ronald E. (1999) 'Artifacts and Paradoxes in New Media', *New Media & Society*, vol. 1, no. 1, pp. 24–32.
Rodriguez, Clemencia (2001) *Fissures in the Mediascape: An International Study of Citizens' Media*, Cresskill, New Jersey: Hampton Press.
—— (2002) 'Citizens' Media and the Voice of the Angel/Poet', *Media International Australia*, no. 103, May, pp. 78–87.
Rosen, Jay (2005) 'Each Nation its Own Press', in Jonathan Mills (ed.) *Barons to Bloggers: Confronting Media Power*, Melbourne: Miegunyah Press, pp. 21–36.
—— (2006) 'The People Formerly Known as the Audience', *PressThink: Ghost of Democracy*, 27 June, <http://journalism.nyu.edu/pubzone/weblogs/pressthink/2006/06/27/ppl_frmr.html>, accessed 13 May 2008.
Roshco, Bernard (1975) *Newsmaking*, Chicago: University of Chicago Press.
Rushkoff, Douglas (2002) 'The Internet Is Not Killing Off Conversation But Actively Encouraging It', in Rebecca Blood (ed.) *We've Got Blog: How Weblogs Are Changing Our Culture*, Cambridge, Massachusetts: Perseus, pp. 116–18.
Salter, Lee (2003) 'Democracy, New Social Movements, and the Internet: A Habermasian Analysis', in Martha McCaughey and Michael D Ayers (eds) *Cyberactivism: Online Activism in Theory and Practice*, New York: Routledge, pp. 117–44.
Savage, Jon (1991) *England's Dreaming*, London: Faber.
—— and Kureishi, Hanif (eds) (1995) *The Faber Book of Pop*, London: Faber.
Scannell, Paddy (1989) 'Public Service Broadcasting and Modern Public Life', *Media, Culture & Society*, vol. 11, no. 2, pp. 135–66.
—— (1996) *Radio, Television and Modern Life*, Oxford: Basil Blackwell.
—— and Cardiff, David (1991) *A Social History of British Broadcasting: Volume 1 1922–1939 Serving The Nation*, Oxford: Basil Blackwell.
Schiller, Herbert I. (1971) *Mass Communications and American Empire*, Boston: Beacon Press.
Schlesinger, Philip (1987) [1978] *Putting 'Reality' Together: BBC News* (second edition), London: Methuen.
—— (1990) 'Rethinking the Sociology of Journalism: Source Strategies and the Limits of Media-Centrism', in Marjorie Ferguson (ed.) *Public Communication: The New Imperative*, London: Sage, pp. 61–83.
—— and Tumber, Howard (1994) *Reporting Crime: The Media Politics of Criminal Justice*, Oxford: Oxford University Press.
Schudson, Michael (1978) *Discovering the News: A Social History of American Newspapers*, New York: Basic Books.
—— (1995) *The Power of News*, Cambridge, Massachusetts: Harvard University Press.

—— (2000) 'The Sociology of News Production Revisited (Again)', in James Curran and Michael Gurevitch (eds) *Mass Media and Society* (third edition), London: Arnold, pp. 175–200.
—— (2002) 'What's Unusual About Covering Politics as Usual?', in Barbie Zelizer and Stuart Allan (eds) *Journalism After September 11*, London: Routledge, pp. 36–47.
—— (2003) *The Sociology of News*, New York: W. W. Norton & Co.
Schultz, Julianne (1998) *Reviving the Fourth Estate*, Cambridge: Cambridge University Press.
—— (2002) 'The Press', in Stuart Cunningham and Graeme Turner (eds) *The Media and Communications in Australia*, Sydney: Allen & Unwin, pp. 101–116.
Sebba, Anne (1994) *Battling For News: The Rise of the Woman Reporter*, London: Hodder and Stoughton.
Shawcross, William (1992) *Rupert Murdoch: Ringmaster of the Information Circus*, Sydney: Random House.
Shirky, Clay (2008) *Here Comes Everybody*, London: Allen Lane
Shoemaker, Pamela J. (1991) *Gatekeeping*, Newbury Park: Sage.
Sigal, Leon V. (1986) 'Sources Make The News', in Robert Karl Manoff and Michael Schudson (eds) *Reading The News*, New York: Pantheon, pp. 9–37.
—— (1999) [1973] 'Reporters and Officials: The Organization and Politics of Newsmaking', in Howard Tumber (ed.) *News: A Reader*, Oxford: Oxford University Press, pp. 224–34.
Sigelman, Lee (1973) 'Reporting the News: An Organizational Analysis', *American Journal of Sociology*, vol. 79, no. 1, pp. 132–51.
Silverstone, Roger (1995) 'Convergence is a Dangerous Word', *Convergence*, vol. 1, no. 1, pp. 11–13.
Sinclair, John, Jacka, Elizabeth and Cunningham, Stuart (eds) (1996) *New Patterns in Global Television: Peripheral Vision*, Oxford: Oxford University Press.
Smith, Anthony (1979) *The Newspaper: An International History*, London: Thames and Hudson.
Smith, Merrit Roe and Marx, Leo (eds) (1994) *Does Technology Drive History?*, Cambridge, Massachusetts: MIT Press.
Smythe, Dallas (1995) [1981] 'On the Audience Commodity and its Work', in Oliver Boyd-Barrett and Chris Newbold (eds) *Approaches to Media*, London: Arnold, pp. 222–28.
Sontag, Susan (1977) *On Photography*, London: Penguin.
Sparks, Colin (2000a) 'From Dead Trees to Live Wires: The Internet's Challenge to the Traditional Newspaper', in James Curran and Michael Gurevitch (eds), *Mass Media and Society* (third edition), London: Arnold, pp. 268–92.
—— (2000b) 'The Panic Over Tabloid News', in Colin Sparks and John Tulloch (eds) *Tabloid Tales: Global Debates Over Media Standards*, Lanham, Maryland: Rowman and Littlefield, pp. 1–40.
—— (2005) 'Media and the Global Public Sphere: An Evaluative Approach', in Wilma de Jong, Martin Shaw & Neil Stammers (eds) *Global Activism, Global Media*, London: Pluto, pp. 34–49.
—— and Tulloch, John (eds) (2000) *Tabloid Tales: Global Debates Over Media Standards*, Lanham, Maryland: Rowman and Littlefield.

Stam, Robert (2000) [1983] 'Television News and its Spectator', in Robert Stam and Toby Miller (eds) *Film and Theory: An Anthology*, Malden, Massachusetts: Blackwell, pp. 361–80.
Standage, Tom (1998) *The Victorian Internet*, London: Phoenix.
Stanyer, James (2007) *Modern Political Communication*, Cambridge: Polity.
Stauber, John and Rampton, Sheldon (1995) *Toxic Sludge Is Good For You! Lies, Damn Lies and the Public Relations Industry*, Monroe, Maine: Common Courage Press.
Stead, W. T. (1886) 'Government by Journalism', *Contemporary Review*, vol. 49, January–June, pp. 653–74.
Steemers, Jeanette (1999) 'Between Culture and Commerce: The Problem of Redefining Public Service Broadcasting for the Digital Age', *Convergence*, vol. 5, no. 3, pp. 44–66.
Stephens, Mitchell (2007) *A History of News* (third edition) New York: Oxford University Press.
Street, John (2001) *Mass Media, Politics and Democracy*, Basingstoke: Palgrave Macmillan.
Tartt, Donna (1992) *The Secret History*, London: Penguin.
Taylor, Philip M. (2003) 'Journalism Under Fire: The Reporting of War and International Crises', in Simon Cottle (ed.) *News, Public Relations and Power*, London: Sage, pp. 63–79.
Thomas, Mandy (1997) '"Beautiful Woman Dies": Diana in Vietnam and in the Diaspora', in Re:Public (eds) *Planet Diana*, Kingswood: Research Centre in Intercommunal Studies, pp. 149–54.
Thompson, Hunter S. (1972) *Fear and Loathing in Las Vegas*, New York: Random House.
Thompson, John B. (1990) *Ideology and Modern Culture*, Cambridge: Polity.
—— (1993) 'The Theory of the Public Sphere', *Theory, Culture & Society*, vol. 10, no. 3, pp. 173–89.
—— (1995) *The Media and Modernity*, Cambridge: Polity.
—— (2005) 'The New Visibility', *Theory, Culture & Society*, vol. 22, no. 6, pp. 31–51.
Thompson, Kenneth (1998) *Moral Panics*, London: Routledge.
Thompson, Matthew (1997) 'Tabloid Whore', *Australian Style*, January, pp. 78–80.
Thoreau, Henry David (1854) *Walden, and On the Duty of Civil Disobedience*, Project Gutenberg, <http://www.gutenberg.org/files/205/205-h/205-h.htm>, accessed 23 July 2008.
Thwaites, Tony, Davis, Lloyd and Mules, Warwick (2002) *Introducing Cultural and Media Studies: A Semiotic Approach*, Basingstoke: Palgrave Macmillan.
Tiffen, Rodney (1989) *News and Power*, Sydney: Allen & Unwin.
Tirohl, Blu (2000) 'The Photo-Journalist and the Changing News Image', *New Media & Society*, vol. 2, no. 3, pp. 335–52.
Todorov, Tzvetan (1975) *The Fantastic: A Structural Approach To A Literary Genre*, Ithaca, New York: Cornell University Press.
—— (1977) *The Poetics of Prose*, Oxford: Basil Blackwell.
Tomlinson, John (1991) *Cultural Imperialism*, Baltimore: Johns Hopkins University Press.

—— (1997) 'Cultural Globalization and Cultural Imperialism', in Ali Mohammadi (ed.) *International Communication and Globalization*, Thousand Oaks, California: Sage, pp. 170–90.
Tracey, Michael (1998) *The Decline and Fall of Public Service Broadcasting*, Oxford: Oxford University Press.
Tuchman, Gaye (1972) 'Objectivity as Strategic Ritual: An Examination of Newsmen's Notions of Objectivity', *American Journal of Sociology*, vol. 77, no. 4, pp. 660–79.
—— (1973) 'Making News by Doing Work: Routinizing the Unexpected', *American Journal of Sociology*, vol. 79, no. 1, pp. 110–31.
—— (1978) *Making News: A Study in the Construction of Reality*, New York: The Free Press.
—— (2002) 'The Production of News', in Klaus Bruhn Jensen (ed.) *A Handbook of Media and Communication Research*, London: Routledge, pp. 78–90.
Tumber, Howard (ed.) (1999) *News: A Reader*, London: Oxford University Press.
Tunstall, Jeremy (1971) *Journalists At Work*, London: Constable.
—— (ed.) (2001) *Media Occupations and Professions: A Reader*, Oxford: Oxford University Press.
Turnbull, Sue (2006) 'Audiences', in Stuart Cunningham and Graeme Turner (eds) *The Media and Communications in Australia* (second edition), Sydney: Allen & Unwin, pp. 78–93.
Turner, Graeme (1996) 'Post Journalism: News and Current Affairs Programming from the Late 80s to the Present', *Media International Australia*, no. 82, November, pp. 78–91.
—— (2000) 'Studying Television', in Stuart Cunningham and Graeme Turner (eds) *The Australian TV Book*, Sydney: Allen & Unwin, pp. 3–12.
—— (2004) *Understanding Celebrity*, Thousand Oaks, California: Sage.
—— (2005) *Ending The Affair: The Decline of Television Current Affairs in Australia*, Sydney: UNSW Press.
—— and Bonner, Frances, and Marshall, P. David (2000) *Fame Games: The Production of Celebrity in Australia*, Cambridge: Cambridge University Press.
UNESCO (1980) *Many Voices, One World: Towards a New More Just and More Efficient World Information and Communication Order* (the MacBride Report), London: Kogan Page.
Volkmer, Ingrid (1999) *News in the Global Sphere: A Study of CNN and its Impact on Global Communication*, Luton: University of Luton Press.
—— (2002) 'Journalism and Political Crises in the Global Network Society', in Barbie Zelizer and Stuart Allan (eds) *Journalism After September 11*, London: Routledge, pp. 235–46.
Wajcman, Judy (1994) 'Technological A/genders: Technology, Culture and Class', in Lelia Green and Roger Guinery (eds) *Framing Technology*, Sydney: Allen & Unwin, pp. 3–14.
Walker, Jill (2003) 'Final Version of a Weblog Definition', *Jill/Txt*, <http://jilltxt.net/archives/blog_theorising/final_version_of_weblog_definition.html>, accessed 27 July 2007.
Wark, McKenzie (1992) 'To The Vector The Spoils: Towards A Vectoral Analysis of the Global Media Event', in Elizabeth Jacka (ed.) *Continental Shift: Globalization and Culture*, Sydney: Local Consumption Publications, pp. 142–60.

—— (1994) *Virtual Geography*, Bloomington: Indiana University Press.
—— (1997) *The Virtual Republic*, Sydney: Allen & Unwin.
—— (1999) *Celebrities, Culture and Cyberspace*, Sydney: Pluto Press.
—— (2000) 'Cellphones and the Cancer of Cellspace', posted to the *Nettime* list at <http://www.nettime.org/Lists-Archives/nettime-l-0011/msg00078.html>, 10 November, accessed 27 July 2007.
—— (2004) *A Hacker Manifesto*, Cambridge, MA: Harvard University Press.
White, David Manning (1950) '"The 'Gatekeeper": A Case Study in the Selection of News', *Journalism Quarterly*, vol. 27, pp. 383–90.
Whitney, D. Charles and Becker, Lee B. (1982) '"Keeping the Gates" for Gatekeepers: The Effects of Wire News', *Journalism Quarterly*, vol. 59, no. 1, pp. 60–5.
Whittemore, Hank (1990) *CNN: the Inside Story*, Boston: Little, Brown.
Williams, Raymond (1958) *Culture and Society 1780–1950*, London: Chatto & Windus.
—— (1974) *Television: Technology and Cultural Form*, London: Fontana.
—— (1983) *Keywords: A Vocabulary of Culture and Society* (revised edition), London: Fontana.
Winner, Langdon (1999) 'Who Will We Be In Cyberspace?', in Paul A. Mayer (ed.) *Computer Media and Communication: a Reader*, Oxford: Oxford University Press, pp. 207–18.
Winston, Brian (2005) *Messages: Free Expression, Media and the West from Gutenberg to Google*, London: Routledge.
Wolfe, Tom (1973) 'The New Journalism', in Tom Wolfe and E. W. Johnson (eds) *The New Journalism*, London: Picador, pp. 15–68.
Woodward, Bob (2002) *Bush At War*, New York: Simon & Schuster.
—— and Bernstein, Carl (1974) *All The President's Men*, London: Secker & Warburg.
Young, Sherman (2007) *The Book Is Dead: Long Live The Book*, Sydney: UNSW Press.
Zelizer, Barbie (1992) 'CNN, the Gulf War, and Journalistic Practice', *Journal of Communication*, vol. 42, no. 1, pp. 66–81.
—— (1993) 'Has Communication Explained Journalism?', *Journal of Communication*, vol. 43, no. 4, pp. 80–8.
Zoonen, Liesbet van (1994) *Feminist Media Studies*, London: Sage.
—— (1998) 'One of the Girls? The Changing Gender of Journalism', in Cynthia Carter, Gill Branston and Stuart Allan (eds) *News, Gender and Power*, London: Routledge, pp. 33–46.

Index

Printed and bound in Great Britain by
CPI Antony Rowe, Chippenham and Eastbourne